Weimar Cities

Routledge Studies in Modern European History

1. Facing Fascism
The Conservative Party and the European Dictators 1935–1940
Nick Crowson

2. French Foreign and Defence Policy, 1918–1940
The Decline and Fall of a Great Power
Edited by Robert Boyce

3. Britain and the Problem of International Disarmament 1919–1934
Carolyn Kitching

4. British Foreign Policy 1874–1914
The Role of India
Sneh Mahajan

5. Racial Theories in Fascist Italy
Aaron Gilette

6. Stormtroopers and Crisis in the Nazi Movement
Activism, Ideology and Dissolution
Thomas D. Grant

7. Trials of Irish History
Genesis and Evolution of a Reappraisal 1938–2000
Evi Gkotzaridis

8. From Slave Trade to Empire
European Colonisation of Black Africa 1780s–1880s
Edited by Olivier Pétré-Grenouilleau

9. The Russian Revolution of 1905
Centenary Perspectives
Edited by Anthony Heywood and Jonathan D. Smele

10. Weimar Cities
The Challenge of Urban Modernity in Germany, 1919–1933
John Bingham

Weimar Cities

The Challenge of Urban Modernity in Germany, 1919–1933

John Bingham

LONDON AND NEW YORK

Routledge
Taylor & Francis Group
711 Third Avenue
New York, NY 10017

Routledge
Taylor & Francis Group
2 Park Square, Milton Park
Abingdon, Oxfordshire
OX14 4RN

First issued in paperback 2014

Routledge is an imprint of the Taylor & Francis Group, an informa business

Library of Congress Cataloging-in-Publication Data

Bingham, John, 1959-
Weimar cities : the challenge of urban modernity in Germany, 1919-1933 / John Bingham.
p. cm. -- (Routledge studies in modern European history ; 10)
Includes bibliographical references and index.
ISBN 978-0-415-95744-1 (hbk)
ISBN 978-0-415-76250-2 (pbk)
1. Cities and towns--Germany--History--20th century. 2. Urbanization--Germany--History--20th century. 3. Germany--History--1918-1933. I. Title.

HT137.B55 2007
307.7609430904--dc22 2006102908

Visit the Taylor & Francis Web site at
http://www.taylorandfrancis.com

and the Routledge Web site at
http://www.routledge.com

For Barbara

Contents

Acknowledgments

It is a great pleasure at the end of this project to be able to acknowledge the enormous help of those along the way. This book began as a dissertation at York University under the supervision of Michael H. Kater. Although neither its direction nor final shape were always what he anticipated, I am grateful for his early interest and continuing support, as well as his exacting eye in reading the various drafts. Of many others who offered advice, encouragement and criticism, I wish to mention particularly Celia Applegate, William D. Irvine, and John Marshall.

My research was initially supported by a doctoral fellowship and, in 2001, an institutional grant from the Social Sciences and Humanities Council of Canada. A Research Development Fund grant from Dalhousie University made possible significant additional work in 1999. The staffs of the Landesarchiv in Berlin, the Geheimes Staatsarchiv Preussischer Kulturbesitz in Dahlem, the Nordrhein-Westfälisches Hauptstaatsarchiv in Düsseldorf, and the Düsseldorf Stadtarchiv were unfailingly patient and helpful. Herr Volker Viergutz at the Landesarchiv was at all times a gracious and knowledgeable guide in my explorations of the vast records of the Deutsche Städtetag and of other communal associations held there. I am particularly grateful to the Landesarchiv staff for generously allowing me to work through renovations in the summer of 1999. The Interlibrary Loan departments at the libraries of York University, the University of Wisconsin-Madison and Dalhousie University were always helpful and patient with my requests for even the most obscure material.

Anthony McElligott and Lawrence Stokes read portions of the manuscript and offered friendly advice at different stages. For generous comradeship, communal endeavor, and kind attention in various measures, I thank Jennifer Jenkins, Sean Kennedy, Kenneth Mouré, James Retallack, Thomas Saunders, and Philip Zachernuk. My colleagues in the Department of History at Dalhousie have patiently heard more, read more, and talked more about Weimar cities than they could have possibly foreseen when they welcomed me in 1998.

At Routledge, two anonymous readers provided excellent comments and suggestions that have helped improve the book. Research Editor Max Novick and his assistant, Erica Wetter, were remarkably efficient, kind, and patient with a neophyte author.

The encouragement and support from friends and family have sustained me far beyond what I had any reason or right to expect. Barbara Clow is the best editor I know; her comments were always sensible and suggestions unfailingly constructive. It is no exaggeration to say I would not have finished without her love and continued faith in me. Both she and Harry are constant reminders to me of what it all really means: they feel like home to me.

Abbreviations

ARCHIVES

BA	Bundesarchiv
DüssStaA	Stadtarchiv Düsseldorf
GSTAPrKB	Geheimes Staatsarchiv Preussischer Kulturbesitz
LAB	Landesarchiv Berlin
NRWHSTA	Nordrhein-Westfälisches Hauptstaatsarchiv Düsseldorf

ASSOCIATIONS

DGT	Deutscher Gemeindetag (1933–1945)
DST	Deutscher Städtetag
LGT	Deutscher Landgemeindetag
LKT	Deutscher Landkreistag
PrLGTW	Preussischer Landgemeindetag West
PST	Preussischer Städtetag
RSB	Reichsstädtebund
VbPrLG	Verband preussischer Landgemeinden
VbPrProv	Verband preussischer Provinzen

GENERAL

BM	Bürgermeister
Mitt. DST	*Der Städtetag: Mitteilungen des Deutschen Städtetages*
NVO	Notverordnung
OB	Oberbürgermeister
PrGS	*Preussische Gesetzsammlung*
PrMdI	Preussisches Ministerium des Innern

RMdI	Reichsministerium des Innern
RWR	Reichswirtschaftsrat
StatJbDSt	*Statistisches Jahrbuch deutscher Städte*
SVV	Stadtverordnetenversammlung

Introduction

Locating cities and modernity in Weimar

The "crisis of modernity" in the Weimar Republic was especially evident in the challenges posed by its cities. Germany's large municipalities in the 1920s were celebrated showplaces of urban power and confidence in technology and progress, exemplars of still resonant associations of the modern metropolis. Competing with each other for prestige, publicity, and resources, they constructed lavish exhibition halls, extended road networks as automobile traffic increased, and built airports for burgeoning air travel; they financed and ran their own electricity, gas- and waterworks, and public transit corporations. Centers of cultural and aesthetic experimentation, they were famous for their musical revues and cabarets, expressionism in the theatre and visual arts, vital artists' communities, and modernist literature. Some cities were sites of quasi-socialist housing cooperatives employing new architectural styles. The famous term, "Weimar culture," invokes immediately the designs of the Bauhaus and architect Bruno Taut, the theatre of Max Reinhardt and Bertolt Brecht, composer Paul Hindemith's early experiments in tonality, the politically provocative art of Otto Dix, George Grosz, and the Dadaists, the cosmopolitan novels of Alfred Döblin, and a host of others. None of the works of these artists, their dozens of peers, or the artistic milieus that nurtured them, are conceivable outside of the urban environment. Weimar culture was to a great degree modern urban culture.[1]

"Culture" of course designates more than just artifacts and styles. More descriptively, it embraces the wider process by which social meaning is negotiated—"a struggle over things, meanings, and positions" between differing, often opposed viewpoints and sensibilities.[2] Contained in the seemingly fragile vessel of the interwar republic were extraordinary tensions and contradictions between the traditional and the modern. In particular, the progressive momentum implied by the power and prestige of the cities was countered by a vehement and widespread rejection of "the Berlin Republic," and of the metropolis and urban modernity in general.[3] Many Germans perceived Weimar first as an "urban republic," founded in the city-based revolutions of 1918–19, fomented by (according to the nationalist right) socialists and urban Jews, and supported by urban workers.

Germany's powerful cities, arguably the most prominent exemplars of industrial and modern progress, also functioned more prosaically as the managers and field agents of Weimar's extensive building and social programs. Whether viewed with pride or hostility, cities were the local face of the republic, and thus barometers of its performance. More broadly conceived, the metropolis has become for German historians one of the primary, defining problems of the period. As a center of artistic and sexual experimentation, of cosmopolitanism, technological enterprise, capital and industrial power, the metropolis (frequently synonymized both then and now with Berlin), its culture and the tensions it generated dominate Weimar's history.[4] Although hostility towards the big city, the *Grossstadt*, can be found almost everywhere on the political spectrum in Germany before 1914, cities came under concentrated attack in what Andrew Lees has called an "explosion" of ideological debate over the value of the metropolis in Germany after the war.[5] Most infamous and extreme in their rejection of cities were the Nazis, who condemned the metropolis as the site of soulless social and artistic experiments, immorality, big capital, crime, rootless anonymity, and racial mixing.[6] Hitler of course famously planned monumental building projects for Germany's cities after the Second World War, but his vision can only be termed "urban" in its sheer physicality. His postwar cities were vast dead spaces of grandiose triumphalism and massive architecture designed expressly to overawe Germans and visitors alike with the power of the victorious Third Reich, rather than accommodate the daily social needs of the millions of urban beings who would live in them. The Nazi seizure of power in 1933 thus marked a temporary but decisive rejection of the metropolitan culture of the Weimar period.[7]

The metropolis, then, whether viewed as a positive development or an intractable problem, was a theme central to Weimar Germans' self-perception and appears to have had at the very least an indirect effect on the republic's political viability. This was a complex historical environment of unresolved social and cultural contradictions—a tension in itself characteristic of the modern condition. If, as Marshall Berman maintains, the rich complexity of modernity can only be grasped by giving equal attention to its opposite, the anti-modern, then the historian's task becomes one of reading the dense, often turgid currents of pro- and anti-modern ideas as part of a larger whole. "Modern" and "anti-modern" tensions and contradictions can therefore help uncover deeper structural fissures in Weimar society and economy.[8]

An important effort to do justice to Weimar's complex multiple dimensions was made by historian Detlev Peukert in the late 1980s, when he insisted on the importance of recognizing that German society enthusiastically embraced certain aspects of modernity while vehemently rejecting others. Uneven economic growth created "sectoral imbalances" that existed in states of tension the weak republic had neither the political nor economic resources to resolve, bringing on what Peukert called "crises of classical modernity."[9] He argued that if "the crucial factor governing a society's stability and survival is going to be the way in which that society deals with these broadly inevitable tensions," then such tensions offer insights into the specific causes, as well as the deeper determinants, of the republic's failure.[10]

Recent criticisms of Peukert's work—his elision of historically discrete periods, as well as omissions and distortions of detail in his emphases on continuities from Kaiserreich to Third Reich—have not diminished the usefulness or relevance of his interest in the role modernity's tensions played in the failure of the republic.[11] The trick, however, has been to find actual areas of such tension and exploit their explanatory potential. Efforts to do so, despite some useful research, have failed either to satisfactorily identify loci of clearly articulated frictions or to address the larger structural and paradigmatic themes on which Peukert focused. Much of this work, very sensibly, has centered on the urban environment.[12] If social tensions arising from the German experience of modernity are important, then surely the city—where time, space, and work are rationalized and old communal ties severed, where aesthetic experimentation, mass housing, urban functionalist architecture, and other "modern" factors are concentrated—is the first logical place to look for them. As usual, the problem lies in the transition from the particular to the general: the very singularities that make case studies promising sites for Peukert's crises also make them resistant to broader generalization. Responses to specifically urban aspects of modernity in Hanover, for instance, differed markedly from those in Düsseldorf and Frankfurt. The distinctive character of local politics and personalities, as well as unique aspects of regional culture, tradition, and experience—especially the concentration of heavy industry and dense urban clustering in the Rhineland, as well as postwar occupation and the rise of a strong particularist movement there—all caution against larger statements about "the way in which [German] society" addressed Peukert's "broadly inevitable" social, economic, and cultural tensions that accompanied the advent of modernity in a specific locale.[13]

To return to Peukert's larger perspective, this study retains the emphasis on cities while stepping back to survey the larger canvas of urban development and its politics across Germany. It considers cities collectively both as the active agents as well as the prominent symbols of social and economic modernization within a country still characterized strongly by older, pre-modern forms and ways of life. The stresses that attended urbanization were not limited simply to direct experiences of metropolitan daily life. Urban concentration created structural, supra-local tensions, as growing cities competed with their neighbors for resources and, via internal migration and tax policies favorable to business, siphoned capital and labor from the surrounding countryside. "Crises of classical modernity," difficult to discern within the borders of the already-modern city, may be more easily seen in the economic, cultural, administrative, and political disjunctures that accompanied modern urban growth and development in Germany as a whole.

The first chapter sketches in the background of German cities' extraordinary growth in the Kaiserreich, and describes their important roles as caretakers and welfare administrators on the home front in the First World War. The founding of the Weimar Republic created a new constitutional, economic, and financial environment that tremendously affected urban centers, especially the metropolises. Most importantly, the Reich's centralization of finance removed their prewar power of determining local spending and taxing; at the same time, the burden of municipal welfare increased after the war. Financially, the result was a frustrating dependence on the Reich's help in times of crisis. Even during the relatively stable years of the mid-1920s, the cities were forced to secure credit abroad in order to hold up their end of the new welfare state's responsibilities. Borrowing made them especially vulnerable politically, and they came under heavy criticism from conservative financial circles, who viewed them as irresponsible borrowers and profligate spenders. Tension between the cities and their critics grew especially pronounced after 1930, when Chancellor Heinrich Brüning's tight monetary policies, aimed at balancing first the budgets of the Reich and then the states, meant that the "heaviest burdens" of austerity were passed down through the Reich's system of finance distribution and "laid on the weakest shoulders" of the municipalities.[14] Yet this was precisely the point where, strained to the breaking point by the weight of long-term unemployment and welfare relief, communal finances reached their nadir, threatening many cities with default and bankruptcy. In Prussia, they were placed under the control of state-appointed commissioners empowered to force through tough budgets, impose unpopular austerity measures, and raise new taxes. By January 1933, local government was widely discredited: undermined by hostile central policies, financially on the ropes, and paralyzed by increasingly polarized communal politics. Many micro studies have shown that the Nazis' activism on the local level played a critical role in their success. But as this chapter emphasizes, the erosion of healthy self-government had older and deeper roots.

Chapter two examines the efforts of the cities collectively to influence their new republican environment through their lobby organization, the *Deutsche Städtetag* (German Congress of Cities, DST). Founded shortly after the turn of the century, the congress played an active role during the First World War as an intermediary between the central government and the cities. Yet its period of greatest prominence was during the Weimar era, and especially in the half-dozen years before 1933. It distributed information and advice to member-cities, collected and collated urban data from across the Reich, lobbied and negotiated with the central and state governments, and published extensively in the popular press in the hope of winning public sympathy for the municipalities' special problems in the 1920s. Ironically, it was only after 1930 that the cities, through Städtetag president Oskar Mulert, gained significant access to policy-makers. Mulert was a frequent visitor at meetings of cabinet ministers during these crisis years. However, it was not as an equal partner, but most often as a supplicant and protestor that he attended, pleading for financial help from the Reich or objecting to the draconian financial measures and administrative interference imposed by the infamous emergency decrees of 1930–32. The Städtetag's record of frustration and disappointment by 1933 parallels the decline of local power and municipal self-government, and in June 1933 the congress underwent "coordination" (*Gleichschaltung*) with the other communal associations of towns, counties, and so forth, into a new National Socialist umbrella organization, the *Deutsche Gemeindetag.*

These communal organizations are the focus of the next two chapters. Similar to the Städtetag, their regional and sub-associations were for the most part founded before the turn of the century, but only managed to consolidate into fully national organizations in the period from the end of the war to stabilization in 1924. Chapter three describes their inner workings, analyzes their understanding of their constituents' interests, and details their jockeying for position and influence in the latter Weimar period. It concludes that they were disadvantaged in their competition with the DST, lacking its financial resources, its connections with decision-making officials in the Reich and state bureaucracies, and the unambiguous clarity of its "modern" urban mandate. Many of the small towns and rural counties, for instance, were poised on the cusp of urban change. They participated indirectly in the urbanization process but nonetheless were strongly affected by it. Chapter four contextualizes their interests and politics along with those of the cities and towns, by examining a specific instance of large-scale urban reform, the redrafting of the administrative map in the Rhineland in 1929. This tremendous reform project entailed the amalgamation of neighboring urban centers, the absorption of small townships by nearby larger ones, and the carving-up of county areas to give cities room to grow and develop. Many rural settlements, strongly attached to local traditions of their *Heimat*, were threatened with becoming, at a stroke, parts of modern urban centers. Given the magnitude of the changes involved, the reform excited considerable public interest and intense debate in professional planning circles. It therefore provides an unusually clear and provocative case study of urban-rural tensions, offering a finely differentiated view of those tensions across the whole spectrum of urban development, from countryside to metropolis, village to middling town.

Reform also is the subject of chapter five, which shifts the focus back to the cities. In the late 1920s, the Städtetag made a number of ambitious proposals to reform Reich administration. With Reich financial and legislative authority centralizing in Berlin, the cities found supervision by the state governments increasingly constrictive and irrelevant. In Weimar, the critical decisions defining the municipalities' responsibilities and determining their financial well-being lay with the Reich ministries and the Reichstag;

as Cologne mayor Konrad Adenauer succinctly put it, "The cities belong to the Länder, while the Reich has the money."[15] Yet the cities' representation at the Reich level had not kept pace with the national concentration of administration. The DST therefore proposed the creation of a number of new central institutions, designed to bring municipal considerations before Reich legislators and administrators, and to coordinate policy more effectively between ministries. The occasion of the proposals was a two-year conference of federal and state representatives, convened in 1928 in order to formulate a comprehensive constitutional, territorial, and administrative reform of the Reich. Such a reform, if successful, would have recast completely Weimar's constitutional structure: local governments with direct connections to Berlin would have had little need of the states' paternalist supervision, and it is certainly conceivable that the state governments would have sunk into increasing moribundity. Unfortunately for the cities, excluded from participating at the conference, their plans received little serious consideration. The proposals that eventually issued from the conference lacked serious commitment from the participants for meaningful implementation, and after 1930 the whole undertaking became effectively a dead issue.

In examining the postwar difficulties of the cities, the mechanisms they chose to represent themselves collectively, and the resulting efforts to assimilate urban modernity more fully in the Reich, this study consciously attempts to avoid equating "modern" with an unhistoricized notion of progress. Weimar's municipal administrators and apologists, not uncharacteristically for their era, believed fervently in continuing social, technological, and economic betterment. They considered well-managed urban development to be one of the clearest indicators of modern progress, and their voices made key contributions to the ongoing debate about the city in Germany. Yet it would be mistaken to categorize them altogether as advocates of a single and unvariegated position in that debate. On the contrary, a close reading of their programs reveals a number of alternative, competing visions of cities. Several insisted, for instance, that a modern state did not necessarily mean one dominated by powerful and independent metropoles, defined by large-scale municipal projects and characterized by urban culture. They argued that Weimar did not have to be the "Berlin Republic." A modern state could also, according to one offered alternative, be composed of powerful district or county governments, with industry decentralized and relocated to rural areas. The aim here is to set in context one aspect of modernity in Germany, the urban, as a way of suggesting the open, contingent and pluralist nature of the larger modern condition. At the same time, the tension between these concurrent and competing visions resulted especially from the pressing, intractable problems posed by the metropolis and ongoing urbanization in a country searching desperately for stability. Confronting the Grossstadt presented Weimar Germans with the most troubling, ambiguous, and inescapable of modern conditions—sudden, drastic urban change. It thus provides a powerful example of the "crisis of classical modernity" in the republic. This study reveals with particular force the insufficient financial, political, and cultural resources available in postwar Germany to meet that challenge.

1 Center and periphery

Cities in Germany, 1900–1933

Urbanization occurred most intensively in Germany over a relatively short span of forty years, from 1870 to 1910. At the beginning of the period, two-thirds of Germans in the new Reich dwelt in the countryside; by 1910, the balance between city and country was roughly equal, and in 1925, the proportions were reversed and two-thirds of all Germans were city dwellers. Similarly, the portion of the Reich population living in the *Grossstädte*, cities with populations over 100,000, had grown by 1910 from 4.8 percent to 21.3 percent, and the number of such cities had jumped from eight to forty-eight, almost equalling those of Britain and the United States, each with a longer history of vigorous urban growth; France, by contrast, had only fifteen. In 1870, only one in twenty Germans lived in a *Grossstadt*; by 1925 it was almost one in three.[1] The brevity of this accelerated burst of urban growth meant that many of the anti-urban critics of the Weimar period could remember personally the time before the Empire was founded in 1866–1871, the *Reichsgründung*, when rural dwellers still constituted two-thirds of the German population.

Naturally, urban growth of this magnitude posed enormous and unprecedented challenges for local leaders and administrators. The growth of industry, and the migration and geographical clustering of labor to support it, led to urban concentration and a corresponding rise in pollution, crime, disease, poverty and disorder. Local governments were forced to devise frequently ad hoc plans to deal with specifically urban problems new in both scope and kind, including sewage and water treatment, refuse removal, housing regulation, and police control. Fast on the heels of these exigencies came demand for infrastructural improvements and secondary services, including roads, bridges, and canals for public and commercial transport; schools, both primary and secondary; and more efficient and effective provision of welfare and health care.[2]

Addressing these and a host of related problems, city administrations increased in size and efficiency from 1875 to 1900. City officials, drawn in the first half of the century from the ranks of local Bürgers voluntarily performing community service, by 1900 were largely career professionals. Mayors were now trained in the law; their staffs included specialists and technical experts such as architects, engineers, and accountants.[3] One response to chaotic, haphazard urban growth was the coordinated effort of administrators and planners to control growth along preconceived lines, laid out according to "scientific" principles of urban expansion. Increasingly sophisticated management of resources, land, and transportation brought spacious boulevards, neighborhood squares, green spaces, and large parks. German cities were widely admired by visitors and administrators from abroad as showplaces of what careful planning, civic spirit, and local initiative could accomplish.[4]

PEACE, WAR AND CRISIS, 1900–1924

From the turn of the century to the First World War was indisputably the era of the German cities' greatest power and freedom, their *Blütezeit.* They were the most energetic growth sectors of the economy, spending and consuming more than the German states or the Reich. By 1914, the cities' total debt amounted to RM 7.5 billion, while that of the Reich was around 5 billion. Largely unsupervised by the Reich and Land administrative bureaucracies, cities enjoyed a virtually autonomous deployment of local capital and exercise of political power. Prussian cities, for instance, set and collected their own taxes, and relied heavily on local revenues for the greater part of their income; the local surcharge on income tax covered almost half of their regular expenditure.[5]

Politically, *bürgerlich* capital and social interests continued to dominate city affairs, and local notables ran the show largely unchallenged by incursions of working-class politics until after the turn of the century. Reasons for this varied across regions and states, but can be characterized generally either as the result of exclusionary property and residence requirements or of a discriminatory franchise. In Hamburg, whose total population amounted to 600,000 in 1892, only 26,000 residents—slightly over 4 percent—retained citizenship and voting rights. In turn-of-the-century Nuremberg, where the cost of becoming a citizen equaled about ten weeks' wages for a worker, only 15.5 percent of the city population could vote in state elections, and only 8 percent for the city council. In nearby Fürth, by contrast, where there were no citizenship fees, the working classes could afford to be more active in local politics; the Fürth council had one SPD member as early as 1871, and ten by 1908. One recent estimate has put average participation in local elections at 13 percent of the Grossstadt population, ranging from 1 percent in Hanover to 20 percent in Remscheid and Spandau.[6]

Similarly, Prussia's three-tiered voting system in some cases relegated more than nine-tenths of a city's voting population to the third class of taxpayers. The most infamous example of the system's iniquities is that of Essen, where industrialist Friedrich Krupp's domination of the first-class voting category allowed him in the 1880s to elect single-handedly one-third of the city council.[7] Despite such institutional obstacles, working-class political activity and representation as a whole increased steadily in municipal politics after 1890. In Berlin, the Social Democrats held only five third-class council seats in 1883; twenty-five years later, they had won thirty-five of forty-eight seats and gained a foothold in the second class. At the outbreak of war, forty-four second-class seats were SPD; the Liberals had 98.[8] These instances of a clearly growing influence of working-class politics in local government nevertheless remained isolated breakthroughs. Overall, Liberal control of the cities remained firm until 1918.

Much changed with the arrival of war in 1914 and the transition to a war-time economy. Cities were the primary caretakers on the home-front, coordinating the distribution of food, dispensing welfare, providing shelter and health care to the wounded, widows and orphans, and functioning as critical administrative links between the central authorities and local conditions on the ground.[9] The increase in activity and responsibility carried a high price, forcing German cities to borrow increasingly large amounts on the domestic money market. Loans to the cities and states constituted 25 percent of loan bureau activity in 1916; a year later they had tripled, to 74.9 percent; and in the last year of the war rose again, to 84.5 percent. As the money market tightened, local governments were often forced to find credit on unfavorable terms, particularly in the stipulation that repayment be in foreign currency.[10] The mounting municipal debt, much of it short-term and burdened with potentially onerous conditions, did not augur well for municipal finance after the war.

NEW POSSIBILITIES

The creation of the Weimar Republic in 1918–19 implied for the cities momentous changes, as legislators, planners and administrators began to come to grips with urban growth and its attendant stresses. With the establishment of a centralized financial and tax administration throughout the Reich, the urban concentration of population and resources, previously a local problem, became an issue of national policy and administration. For the first time, urban modernity—the evolved *fact* of cities in Germany—had to be addressed consciously as a large-scale problem: how to define the cities' roles regionally and nationally so as to integrate them into the economic and constitutional fabric of the Reich?

Articles 8 and 11 of the Weimar constitution granted the Reich sole authority to levy taxation within Germany, and to set the taxes of the individual states.[11] In the late summer of 1919, Reich Finance Minister Matthias Erzberger proposed to create a "hierarchically structured Reich finance administration" whose orders of jurisdiction would descend from the Reich finance ministry to the ministries in the states, and finally to local finance agencies in the municipalities.[12] These powers were soon codified in more detail in the States' Tax Law (*Landessteuergesetz*) of 30 March 1920, which prohibited local and regional authorities from levying taxes independently.[13] With all the strands of public revenue in its hands, the Reich financial administration became, in the words of admiring American observers, "a gigantic tax machine."[14] As cogs in the machine, the cities lost their key source of income from the prewar period, the local surcharges on income and corporate taxes. Taxes were now set by the central authorities and collected by field representatives in local and district offices. Revenue was then distributed from the center outwards: from Reich to state, state to municipality. In addition to putting cities last in line for revenue distribution, this legislation tied them into a web of financial interdependence in which their own fiscal well-being depended on the healthiness of communal and state finances elsewhere in Germany. Poorer cities and towns were dependent on those that were better off, an obligation that caused considerable resentment in the latter.[15] Observing in 1930 that the expansion of city interests had "covered the country with a net of supra-communal cooperation," the German Congress of Cities (Deutscher Städtetag, DST) declared, "The time of strictly individual administration and economy is past."[16] The cities' glorious isolation was gone. But as municipal financial difficulties mounted through the Weimar period and continued into the early years of Nazi rule, it became clear that their old isolation had been replaced by a new one that denied them necessary room to maneuver and make their own decisions.

Erzberger's centralization of Reich finance in 1920 has been ranked with the *Reichsgründung* as "a great modernizing step," and "probably... the most revolutionary act in the history of the Weimar Republic."[17] But even as we acknowledge the importance of the reform, it is important to bear in mind its limits. The issue of greatest importance for the cities was whether the new system of collecting and distributing revenue realistically reflected their responsibilities and needs and, more fundamentally, their economic and constitutional positions in the Reich. Although local variations in bookkeeping practices make it risky to draw firm conclusions from the statistics available, it would appear on balance that it did not. This can be seen most clearly in the contrast between pre- and postwar levels of public spending and income. Before 1914, Reich, Land, and communal shares of public spending were 41.9, 21.8, and 36.2 percent, respectively. After 1918, the Reich, at 70 percent, became by far the biggest single public spender; the states and municipalities declined to 10 and 20 percent.[18] Cities and towns now ranked second in spending behind the Reich, yet they were below the states, or *Länder,* in the tax hierarchy, and were thus "fed with the crumbs left over" after Reich and state finances were secured.[19] Significantly, their share of total tax revenue fell from 44 percent in 1913–14 to 32 percent in 1925–26. From the cities' perspective, therefore, the overhaul of national finance in early Weimar did not reflect public spending needs, but was in reality a political holdover from the prewar days, merely a "partial centralization, superimposed on the Länder's continued authority."[20]

Constitutionally, the municipalities' position in 1920 was just as uncertain as their finances. Again, the problem can be traced to the backlog of intensive urban growth after 1870, unattended in any systematic or comprehensive way by central authorities. After the reforms of 1848 were undermined or overturned in the reaction of the following years, the rest of the century saw little or no state attention directed to the problem of communal legal reform. A survey of the charters for city, town and county governments (*Städte-*, *Gemeinde-*, and *Kreisordnungen*) in 1920 reveals a bewildering variety of legal concepts, jurisdictions, and types of communal government across the Reich and even within individual Länder—twenty-five different sets of municipal regulations in effect in Germany, nine in Prussia alone—all surviving from piece-meal local reforms in the nineteenth century.[21] No overarching standards or procedures specified forms of local government or defined the relationship of communes to the states and Reich. Supervision of communal affairs was the business of the Länder. Although local governments claimed the hallowed "right of self-administration" that dated back to the Stein reforms of the Napoleonic era, in practice this amounted essentially to little more than doing what they pleased unless otherwise prohibited by law or a higher authority.[22]

In 1919, great constitutional changes for the municipalities appeared possible. Hugo Preuss, the legal theorist and Berlin city councillor commissioned to prepare the new constitution, envisioned a Reich radically different from that of the imperial period. Strongly influenced by his teacher, the legal scholar Otto von Gierke, Preuss viewed local communities, the *Gemeinden*, as cells within a living organism. The communes would be the fundamental political and administrative building blocks of the Reich: "the state coalesces from the organic collectivity of its parts, its individuals, its members." The political challenge posed to a central state by the rapid growth of powerful cities could be answered, in Preuss's view, by strong local self-government (*Selbstverwaltung*), based on "*bürgerliche Freiheit.*"[23] Bürgers participating as local representatives and committee members would acquire the political awareness and experience necessary to make the democratic process work. Education in local political issues and experience in administering affairs at home would mold politically responsible, self-reliant citizens—locally "embedded, determined, limited social being[s]" who, learning the art of politics and the business of administration in their immediate environs, could then participate competently in the states and the Reich: "from participation in local affairs will come the impulse to participate in the state as a whole."[24]

Preuss's conception of the citizen as a geographical being provided the basis for his far-ranging proposals for constitutional reform of the individual states' powers. The thorniest problem was the division of Prussia, whose possession of almost three-fifths of Germany's territory and population created an internal power imbalance. To counter Prussia's domination of the Reich, Preuss proposed a German republic of eleven states of more or less equal size. Prussia was to be divided into provincial units; the smaller states were to be either absorbed completely by their larger neighbors or else built up into larger areas through allocation of additional territory; Austria would be a part of this new republic, with Berlin and Vienna providing the capital poles. Behind the mechanics of border shuffling lay a grander vision: a republic "built on the particularism of persistent local loyalties and provincial identities," in which the critical basic cells, the communes, enjoyed a direct relationship with the whole organism, unmediated by interference from the increasingly anachronistic state governments.[25]

Obviously, a reform of such revolutionary extent was going to encounter stiff opposition. In fact, none of Preuss's ideas survived unaltered. His draft for the new constitution fell under a revisionary assault by the states, who flatly rejected such a diminution of their power. For different reasons, delegates to the National Assembly in Weimar shrank from subdividing Prussia. The Reich needed the states whole and healthy in the postwar period of violence and upheaval to maintain order. Prussia's Social Democratic strength offered the troubled new republic stability and a firm commitment to democracy.[26] Communal self-administration thus remained constitutionally fixed in its prewar limbo. Article 127 of the Weimar Constitution did no more than describe the prevailing situation: "Communes and communal associations have the right of self-administration within the limits of the laws."[27] No further constitutional guarantees were forthcoming, and local affairs remained under the supervision of the individual states. The republican compromise did not include Preuss's most extensive reforms: Reich centralization was limited by the states' continued power; and the problem of providing for and governing Germany's increasingly powerful cities remained unaddressed.[28]

Although unclear at the time, these fiscal and constitutional developments foreshadowed the political isolation and marginal financial status that would undermine the cities' ability to stabilize and support the republic. Many municipalities came out of the war with budgetary deficits and significant levels of debt—the result of increased wartime social responsibilities, costly demobilization, the difficult transition to a peace-time economy, and inflationary depreciation of their real tax income. Greater local demand for municipal services and increasingly straitened finances left the cities no breathing-space in which to dig themselves out. Their burdens multiplied with new welfare duties in the postwar inflationary crisis. Other expenses skyrocketed too: for example, salaries of municipal civil servants and employees increased thirty-one-fold in real terms between 1918 and 1922.[29]

The cities' many new legislated social obligations in the 1920s included housing aid, support for wounded veterans, and aid to low-scale renters. The most socially significant and financially onerous of their duties, however, was caring for the poor and unemployed.[30] Prior to 1924, the Reich, states, and communes provided relief support in proportions of 3:2:1, respectively, in one of two forms: either as outright payments, or through emergency work projects (*Notstandsarbeiten*). Neither was especially satisfactory for the cities and towns that administered them. In the case of support payments, municipal administrations came under direct pressure from local unemployed workers, trade unions, and the soldiers' and workers' councils to raise relief ceilings to more realistic levels. But municipalities also had to follow strict federal guidelines when distributing relief if they wanted to receive supplemental funds from the Reich, which was thus in a good position to resist efforts by the localities to increase relief payments. In addition, after November 1921, emergency funds were funneled through the Länder, who then determined how they would be allocated to the cities on the basis of local need. According to Gerald Feldman, "The Reich was treating the municipalities in the same manner as the municipalities were being compelled to treat its citizens on poor relief; namely, require them to undergo a means test and humiliating and ungainly procedures in order to get assistance."[31]

Emergency work projects, initiated and run by the cities, made more political sense than paying relief outright. They gave work to the potentially restless and troublesome unemployed, and the authorities could be seen actively and productively engaged in reconstruction. In Berlin, a large influx of veterans and refugees in 1919–20 exacerbated an unemployment problem made already acute by the disruptive transition from a wartime to peacetime economy. As many as sixteen thousand unemployed worked on a massive project to expand the city's public transit system. In late 1923, even small towns put the long-term unemployed to work cleaning and maintaining streets, squares and graveyards, sprucing up and planting public parks, directing traffic, doing office work and, for women, cleaning and cooking in municipal soup kitchens. The municipalities downplayed both their coercive aspects and the hours of work, and uniformly reported themselves satisfied with the results, despite the fact that emergency projects made little economic sense. Employing workers on projects cost more than supporting them with relief payments.[32]

At its height in late 1923, the hyperinflation brought daily uncertainty, anxiety, and misery to metropolitan and small-town inhabitants alike. In the industrial Ruhr district, unemployment in October and November exceeded 50 percent. By the end of the year, one in four Berliners was on social relief of some kind. Even those with income had little reason to feel secure. The timing of financial transactions was so critical, that being paid in the morning rather than the afternoon could make a difference in real-wage value of 100 percent. The "pressure to spend the money received quickly and correctly" for even simple purchases could be enormously stressful.[33]

City administrations also experienced lasting traumatization as they tried desperately to create order out of economic chaos. According to Paul Mitzlaff, who in 1923 was managing director of the *Deutsche Städtetag*

(German Congress of Cities, DST), "Tax payments, fixed on one day and paid another, were not worth the paper on which the tax bill was written."[34] City budgets during the Weimar period as a rule were neat and orderly affairs, printed and published in bound volumes. But for 1923 no budgets appeared—a lapse unrepeated in even the darkest years of the Depression. According to urban historian Jürgen Reulecke, it is still impossible to obtain a clear picture of the effect of the inflation on municipal finance. The extreme and unprecedented volatility of the inflation made it impossible to pinpoint its causes accurately, let alone formulate effective countermeasures. Uncertainty over what the mark would do daily, even hourly, rendered futile all efforts to chart current finance or plan for the future.[35]

Faced with rising costs, an increasing welfare burden, and a depreciating mark, the municipalities had a number of possible ways to raise revenue, and they tried them all: raising the communal taxes they still controlled; calling on the Reich for help; borrowing on credit; and printing their own emergency currency. At first, the weight of their efforts lay in trying to regain their old right to add a communal surcharge on income tax.[36] But the time-lag was too great between the assessment and collection of taxes and the redistribution of revenues by the Reich and Länder. Even with the switch in 1921 from yearly to quarterly assessments of income and corporation taxes, yields continued to lag behind inflation. The Reich was also frequently late making distribution payments. Berlin received seven-eighths of its 1920 transfer sum only in 1922; transfers slated for 1921 were not paid out until May and August 1922.[37] With the realization that any time-lag would work to their disadvantage in a calculated tax on income, and since consumer spending did not slacken in the inflation, the cities altered their taxation policies in favor of those taxes that were keyed to consumption and so regulated directly by the economy itself. The central element in this scheme was the turnover tax (*Umsatzsteuer*), viewed increasingly by the municipalities as the "flexible factor" they needed to compensate for the vagaries of the economy.[38]

Added to the main taxes on income, sales, and business, came various taxes on consumption and sundries, including dogs, entertainment, beer, and hotels. Before the First World War, in 1913, taxes on the private sector made up 12.3 percent of Berlin's municipal revenue; by 1921, they had jumped to 38 percent. Even then, the increase fell short of the cities' needs. Moreover, what was widely perceived as tax-gouging brought local governments lasting hostility from taxpayers. The municipalities' relations with private business also soured as they desperately tacked ever-increasing communal surcharges on trade and property taxes. More than one urban historian has viewed the increased municipal tax burden as the "principal factor" in the fierce public criticism directed at city finance later in the 1920s.[39]

The second option, that of covering municipal deficits with emergency subventions from the Reich (*Reichshilfe*), was beset with drawbacks. The cities objected that such a course ran counter to the twin tenets of financial self-sufficiency and independent local self-government. They saw in Reich subventions a dangerous centralization of financial power and decision-making. In any case, the areas of heaviest municipal expense not covered by ordinary supplements—including construction and employee salaries—when combined with the depreciation of funds "between payment and receipt of the subsidies," undercut any real aid that Reichshilfe might have offered. Nonetheless, when many cities faced default on their salary- and bill-payments in October 1922, desperation forced them to petition for help, which they received in a one-time emergency grant of RM 14 billion.[40]

Unable to obtain sufficient funds either locally or from Berlin, the cities were forced to print their own money or to borrow it elsewhere. In the first instance, emergency currency or *Notgeld*, printed by city and district authorities, by the Länder, and by large private firms such as Krupp, had played an important role both during and after the war in making up cash shortfalls and keeping local finances liquid. In early 1923, the cities estimated that approximately 12.5 billion marks of municipal Notgeld were in circulation, a sum equivalent to 7.6 billion gold marks. Although not officially sanctioned prior to the inflation, emergency money was acknowledged as a necessary evil by the Reich Finance Ministry and Reichsbank after 1914. With the inflation, however, its use got dangerously out of hand and was forbidden by law on 17 July 1922; the law was unenforceable. Aware of the inflationary damage that uncontrolled local money production could inflict, the cities acknowledged that notes should not be issued without backing and, as a rule, cooperated with the Reich Finance Ministry to ensure that scrip production was centrally supervised. But printing nevertheless got out of hand, especially in Rhenish cities, where French troops occupied printing offices and seized money shipments from Berlin. There were also, of course, local risks in producing money. Printing Notgeld indeed brought quick relief to constricted local finances, but the relief was temporary and, in the long term, added to the cities' reputation for irresponsible financial practices. The quick currency fix was not always available when needed, either, as cities desperate for cash waited for permission to print from the Reich Finance Ministry.[41] Unfortunately, they often had no choice: with no help forthcoming from the Reich, or when it came too late, "simply nothing remained for the cities except to produce emergency money, be it without permission and without backing."[42]

Such a course was therefore one of last resort for desperate local authorities. Cities more usually turned to borrowing in Germany and abroad. Before the war, the purpose of municipal borrowing was to cover "extraordinary" budget items, defined as those paid for through loans or bond issues and spread over a number of years, hence falling outside the annual flows of income and expenditure.[43] Especially prominent in this category were large-scale construction projects. After the war, however, local administrators turned increasingly to loans simply to cover "ordinary" expenses such as welfare and salaries. According to statistics compiled by the Städtetag, the municipal floating debt in February 1923 stood at RM 33.8 billion, with an additional RM 53.2 billion pending in projected loans.[44] On balance, this appears moderate. Although it was relatively easy to obtain foreign loans in the early 1920s, municipalities were cautious borrowers, circulating warnings amongst themselves about the dangers of easy foreign credit and on the whole exerting collective self-restraint.[45] It should be remembered, too, that Reichsmark numbering in the billions meant little during the hyperinflation. In June 1923, for example, the city council of Frankfurt am Main approved a seemingly phenomenal municipal budget of 210 billion marks; five months later, the same sum could be earned by one skilled worker in twenty minutes.[46] It is thus difficult to assign meaning to such figures.

Indeed, the chaos of the hyperinflation makes any conclusion about its effects speculative and impressionistic.[47] A number of tentative points can be made, however, concerning its long-term resonance in municipal finance later in the 1920s and early 1930s, and what it reveals about the collective status of cities in the republic. First, the economic catastrophes of the early 1920s showed the Erzberger reforms at their worst. The cities' constitutional and financial isolation erected barriers of distrust between them and central authorities on one hand, and the German populace on the other. Even at the height of the crisis in 1923, Reich financial authorities were unwarrantedly dismissive about the cities' efforts to cut local spending.[48] Believing municipal administrators to be profligate spenders, reckless borrowers, and irresponsible money printers, they scathingly criticized the cities' "unhealthy financial practices."[49] Similarly, increased taxation by municipal authorities desperate for more income gained them enduring antipathy from local inhabitants and hostility from business circles.[50] Moreover, the latter phases of hyperinflation allowed most cities to pay off their creditors, principally communal savings banks (*Sparkassen*), with depreciated paper currency. Many emerged from the crisis relatively debt-free, but at the expense of their own credit institutions and account holders.[51] Popular animosity was not lessened by the widespread impression that the cities had profited by the inflation, escaping relatively unscathed and with their coffers full.[52] Official mistrust of local finance emerged full-blown in 1927, when the Reich Finance Ministry and the Reichsbank blocked the cities' access to foreign money markets, and reached its extreme in the infamous public attacks on municipal borrowing and spending by Reichsbank president Hjalmar Schacht.[53]

For their part, the cities brought away hard lessons. Dealing on their own with financial crisis and hyperinflation hammered home their isolation and essential powerlessness. Municipal administrators consequently came to adopt an everyone-for-himself mentality that, despite their collective challenges, seriously eroded inter-city solidarity. Thrown back on their own resources by a central government with little sympathy for their plight and less aid to offer, they were forced to borrow. As reconstruction began in earnest in 1924, municipal spending and borrowing rose sharply. "No spending without funds," an axiom of communal finance before the inflation, was replaced by a fatalist acceptance of high levels of spending and debt.[54] For the rest of the 1920s, borrowing became the "flexible factor" covering the cities' deficits.

THE AGENTS OF THE NEW REPUBLIC

One of the German Revolution's cardinal weaknesses in 1918–19 was that although its first practice was the seizure of power from local authorities, its aims remained largely national in scope. In the critical words of one historian, "Weimar democracy was not perceived to be based on local foundations."[55] Rather than overturning the old order's local bases of power, the soldiers' and workers' councils interfered little in the day-to-day business of local government, choosing instead to collaborate with local authorities. For their part, municipal administrators exhibited astute flexibility in dealing with the councils, adapting and cooperating where necessary to avoid damaging confrontations, revealing a spirit of "civil corporatism" that dampened the local effects of the postwar political upheaval.[56] By early 1920, most of the councils were gone, leaving little imprint on municipal administrations. Many localities thus retained personnel and perspectives that dated from the imperial period.[57]

In local politics, the principal change wrought by the revolution and the founding of the republic was the extension of voting rights to all Germans over the age of twenty. The lifting of the restricted prewar franchise, one of the Liberals' most effective tools for maintaining their hold on local governments before the war, naturally suggests a shift of local power from the old elites to working-class parties of the left. A survey of party affiliations of municipal council members in 1920 shows, however, that despite considerable numbers of SPD and USPD representatives in the Grossstädte, especially in Prussia, political strength in the smaller cities and towns was more evenly divided. The presence of new special-interest parties devoted to civil servants and employees, veterans, and agricultural reform, as well as regional groups like the German-Hanoverian Party, highlights a new openness in local political life and a corresponding increase in the importance of public opinion.[58]

The new presence of parties hitherto excluded from the city halls must be viewed within the context of an overall continuity of personnel within municipal administrations. Largely unaffected by the revolution, local administrations exhibited a remarkable degree of continuity before and after the war. Mayors and their staff-members served considerably longer terms than councillors, from six to twelve years, and many of the most prominent Bürgermeister from the imperial period continued in office through the twenties and early thirties.[59] For mayors, in particular, the republican period was one of extraordinary power and prestige. Largely independent of state supervision and free of restraint by political parties, they chaired meetings of municipal councils, whether unicameral or bicameral. Many served on important regional and state committees. Gustav Stresemann noted famously in his diary:

> The mayors of today's Germany are in reality, after the big industrialists, the kings of the present age. Elected for long periods, many undismissable, they are more powerful than ministers and also currently function essentially as legislators and political leaders.[60]

Being elected Oberbürgermeister of an important city also provided a convenient springboard to prominence on a larger stage. Konrad Adenauer (Cologne), Hans Luther (Essen), Wilhelm Külz (Dresden), Carl Goerdeler (Königsberg and Leipzig), and Franz Bracht (Essen), to name a few, all went on to play more or less pivotal roles in state and Reich politics.[61]

If Weimar "never really made the transition from a 'war society' to a 'peace society,'" as Richard Bessel has suggested, then inter-party cooperation and agreement in municipal politics—fostered during the Kaiserreich by a common familiarity with local problems and during the war by a declaration of social truce, or *Burgfrieden*, on the home front—would seem to have persisted well into the Weimar period.[62] Parties of right and left were at their most reformist and cooperative at the local level. This was evident even in the 1890s, when after the SPD's 1893 congress in Cologne, the party lifted its ban on socialist participation in local politics. Party theorists judged local administration and politics to be somehow unpolitical: whereas the state was "above all an institution of domination, a mechanism for the domination of *men by men*," municipal government was simply "an administrative organization, a mechanism for the administration of *things by men*."[63] The pragmatic willingness of socialist council members to work with liberal municipal administrations suggests that a truce was already operating in the cities when war broke out in 1914, as local SPD organizations provided the social grease to smooth relations between workers, trade unions, local governments and military administrators.[64]

In Weimar, the sense of community and the magnitude of obstacles to be overcome for postwar recovery made it easier to identify problems and agree on courses of action, and made pragmatism a virtue in local government. Paul Mitzlaff, for instance, who led the Städtetag in the first half of the 1920s, characterized a city administration's "daily necessity of discharging detailed practical duties," as "a school of training in the exercise of reason, tolerance, and compromise."[65] Ben Lieberman argues that a broadly based "consensus of recovery" prevailed in German cities, encouraged "municipal activism," and fed "a wide range of ambitious and sometimes successful programs in pursuit of recovery."[66] This may be too easy: nothing encourages consensus more strongly than prosperity. Yet within the political frame created by the wider postwar franchise, the evidence suggests that a Burgfrieden of sorts did exist in local governments and continued to hold after the war ended—a consensus (or, more properly, a willingness to compromise) of left, right, and center in municipal politics concerning the proper direction of economic, social, and governmental energies to build after the war and establish stability in the republic. Political interests and parties at the local level, despite their differences, agreed on the broad goals of recovery and reconstruction.[67]

Those goals were laid out in detail in *The Future Tasks of German Cities* (1922), a book edited by Städtetag director Mitzlaff and his more famous predecessor, Hans Luther, along with the chairman of the Association for Communal Economy and Communal Politics, Erwin Stein. Many of the authors were prominent local leaders and theoreticians of communal law; some had risen to state and federal office in the republic.[68] The essays covered every conceivable aspect of communal activity—from constitutional issues to internal administration, municipal finance to education, housing to fire brigades and police, public utilities to puppet theaters. The essayists presented cities as energetically impatient to tackle the tasks they catalogued so thoroughly. Confidence and optimism for the future were summed up clearly in the book's rallying cry: "Cities forward! (*Städte voran!*)."[69]

It has become commonplace to refer to the years after the inflation as ones of "relative" and even "deceptive" stabilization, in that they "seem stable only by contrast with the periods of crisis that preceded and followed them."[70] The same conditions held for the cities. In simple physical terms, many grew in size and population as they absorbed land and communities around them—most spectacularly in the consolidation of metropolitan Berlin in 1920, and in the even greater administrative reform of the Rhineland in 1929.[71] Costly, large-scale municipal building projects were also undertaken in this period. Underground transportation systems in Berlin and Hamburg were underway by the mid-1920s; Cologne opened a new harbor on the Rhine; Berlin, Düsseldorf and Stuttgart built municipal airports. Düsseldorf Oberbürgermeister Robert Lehr exhorted his city council in 1925, "We must do everything to see that this cultural progress does not pass us by. We must take part wherever currently possible."[72] In an atmosphere of marked inter-city competition, many Grossstädte erected lavish exhibition halls. Berlin, Cologne, Düsseldorf, Essen, and Stuttgart all financed and hosted giant exhibitions, each requiring years of financial planning and local construction work.[73]

Less ostentatious but of greater significance was the broad spectrum of city caretaking activity and municipal enterprise: in other words, the maintenance and expansion of the built urban environment, and provision for the welfare and prosperity of local inhabitants. Most prominent and expensive were the funding and management of public transportation and utilities, and the construction of affordable housing. By 1927, the great majority of streetcar concerns were controlled, either directly or indirectly, by the cities.[74] Public transportation also underwent extensive rationalization. Berlin in 1927 unified its subways, streetcars and buses into a single transport system, and two years later created the Berliner Verkehrs-Aktiengesellschaft as a commercialized utility company.[75] All told, the municipalities were responsible in the latter half of the twenties for over four-fifths of water, gas, and electricity output in Germany.[76] Production of electricity, in particular, grew steadily after 1900, and slackened only in 1930 when demand fell and financing grew scarce.[77]

Housing too, after a long-standing shortage, and a virtual halt in construction during the war years, was a first priority after stabilization. Most estimates after 1923 placed the shortage at around 600,000 units; according to a housing census of May 1927, one in ten German families was without a dwelling of its own.[78] To remedy this, landlords who had paid off mortgages with low-value paper currency during the inflation became subject after 1924 to a Reich Property Equity Tax on buildings constructed prior to 1918. The tax was collected by the Länder, who then passed on a portion to the communes to subsidize local building.[79] All told, housing construction and renovation costs absorbed 17.8 percent of German gross domestic investment from 1925 to 1929, with public authorities providing between 40 and 60 percent of the financing. The number of new and converted units increased every year from 1924 to 1929, and total output tripled over the period.[80] At the peak of construction in 1929, 80 percent of new houses were financed to some degree with public funds.[81] Within the financial constraints imposed on the communes and states, therefore, the undertaking was a qualified success.

In sum, the principal characteristics of the myth of an urban republic—the growing independence, financial and political power of cities and a predominantly urban, cosmopolitan culture—emerged most clearly in the half-decade between the inflation and the Depression. That the cities' golden era corresponds to the republic's most productive and crisis-free years in the mid-twenties says much about the larger structural and economic factors outlined here as determinants of urban productivity and the viability of the Weimar constitutional and financial environment.

Cooperation and consensus within municipal administrations broke down in the later 1920s not over the ultimate goals of reconstruction, but over methods and means. Competition for the political and cultural authority to determine which direction a renascent Germany should take, led to struggles for access to funds and control over their use. Narrowing definitions of success meant less room for compromise. Utility rates, for instance, were one of the few sources of income wholly controlled by the cities. They played an increasingly important role in balancing municipal budgets, in some cases compensating for shortfalls by as much as 25 percent.[82] Not surprisingly, the cities' reliance on profits from publicly funded, tax-exempt utilities drew complaints of unfair competition from the private sector. Since high rates and public funding smacked of creeping socialism, the right favored hiking user rates while the left, concerned about working-class customers having to pay higher rates, favored raising taxes instead.[83] Similar disputes, some aesthetic and ideological, others focusing on favoritism and exorbitant spending, arose in many areas of municipal activity, especially in the design of publicly funded housing and the municipal patronage of modernist architecture and art.[84] The erosion of consensus took on ominous tones with the onset of the Depression, as narrowing reconstruction possibilities encouraged factional strife in municipal politics. Polarized city councils unable to pass their budgets in the early 1930s inclined many exasperated municipal executives to favor more authoritarian schemes of city government, brought emergency decrees and state intervention, and discredited communal self-administration in the eyes of the public and the central authorities.

THE WEAKEST SHOULDERS

The cities' isolation, however—the lack of clearly defined constitutional rights and powers, and their financial dependence on the central administration—points to a larger problem: municipal challenges received little or no acknowledgment at the central or state levels of government. In other words, urban modernity remained unassimilated during the republican years. The inflationary period set the pattern. The cities possessed a modicum of cultural and political prestige, were run by pragmatic local governments, and wielded considerable economic power. But they remained financially hamstrung or, in their own bitter phrase, "pensioners of the Reich"—dependent on borrowing, subventions, and handouts, even as they suffered damaging criticism from conservative administrators and representatives of the private sector.[85]

One of the critical issues of municipal finance after the Erzberger Reform became the setting of distribution payments, codified in a complex system of Reich regulations and laws known collectively as the *Finanzausgleich*. In principle, the Länder received from the Reich set percentages of the revenue from various taxes—the most important being the taxes on income and corporations—and then subdivided the funds between their districts and municipalities. Depending on which state and tax was involved, the amount transferred to the cities was determined partly by general guidelines laid down by the Reich, partly by the size of the municipality and its consequent spending burden, and partly by each state's past practice in distributing its tax revenues. Income from some taxes was earmarked for specific purposes. Yields from the tax on motor vehicles, for instance, went towards maintaining public roads and bridges, with the funds going to the authorities responsible in the cities, counties or provinces.[86]

The main problem with the *Finanzausgleich* was that it never firmed up into a stable system of revenue distribution. As a "permanently temporary" arrangement, it was the subject of a continuous and ultimately fruitless tug-of-war between Reich, Länder, and municipalities. In the course of currency stabilization, the Third Emergency Tax Decree of February 1924 increased the states' and municipalities' percentage of the key taxes on income and business from 75 percent to 90 percent.[87] As the crisis abated and the economy picked up speed, the Reich naturally pressed to regain its lost ground; the Länder and the cities just as naturally wished to hold onto the extra income as expenses rose.[88] This deadlock, and the general erosion of goodwill between center and periphery during and after the inflation, resulted in a series of stopgap measures from 1924 to 1929 that left the issue unresolved.[89] The entire question became moribund after the Emergency Decree of 1 December 1930, which regulated the distribution of finance until 1933. The problem was thus never settled, but it retained ominous significance for the cities. Total municipal income from taxes after 1925—the period when expenditure for reconstruction skyrocketed—rose only in small increments.[90] In 1930, it began to drop steeply and by 1933, was at two-thirds of its 1929 level. Even though the cities undertook draconian savings measures and by 1933 had cut expenditures by roughly the same margin, the resulting layoffs in municipal employment, combined with unprecedented increases in unemployment support, pushed many of them to the brink of bankruptcy.

The cities' assumption of tremendous social burdens, combined with their extensive reconstruction projects after stabilization, made finding operating capital their first priority. A comparison of municipal expenses between 1911 and 1925, the first year for which comprehensive Reich statistics were collected, shows an average increase of 183 percent for all municipalities with a population over fifty thousand; by contrast, expenses not covered in the regular budget (known collectively as the *Zuschussbedarf*) grew an average of 255 percent.[91] As the Zuschussbedarf shows specific areas where municipal spending increased or declined, it provides a useful illustration of how the cities used their resources.[92] Municipal budget figures show, not surprisingly, that the categories of expenditure experiencing the greatest increase after 1925 were welfare and unemployment support—in Frankfurt's case, for example, by a reported factor of five in 1927–28.[93] The "Labor Exchange and Unemployment Law" of 1927 was designed to relieve the burden by establishing a system of unemployment insurance based on employer and employee contributions, and seemed initially promising. But with the advent of the Depression however, the relief setup of 1927 in fact ended up *increasing* the municipal burden. The critical factor was "crisis relief" (*Krisenfürsorge*), which covered workers whose eligibility for unemployment insurance ran out after the allotted fifty-two weeks. After 1927, the cities carried one-fifth of this cost.[94] Once crisis coverage expired, the long-term unemployed were wholly dependent on local welfare. The shortcomings of this arrangement were soon evident. Forecasts for unemployment after 1927 remained consistently low and the new central welfare agency, the Reich Board for Labor Exchange and Unemployment Insurance, was in the red from the beginning. The full extent of the failure to better understand the conjunctural causes of unemployment, and to compensate for it more effectively through local relief and municipal finance, became clear with the arrival of the Depression three years later. With the cities deep in financial crisis, suffering under emergency decrees and on the edge of bankruptcy, the Städtetag observed with admirable understatement that "developments from 1927 to 1932 were completely different than expected."[95] The relief structure set up in 1927 had in fact ended up laying "the heaviest burden of the unemployment crisis... on the financially weakest shoulders."[96]

The inflation years had undermined the cities' finances and left them keenly aware they could expect little help from state and federal authorities; the *Finanzausgleich* showed itself to be chronically inadequate for their growing needs. They thus turned to borrowing, both domestically and abroad. Many of the Grossstädte got so used to foreign credit in this period that they spent the money before the loan received state approval.[97] In total, German municipalities assumed domestic and foreign loans between 1924 and 1930 amounting to roughly 7.5 billion marks, about 60 percent of which was spent on transportation, utilities and housing—far and away the most socially significant of the communes' economic activities.[98] This level of municipal indebtedness was fairly moderate: just prior to the war the cities had accumulated a much larger debt of RM 10.5 billion, while in England and Wales, both before and after the war, municipal debt was comparable to or greater than that in Germany.[99]

Relative moderation in local borrowing did not keep industrial and business circles from protesting vehemently against the ostensible favoritism accorded the cities, however. Industry, private banks, the Reichsbank, and to a lesser extent Reich government officials, felt that American credit should go first to German business.[100] They argued that cities irresponsibly ignored the larger financial implications of their actions as they focused on their immediate needs and local projects, borrowing exorbitantly, spending extravagantly, and sapping Germany's economic strength. To control local borrowing abroad, a decree of Reich President Ebert on 29 January 1925 established a special Advisory Board for Foreign Credit (*Beratungsstelle für Auslandskredite*) to advise the Länder whether to approve the borrowing proposals submitted by their local governments.[101] The board consisted of five members: two bank representatives from Prussia and Bavaria and one from the state in which the proposal originated, as well as one representative each from the Reichsbank and the Reich Finance Ministry; the board was chaired by the latter. Despite the fact that the majority of all loan proposals originated with the municipalities, no communal representative sat on the board. This reflected its underlying purpose: to restrict borrowing abroad by local authorities, and so favor the German private sector in the competition for foreign credit.[102] In this aim the board was largely successful. Only 65 percent of municipal loan proposals were approved during its first two years in operation, compared to 89 percent for the Länder, a gap that widened even further in subsequent years.[103]

The Advisory Board's decisions were based on liberal economic conceptions of the measures and conditions necessary to return the German economy to health and, more immediately, to meet and overcome the challenge posed by the reparations burden. The board approved municipal loans only if the funds were for demonstrably "urgent, necessary, and productive" purposes. The key criterion underlying its assessments was "productivity"—in actuality a cluster of concepts that came to have special resonance in debates over public finance in the latter half of the decade. Productive loans were those that directly improved industrial production, increased German exports, and could be paid out of the regular budget and required no further financing.[104]

Finding agreement on the meaning of "productivity" was complicated by pressure from the Allied powers to maximize and speed economic recovery so that Germany could pay war reparations. The Dawes Plan of 1924, for example, provided for an "Agent-General for Reparations," American banker S. Parker Gilbert, whose supervisory duties were to exact as full a measure of reparations as possible without destabilizing the German economy.[105] Gilbert's periodic reports on German productivity and finance received the closest attention in Germany and abroad in the mid-1920s, and his opinions exerted considerable influence in German banking and financial circles.[106] As his reports grew increasingly critical of municipal spending, and of the cities generally as loose cannons in the German economy, foreign and internal pressure mounted on the German government to control the cities' spending and exclude them from foreign loan markets. The cities, for their part, countered that Gilbert considered virtually all cultural expenditures to be "Luxusausgaben," and complained that he showed little understanding for the peculiarities of Germany's situation or the burdens of postwar reconstruction.[107]

These two threads of hostility to municipal finance—one domestic, emanating from German industry and private banks, the other foreign, issuing from Gilbert and, by extension, the Dawes Plan guarantors—came together in Reichsbank President Hjalmar Schacht, who aspired to centralize the control of German public finance in the Reichsbank. After 1924, the bank's power and influence were such that it functioned as a quasi-independent, shadow government within the Reich.[108] Control of Weimar financial policy became a contest for power between the federal government and the Reichsbank—a struggle that relegated cities to hapless third parties caught in the middle. In a widely-noted speech at Bochum on 18 November 1927, Schacht claimed they possessed neither the self-control nor the larger perspective necessary to keep from borrowing exorbitantly and irresponsibly. He declared that "each individual city administration sees only the expenses within its own narrow realm of activity," and contrasted the cities' limited vision with that of the Reichsbank, which had to "keep in view the entirety of economic and currency questions."[109] Schacht focused the weight of his criticism on what he called the cities' "luxury spending" (*Luxusausgaben*) on construction and development projects, including sports stadiums, swimming pools and parks, exhibition halls, office buildings, hotels, museums, and airports. Although Schacht admitted that he did not have complete figures on these expenditures, he claimed that what he did have justified his conclusion that they amounted to almost all of the municipal foreign debt.[110]

The cities responded immediately and with vigor. One day after Schacht's speech, Oskar Mulert, president of the Städtetag, criticized Schacht sharply: "It is hard to understand how a public figure who occupies a responsible post in German economic life could raise such grave accusations without firm foundations."[111] In a lengthy article several weeks later, Mulert rejected Schacht's "baseless attacks on the cities," countering categorically, "No dollar, no guilder, no pound of foreign loans has been used for so-called unproductive purposes!" Mulert pointed out that in terms of the overall long-term indebtedness of German municipalities in 1927, foreign loans comprised a mere 10 percent of the 5.5 billion mark total. Of forty-two German Grossstädte, twenty-one had foreign long-term debts totaling RM 406 million; of that figure, only RM 77.4 million, or 19.1 percent, had been allocated for anything other than "urgent" purposes.[112] Many of the latter "non-essential" expenses, such as the construction of halls and stadiums, were in fact continuations of postwar emergency work-creation projects undertaken at the orders of the Reich government.[113] Obviously, the cities' definition of "productive" economic activity was necessarily more expansive than that of the Advisory Board or the Reichsbank, based on local experience of what promoted production and economic strength in real but often indeterminate terms. Mulert accused Schacht of ignoring Germany's most valuable resource, people: "Germany is poor in resources, poor in capital. The capacity for labor of German workers forms the most valuable foundation of our economic productivity." In building healthy housing, providing facilities for leisure and sports activities, and supporting youth programs, the cities were developing a healthier environment and nurturing a more productive working class, so contributing tangibly and directly to German economic productivity.[114] Mulert predicted that Schacht's agenda to centralize public finance would turn the process of assessing local spending and borrowing into a bureaucratic morass in which direct knowledge of and input from the localities would play no part. Finally, he warned that excluding the cities completely from foreign money markets would increase unemployment. Laid-off city workers would require unprecedented levels of relief support—inarguably an unproductive way to spend public money.[115] The debate between advocates of public and private spending remained unresolved. The Advisory Board's activities continued until the onset of the Depression, when energies were turned to holding off creditors rather than controlling access to credit.

The cities' weakness compared to both the private sectors and the agencies of Reich economic and financial management throws into high relief their lack of integration in Weimar's administration and economy. Both the exigencies of the inflation and the tasks of reconstruction afterward required tremendous increases in public spending, and "the main burden, both of work and expenditure, fell upon the cities."[116] Unfortunately, this was just at the point when renascent Weimar conservatives in industry and finance were again in a position to make such spending a political liability. The Reichsbank's greatest hope for increased power lay in extending its financial jurisdiction into other realms of policy and management by defining social and political problems in terms of finance. Accusations of municipal corruption and irresponsibility thus played a key role in Schacht's campaign to arrogate to the Reichsbank control over public spending.[117]

In the legal realm, too, Weimar constitutional scholars questioned, and ultimately undermined, the cities' position within the state. Roland Brauweiler, for instance, followed Otto von Gierke in noting the dual nature of the commune as both "part of a higher organism" and "an organism in itself." This dualism was inherent in the functions and activities of local governments, who looked after their own affairs (*Selbstverwaltungsangelegenheiten*) while simultaneously performing services delegated by state and federal authorities (*Auftragsangelegenheiten*). Brauweiler contended that with so much overlap between the jurisdictions and duties of central and local governments, it was impossible to divide realistically the realm of local and state affairs.[118] Going further, conservative critics Ernst Forsthoff, Arnold Köttgen, Carl Schmitt and Hans Peters expressed serious reservations about city power.[119] Identifying the fundamental issue as one of plurality within a democratic state, each of these writers compared a (highly inaccurate) portrayal of a prewar public administration untainted by politics with the postwar "politicization" of public life and administration. They concluded that increasing activism by powerful municipalities posed a threat to the internal stability of the Reich and Länder.[120] Cities continued to run a distant third in the Reich-Land-Stadt triad.

IN THE DEPRESSION

Because the three-tiered system of unemployment, "crisis," and welfare support set up in 1926–27 was predicated on chronically low estimates of unemployment, and the final safety net for the long-term unemployed remained the local welfare rolls, the arrival of chronic economic crisis revealed the system's structural shortcomings in a fashion especially brutal for the cities. As the Depression persisted after 1930, the unemployed fell back on crisis relief in increasing numbers as their eligibility for regular insurance payments ran out. Once that was exhausted, they had no option but to turn to local welfare. In December 1930, 2.1 million unemployed were receiving insurance, 0.6 million crisis relief, and 0.7 million welfare. In October of the following year, the number of unemployed on the municipal welfare rolls, roughly 1.3 million, for the first time surpassed those on unemployment insurance and crisis relief. In December 1932, the positions were fully reversed, with 0.8 million on unemployment, 1.2 million on crisis relief, and 2.4 million on welfare. According to the Städtetag, total municipal annual expenditure on crisis relief and welfare more than quintupled during the period 1929-32—from 0.3 billion to 1.6 billion marks.[121]

As expenses rose, municipal income dropped drastically. Transfer payments decreased by half, and revenue from local taxes by slightly less than one-third. In sum, the extraordinary expansion of municipal finance after 1925 was followed by an even swifter contraction after 1930. The critical factor was welfare expenditure. Continuing to rise even as the communal economy shrank, it consumed an ever greater percentage of the municipal budget. Profits from municipal utilities were diverted to make up the welfare deficit, but it was not enough.[122]

The cities were aware from the start of the potential danger that local fiscal distress posed to their autonomy. Their greatest fear was that the Reich and Land governments would take the opportunity to institute harsh supervisory measures to forcibly balance municipal budgets. The resulting damage to local self-government would long outlast the immediate crisis.[123] High pressure was exerted centrally by the Städtetag on its city-members to police themselves, impose their own spending cuts, suspend building projects, cut salaries and—above all—abstain from further borrowing. DST president Mulert reminded the cities of the fiscal and moral extent of their care-taking obligations in emergencies, but also warned of their vulnerability to central fiat and public criticism in times of crisis. He called on city administrators to exercise the greatest care and sobriety in managing municipal affairs, and to impose the severest spending cuts on themselves. Only in this way could they avoid negative publicity, public censure, and possible state or federal intervention.[124] The resulting local saving measures cut city spending overall from RM 750 per person in 1929 to RM 700 a year later, and RM 630 in 1931.[125] All told, the cities claimed by 1932 to have saved a total of 1.7 billion marks.[126]

But the cuts were insufficient. By 1932, many cities were in default on their loan payments, among them Cologne, Gelsenkirchen, Dortmund and Altona.[127] The same polarization in national and regional politics was evident in local city halls as the councils, hamstrung by particularist protest parties and beset by increasingly trenchant left- and right-wing radical demands, were unable to pass legislation or manage finance.[128] As the crisis worsened, municipal fears of central intervention proved justified. Emergency Decrees (*Notverordnungen*, NVOs) imposed in the early 1930s by the Brüning government aimed to increase revenue by raising taxes and decreasing spending by cutting social benefits.[129] Several decrees clustered in mid-1931 were directed specifically at the cities. A decree of 5 June cut by 5 percent the unemployment and crisis benefits administered by local governments, and imposed new "crisis supplements" as direct Reich taxes to which the Länder and cities had no access, thus further depleting local revenue.[130] On 5 August, a new decree prohibited cities from borrowing from their own communal savings institutions (*Sparkassen*). The impetus behind this drastic move came from the Reichsbank, which stipulated that it would grant credit to the Sparkassen only if the funds did not go to the cities.[131] The infamous *Dietramszell* decree of 24 August for "Securing the Budgets of Reich, Länder and Communes," empowered the state governments to cut spending without consulting their parliaments, and extended their powers of supervision and interference in local affairs.[132] Taking their cue from the Reich, the Länder followed suit. In Prussia, a decree of 12 September allowed Oberbürgermeister to ignore city councils when implementing spending cuts. Finally, the decree of 31 October 1931 cut transfer payments to the Länder and communes, without consultation in either case. The cities, who had worked to establish a closer relationship with the Reich constitutionally and financially, naturally perceived the decrees of mid-1931 as catastrophic attacks on their autonomy.[133]

The second aspect of increased central control took a more direct and personal form. Beginning in late 1930, Prussia installed state commissioners to oversee municipal finances in towns experiencing financial trouble—especially those holding back state tax revenues in order to pay their own expenses first. The commissioners were empowered to force the approval of budgets and, more generally, to ensure that cities and towns were financially viable and capable of providing basic services. The commissioners were authorized to increase existing taxes or impose new ones if they or their superiors deemed it necessary to restore fiscal order.[134] Unpopular taxes on beer, alcohol, and polls were introduced in over 90 percent of the 541 Prussian cities and towns that had commissioners by December 1930.[135]

The emergency decrees and the state commissioners pose difficulties of interpretation and perspective. Just as it is difficult to avoid determinism in assessing the republic's fall to Nazism, it is hard not to see the decay of municipal self-government during the Depression as part of a more comprehensive breakdown of republican institutions. Some postwar historiography has balanced contemporary protests against state infringements on local power by stressing the severity and extent of the crisis, and by pointing to the limited nature of the decrees and the commissioners' powers. Harold James, for instance, is at pains to emphasize that despite their desperate situation, some German cities still showed themselves stubbornly unwilling to change their borrowing and spending practices even in the deepest point of the crisis. While he gives due weight to the constitutional damage wrought by the emergency decrees and acknowledges their more draconian aspects, he nonetheless presents them as the logical fallout of any policy centralizing control over spending and taxing during a fiscal crisis. The NVOs were the only way to protect—in a much-used contemporary phrase—the "general welfare" once "the financial foundations of the commune" were in jeopardy.[136] Following the same reasoning, others have pointed out that the installation of commissioners was designed merely to restore fiscal responsibility and confidence in municipal administrations. The commissioners' activities and powers of interference were restricted to problems of finance and the budget, and did not pose the threat to local self-government they were believed to be at the time.[137]

Considering the extremity of the Depression, these comments make sense. But when the focus is expanded to include the constitutional and financial weaknesses of the cities in the 1920s, their experience of actively inimical supervision by the federal and state governments after 1930, and the key role that communal governments played in the Nazi acquisition of power, then the erosion of local power assumes a larger and more ominous pattern. The political parties' secondary attention to the local scene, combined with the cities' financial and constitutional isolation, made local governments vulnerable to a striking degree. That the decrees and commissioners even existed undercut and dangerously discredited local governments. City administrations were widely perceived as corrupt and inefficient havens of political favor-mongering and infighting, an impression given credence by the generally pugilistic atmosphere of the city councils, as well as by high-profile municipal scandals in Berlin and Frankfurt in the late 1920s.[138] Local authorities' ongoing inability to negotiate a reasonable plan with the Reich for the distribution of tax revenues, the attacks of Schacht and others on their alleged luxury spending, and the central government's willful ignoring of the communes' proposals for combating the fiscal crisis after 1930, all combined to undermine critically the legitimacy and efficacy of German local government.

In January 1933, the finances of over six hundred Prussian cities were under the direct supervision of commissioners, of which there were rumored to be two thousand or more.[139] The Nazis found smoke sufficient to assume there was fire, citing the commissioners as evidence of corruption while conveniently ignoring the fact that they were short-term appointments that had come and gone periodically since first instituted in 1930 and possessed limited fiscal powers.[140] But as the Nazis of course knew well, quibbles about details of fact were less important than appearances. In this vein, Dieter Rebentisch has persuasively shifted the ground for assessing the "crisis of self-government" of the later Weimar years. When the legitimacy of representative government is in question, apparent and real crises are hard to tell apart.[141]

What is clear, however, is the remarkable swiftness with which the National Socialists took over the machinery and reshaped the principles of communal administration. With the partial exception of the SPD, none of the Weimar political parties were especially attentive to the nuances of communal politics, and had little apparent conception of its importance.[142] Admittedly, the Nazis were no better in this regard; but what they lacked in theory they made up for in practice.[143] Where the workers' and soldiers' councils of 1918–19 had failed to secure the local basis of Weimar democracy by replacing local administrative personnel, the Nazis, despite their anti-urban rhetoric, were well aware that a critical key to power lay in the political control of towns and cities.[144] Following the local elections in Prussia of 12 March 1933, the NSDAP became the largest party in virtually all Prussian Grossstädte. In the other Länder, the "Gleichschaltung" decree of 31 March reorganized local councils, keying party representation to Land election returns for the Reichstag, and reduced the number of seats to reflect population. A subsequent rash of public attacks in the press on the old communal leaders and their administrations led to the resignation or forced retirement of many Oberbürgermeister and their staffs. After promulgation of the "Law for the Reconstitution of the Bureaucracy" of 7 April, many Nazi-appointed Bürgermeister appeared, and the purge of local administrations began in earnest. By January 1934, only 14 percent of the Grossstädte had the same Oberbürgermeister of the January before.[145]

Centralization of control over the municipalities continued in the Prussian laws for communal finance and constitutions of 15 December 1933. This legislation replaced the different sets of city and town ordinances in Prussia with a single set of regulations, increased the authority of the communal executive over that of the representative council, and gave greater powers to state supervisory authorities.[146] A little over a year later, the German Municipal Charter (*Deutsche Gemeindeordnung*, DGO) of 30 January 1935 followed suit for the rest of the Reich. Abolishing the many existing municipal constitutions, it established a single system of regulation for all cities, from town to metropolis. The new arrangement consolidated power in the office of the Oberbürgermeister, who was appointed by a local NSDAP deputy. Communal administrations generally had the freedom to conduct their business unhindered; no party official could wilfully interfere in the everyday affairs of local government. Local officials could appeal the decisions of their party superiors to central authority, which the DGO centralized in the Reich Ministry of the Interior.[147]

The DGO in the end was a compromise, aimed at pleasing both discontented Nazi reformers as well as local officials. The right of appeal undoubtedly strengthened the power of self-administration; the cities previously experienced frustration at having to send their requests and complaints laboriously through the proper channels in order to get the attention of the relevant ministry.[148] But by the same token, of course, opening administrative channels to complaint from local authorities meant little when consensus was managed from above and complaint forcefully discouraged.

In many ways, this contrast applies to virtually all developments in communal law and finance from 1930 to 1935. The Emergency Decrees cleared away the jungle of central, state, and local tax codes.[149] They and the commissioners, as well as the new municipal charters in Prussia in 1933 and the Reich in 1935, cumulatively strengthened executive authority at the expense of fractious local councils. As commentators then and historians since have pointed out, Weimar communal leaders themselves had demanded many of these reforms, the most obvious being a desire for greater executive authority.[150] The new charters cut through the particularist pressures that had maintained so many different systems of communal regulation. And finally, the centralization of power in Berlin was reflected in the cities' desire to restrict constitutionally or even escape completely the states' power in favor of a "decentralized unified state" (*dezentralisierter Einheitsstaat*) whose principal organic elements would be powerful cities. There were of course fundamental differences between the cities' aims to simplify and rationalize administration and the Nazis' consolidation of power in 1933. These differences at least initially went largely unrecognized by the reforming mayors. Speaking to the Leipzig city council in March 1933, mayor Carl Goerdeler noted with approval: "For the first time since the founding of the Reich by Bismarck, there exists the possibility of integrating centrally the Reich and state constitutions, communal law, and the special bodies of self-government in a way that reflects the experiences of the last sixty years, the fundamental interests of the German people, its character, its national desires, and its honor."[151]

2 The congress of cities

In 1930, the Deutsche Städtetag (DST), or German Congress of Cities, marked its twenty-fifth anniversary by publishing a short volume surveying its history and current work. The book presented the "cooperative work of German cities" as having evolved naturally in the latter decades of the nineteenth century, as urban centers increased in size and density, extended new transportation arteries, and proliferated their economic ties. Cities recognized their common interests and formed loose working relationships, culminating in the founding of a national association in 1905. Representing everything from the middling town to the biggest metropolis, the DST coordinated the activities of branch organizations of towns in the German states and Prussian provinces, and lobbied energetically for municipal interests in national, state, and regional governments, as well as with industry and business. Its tri-annual congresses in the 1920s brought upwards of a thousand municipal delegates together with the republic's most prominent officials and ministerial personnel, providing high-profile forums for urban issues as well as giving city officials the opportunity to share information and experiences. In the monthly newspaper, *Der Städtetag*, mayors, technocrats, urban planners and economists from across the country wrote on every conceivable aspect of municipal and national affairs. In the urbanized Germany of 1930, few issues did *not* affect the cities. The DST asserted with some pride the importance of its national role as the collection point, clearing house, and publicist of every kind of information about municipal activity: "From the requests, concerns, and desires of the cities, a comprehensive picture of communal life emerges and constantly renews itself as a mosaic that the work of the Städtetag gives vitality, direction, and drive."[1]

Contemporaries' perceptions of the cities' importance as centers of industrial, financial and political power have persisted. Given the wide range of the cities' interests and activities, their apparently tremendous financial resources and the prominence within the DST of high-profile mayors such as Gustav Böss (Berlin) and Konrad Adenauer (Cologne), it has become a commonplace that the Städtetag exerted a singularly powerful influence during the Weimar years, in particular acting as an effective buffer between vulnerable municipalities and the hostile, intervenionist German state.[2] Yet the cities' ability to shape their environment was more apparent than real. As seen in the preceding chapter, local governments occupied the bottom rung of the Reich's system of revenue redistribution; securing funds sufficient for their needs was their gravest problem and showed little change during the period. Their complaints that local finances were in a "state of emergency" occur with equal frequency regardless of their "good" and "bad" periods.[3] The urgency of rescuing municipal finances from imminent collapse appear to slacken as "relative stability" took hold in the mid-twenties, but is traceable not so much to the Städtetag's ability to lessen the burden as to the cities searching out and borrowing funds on their own from outside Germany altogether, especially in the United States. Financial need drove their initiatives and colored their rhetoric. Their continuing concern to protect their powers of self-government from intervention by the Reich and states, for instance, while spirited and sincere, also began and ended with the municipal treasury. When the Depression hit cities especially hard, their financial independence and powers of self-administration deteriorated steadily under a barrage of national emergency decrees that contained little provision for their needs. Finally, National Socialism's success was due in no small part to the party's emphasis on securing power locally as well as nationally. The dissolution of local city and town councils in March and April 1933, their subsequent reformation under Nazi control, and the dismissal or forced retirement of upper municipal officials during the remainder of the year, were all accomplished with what, in retrospect, appears to have been stunning ease.[4]

In contrast to the power and independence that marked their *Blütezeit*, their golden age before the First World War, Germany's cities and towns were singularly vulnerable in the republic. A core assumption of this book is that they occupied, in both real and symbolic terms, positions of both pivotal importance and unusual weakness throughout the Weimar period. They were caretakers of local populations: administrators of an extensive but rigid and short-sighted system of welfare and unemployment support that for many Germans defined the new interventionist state of the republic; local managers of massive postwar recovery and reconstruction programs; and (not least) the power-centers of the working-class political parties. Cities were among the most modern, dynamic, and ostensibly powerful of the republic's constituent elements. Yet they simultaneously lacked the capital and political resources to fulfill these roles. In other words, to an even greater extent than their weakness, it was the disjunct between weakness and power that undermined fatally their ability to provide the stable foundations the republic so desperately needed.

COMMON DESTINY

Prior to the DST's founding in 1905, German cities belonged to associations in Prussia's provinces whose founding dates are clustered in the years of German unification, the *Gründerzeit*, from the mid-1860s to the mid-1870s, reflecting the acceleration of urbanization and the growing civil and economic power of the German *Bürgertum* in cities and towns.[5] Members met as loosely grouped *Städtetage*—literally, congresses of cities—occasional meetings of municipal leaders rather than regular functions of firmly structured organizations. Until the creation of the Prussian Städtetag (PST) in 1896, their networks had no permanent home, business office or administrative personnel. The managerial and clerical work for each meeting was handled by the prospective host-city, with the result that the cities' collective projects lacked long-term planning and clear definition by a central, coordinating authority, and received little of the guidance and energy necessary to see them through to completion. There was little effort to engage in affairs outside their own provincial and state borders.[6]

The fluidity of these beginnings makes it difficult to discern the real impetus behind the creation of the associations and the true nature of their collective interests in this early period. Urban historian Christian Engeli cautions against easy conclusions about their activities, which could be makeshift and sporadic.[7] Otto Ziebill, himself managing director of the Städtetag from 1951 to 1963, published its first comprehensive history up to the period just after the Second World War. Ziebill traced the founding of these early associations to the largely urban revolutions of 1848–49 and the subsequently frustrated social and political ambitions of the Bürgertum. In this view, the cities coalesced into "political fighting associations" ranged against conservative rural and agrarian economic interests as well as the administrative interference of an increasingly centralized, interventionist Bismarckian state. Cities banding together against state power symptomized what Ziebill perceived as the growing economic and political influence of the urban Bürgertum in the latter nineteenth century.[8] It can be argued, however, that this view too simplistically ranges the cities' interests against those of their "opponents." In fact, the state and Reich governments, though distrustful of the political motives of such large and potentially powerful organizations, nonetheless had considerable interest vested in the municipalities' welfare, especially after Germany's urban and industrial take-off in the 1880s. State interests to an increasing extent converged with city interests. The cities, for their part, expressed the desire to work loyally "hand in hand with the state and its administration."[9] The records and proceedings of the regional associations contain no overt hostility towards state activity or intervention. Naturally, some differences of emphasis and intent were inevitable, given the specialized particular needs of urban centers and the more general imperatives of state policy. Yet it is important not to overestimate such differences. Bürgermeister and other communal leaders who assembled in the congresses were all beneficiaries of the highly restrictive local franchise that prevailed before the First World War. Predominantly lawyers, civil servants and local notables of *bürgerlich* backgrounds, they had little interest in promoting sudden social and political change. Many of them, while elected locally, had to be confirmed by state authorities before taking office. Owing allegiance to both local and central governments, they could ill-afford to antagonize either.[10]

The Prussian and Bavarian Städtetage, both founded in 1896, were the largest and most powerful of the state groups, bringing together individual cities as well as, indirectly, the town associations from Prussia's provinces.[11] The same structure was adopted by the German national Städtetag, founded in 1905 at the suggestion of Dresden Oberbürgermeister Otto Beutler, after an exhibition celebrating urban progress was held in his city in 1903. When the founding congress convened on 27 November 1905 in the Reichstag building, 159 German cities with populations over 25,000 were represented—a fact taken as evidence by the DST that "in all cities the awareness of their common destiny had spread beyond state borders." The delegates pledged "to protect the collective interests of the cities and increase awareness and knowledge of administrative institutions," focusing their activities especially on lightening their municipalities' social burdens.[12]

During the years of the First World War, the "social truce" (*Burgfrieden*) on the home front merely put a name to a tradition already common in municipal governments, in which ostensible political enemies nonetheless cooperated to solve commonly recognized local problems.[13] In 1914, local governments took over numerous new social responsibilities, the most important of which was managing food distribution. The pragmatic spirit of local cooperation, combined with the expertise of municipal administrators intimately familiar with their towns' transportation logistics and local commercial relations, ensured that the wartime military régime gained maximum responsiveness and flexibility in easing local food pressures and forestalling civilian discontent arising from scarcity.[14] The DST provided a convenient mediating point between central authorities on the one hand and the local governments on the other. The war

> brought the Städtetag and the cities into direct, constant contact and cooperation with Reich institutions and Reich authorities and made communal politics a decisive part not only of the internal politics of the states, but now also of the internal politics of the Reich.[15]

The DST thus emerged from the war in 1918 with an enhanced profile. City governments, their mayors and technical staffs had become valued partners in national social and economic management, and the Städtetag's expertise and cooperation confirmed the importance of local affairs "on the ground" even as administrative and governing power in the Reich centralized.

Political and economic turmoil after four years of war presented cities with unprecedented challenges. More active intervention from national and state governments, along with the DST's increased influence and fields of activity, expanded the scope of its interests and made more pressing the need for effective organization. The correspondence of the DST's business office in 1920 was five times that of 1913.[16] Yet balanced against the cities' need for more efficient representation, information gathering and resource management was the Städtetag's growing difficulty in representing the full spectrum of its constituents, stretching from town to metropolis. Tensions between the smaller municipalities and big cities indeed went back to the previous century. Bürgermeister of large towns and cities occupied central positions in the associations from the beginning; urban delegates held more voting weight in the congresses and a clear majority in the Council. Big city administrations were focused increasingly on problems of urban technology and mass welfare: transit, large-scale modern utilities such as electricity and water treatment, construction of housing developments and maintenance of large urban infrastructures and social programs. The tremendous scale of such problems in the Grossstadt reached an order of magnitude wholly different from that of the towns, preoccupied with alleviating the cost of local education and police through increased state subvention, and gaining independence from the administrative and fiscal control of the surrounding county.[17]

The gap between town and city, if anything, had widened during the war. Increasingly in the postwar years, the Städtetag's activities were directed not by the democratic input of all members, but by the personal influence and connections of its leaders, especially those of Managing Director Hans Luther, then Oberbürgermeister of Essen.[18] In 1921, an Executive Committee was created to lead the national and Prussian associations. Over the next decade, its members were Germany's most powerful mayors: Hans Lohmeyer (Königsberg), Konrad Adenauer (Cologne), Ludwig Landmann (Frankfurt am Main), Karl Scharnagl (Munich), Hermann Beims (Magdeburg), Karl Jarres (Duisburg), and Max Brauer (Altona).[19] The Grossstädte thus retained authority over national, state, and regional urban associations and so over the direction and expression of the cities' aims throughout the republican years. Politically, the members were moderates, situated largely from the center to the moderate left, though all showed in their dealings the same pragmatism that dominated city halls. Party politics as such did not play a role in the Committee's business. Until 1933, the big-city mayors wielded such extensive control over the national Congress that Ziebill called the Committee "one of the most important administrative-political bodies of the Weimar era."[20] That other DST members agreed with this judgment is clear: when a seat came vacant in 1931, petitions requesting it arrived from prominent mayors from all parts of the country.[21]

The second major organizational change had its origins in the increased politicization of local government after 1918–19. Following the lifting of local franchise restrictions, city councils with new political complexions appeared.[22] Social Democrats gained the upper hand in many of the larger cities. Town councillors demanded that more representatives to the Städtetage be chosen from their ranks. Amendments to DST regulations in 1918 specified that the number of a city's delegates be determined by its population, leading to a substantial increase of councillors in Städtetag assemblies.[23] When councillors also pressed for a greater role in Congress decision-making, regulations were altered in 1922 to require that they comprise one-third of council delegates.[24] These changes did not devolve significant power to the smaller towns, however: in 1925, the largest cities (over 250,000 inhabitants) still dominated the councils of both associations with majorities of 60 percent or better.[25]

For the rest of the Weimar period, proceedings at the annual meetings and, even more, at the larger tri-annual member-congresses of 1924, 1927, and 1930 resembled full-blooded national and state parliaments. Participants made formal speeches, debated and made declarations openly in the name of their political party.[26] Policies and positions tended to parallel platforms and ideologies on the national level. Deputies from the SPD, for instance, strongly supported a thorough-going constitutional and territorial reform of the Reich towards a unified central state, while the Nationalists were resistant and the Bavarian People's Party unremittingly hostile to the idea.[27] The Communists (KPD) also became an important presence in local politics. The KPD's hubris in political assemblies was infamous. KPD councillors in the Städtetag, though relatively few in number, followed their practice in town councils of exceeding the limits of their allotted speaking time, going out of their way to violate the proprieties of parliamentary order, and generally exasperating the assemblies with openly oppositionist positions. In 1924, councillors and lawyers both in city halls and in the Städtetag began discussing how to keep order in their meetings. According to DST records, alterations to council regulations that allowed the chair to throw out and censure uncooperative or disruptive members, first passed in Cologne, were generally adopted where expedient. In May 1924, new KPD city councillors in Düsseldorf refused the ceremonial inaugural handshake that finalized their swearing-in. By order of the Prussian Interior Ministry, no representative could assume her or his seat without the ceremonial *Handschlag*, a requirement acknowledged in all regional and state communal charters. The Chair of Düsseldorf's Council, Bürgermeister Karl Geusen, ruled that without it the new members were not representatives and would have to leave. To their protests he replied simply, "You are not city council-members; you have nothing to say here." After a short recess, the Communists returned and sulkily came up to shake hands. One of them muttered (with an obvious lack of prescience), "You are not going to have any fun with us."[28]

Historians have chosen to follow the Städtetag's cue in downplaying such political tones in its internal debates.[29] For most issues on which members voted, a clear majority was usually available, indicating a deep and pervasive sense of common interest among Weimar's cities and towns. Yet this focus on function and its recorded result misses much that was divisive and contradictory in the cities' strategies and tactics. The delegates' debates could reach a high level of invective, especially against the KPD members: hoots, catcalls, and worse were not uncommon. In 1924, KPD delegates to the all-member Congress in Hanover discovered that Gustav Noske was in attendance. Now a high-ranking regional official in Prussia (*Oberpräsident*), Noske, while SPD Minister of Defence in 1919–20 had used extreme, lethal force to maintain order, brutally quelling uprisings by leftists and militant workers. The Städtetag KPD fraction now furiously claimed that he had acquired his current position only by slaughtering fifteen thousand workers, and demanded that he be ejected from the building. To the outraged retorts and insults that exploded around them, the Communists cried, "Raus, Noske!" and "Cain, where is your brother, Abel?" Gustav Böss, chairing the congress, restored order only with difficulty.[30] If such in-fighting was only posturing, then prevailing emphases on cooperation and consensus appear justified. Yet again and again, the delegates expressed firmly and convincingly views that were undeniably sincere and deeply felt. Indeed, they frequently exhibited a pugnacity consonant with the tempestuousness of other political assemblies in the republic.[31]

THE PROTECTION OF CITY INTERESTS

Political upheaval and inflation in the early 1920s presented the municipalities, especially the large metropolitan centers, with emergencies of such magnitude and severity that they had little energy for other business. Local governments were completely occupied with unemployment, currency inflation, demobilization, work-creation projects, and new and extensive welfare provisions. The same preoccupation is reflected in the activities of the DST, which spent little time on business not aimed at alleviating the crisis in one way or another. Only with the return of what historians term "relative stability" to Weimar's economy and finance—marked by the end of hyperinflation and passive resistance in the Ruhr, followed by the formulation in 1924 of the Dawes Plan—were the cities and their associations finally able to look beyond the procession of continuous postwar crises and begin planning for the longer term. As described in chapter 1, postwar urban reconstruction began in earnest, financed largely via loans obtained abroad.

The Städtetag embarked on a program of internal reform to strengthen its influence on government policy-making, firstly by appointing a managing director whose authority would equal that of the chairman.[32] The committee's choice, Oskar Mulert, came with the highest qualifications short of actual service in a municipal administration. A meteoric rise through the ranks of Prussian government by mid-1920 had brought him the directorship of the Prussian Interior Ministry's section on communal affairs.[33] During his five years there, he exhibited a tremendous capacity for work, formidable diplomatic skills, and penetrating expertise in all areas of city finance, planning, and management. His experience in state administration gave him a keen sense of the necessity for cooperation between the two levels of government, central and local, and he worked closely with the communal associations, as well as the prominent Association for Communal Economy and Politics.[34] His lack of direct experience in communal administration was offset by the "objective" principles and "larger perspectives" prevalent in the ministry—that is, a familiarity with state imperatives and policies. In an affectionate farewell note to Mulert upon his departure in 1926, his boss, Interior Minister Carl Severing, admonished him to remember, "City and state interests should not be opponents, and where misunderstandings arise, they can be eliminated easily by a man who does not see in the state an enemy of self-government."[35]

In late October, DST chairman Gustav Böss, Lord Mayor of Berlin, offered Mulert the directorship. Mulert, doubtless perceiving the weakness of dividing power equally between two leaders, proposed instead consolidating directorial control in the new office of a president with wide-ranging powers of discretion in running the organization's business office and its general affairs. The chairman's role, by contrast, would diminish in equal measure; indeed, his only significant duties would be reduced to chairing the large annual meetings and the tri-annual member-congresses. Although Böss naturally fought these changes, it was soon clear that Mulert had the support of the Council. There was little Böss could do, and Mulert assumed the office of Executive President in early March 1926.[36] From this point, every area of Städtetag activity and policy-making bore the mark of his influence, and he quickly assumed the role of the DST's first representative.

Just as the creation of the Executive Committee had earlier placed control of the Städtetag firmly in the hands of the big cities, so instituting a president concentrated administrative power in the hands of a single figure. That the new president was Mulert was doubly significant: his energy, forceful personality, and close connections with ministerial and political figures in the Prussian and Reich administrations made for a formidable combination. Gotthilf P. Bronisch, the DST's expert on city construction in the late 1920s and early thirties, functioned as Mulert's personal assistant for a time. Bronisch remembered that when he first went to work there, all he knew of Mulert was "that he was an eater of men [*Menschenfresser*]" who had consumed a large number of assistants in the Interior Ministry.[37] He remained close to his successor in the Prussian communal affairs section, Viktor von Leyden, and stayed on good terms with his old chief in the Prussian Ministry of the Interior, Carl Severing.[38] The latter relationship took on added significance during Severing's tenure as Reich

Minister of the Interior from 1928–30, when the DST was promoting an ambitious program of constitutional reform.[39] The associations of towns (*Reichsstädtebund*), rural townships (*Landgemeindetag*), and counties (*Landkreistag*), were taken by surprise by Mulert's appointment and grew uneasy, as it presaged for them stiffer competition for official influence and public attention.[40]

Nor did they have long to wait. A new charge in the atmosphere was evident from the start, when Mulert became chair of the Executive Committee. Although he made few lengthy interventions, it was he who at the end did the final summing-up; he also edited the final version of the minutes, which after he took office became clearer, more focused, and more comprehensive synopses of transacted business. Not surprisingly, these final records also reflected his personal preferences and perspectives, and at times reported a unity of opinion and singleness of purpose that in actuality were not always evident.[41]

These last points suggest that both Mulert's presidency and his person were more problematic than is commonly believed. The co-worker who knew him best and worked with him most closely, DST vice president Fritz Elsas, tellingly judges him most harshly.[42] Previously a city administrator and then councilman from Stuttgart, Elsas's extensive activities as DST second-in-command from 1926 included representing the cities on numerous committees of outside organizations—seventeen by the time he left in 1931—the most important of which were as chair of the German Employers' Association and as member of the governing council of the Reich Office of Labor Exchange and Unemployment Insurance.[43] Entrusted with sensitive negotiations at the ministerial level (though restricted largely to Prussia), he conducted them with sobriety and firmness.[44] His area of greatest expertise was the film industry and its role in the urban economy, a subject on which he gave speeches and published numerous articles.[45]

Of serious disagreement between Elsas and Mulert the official record shows no trace. Historians until recently concluded that the two worked well together.[46] But excerpts from Elsas's diary published in 1999 show clearly that he was deeply dissatisfied with Mulert's leadership almost from the beginning. The president's "personal conceit" was so great, he felt, that dealings with him required the greatest care both within and outside of the Congress. Mulert had "no notion of well-regulated business":

> Mulert continually disrupts the normal course of business, lets the most important correspondence go unattended, doesn't inform me about the most important matters... he reads everything of no importance, takes six weeks and more [to prepare] the simplest records and contributes neither a thought-through idea nor anything productive![47]

Elsas left the DST in 1931 to take up a post as second Bürgermeister in Berlin, but remained a member of the DST Council. Though no longer working under Mulert, his strong dislike remained. In February 1933, at the Council's last meeting before the Nazi Gleichschaltung, he sat through an "endless and boring" speech by Mulert reviewing the "Situation of the Communes in 1932" (which admittedly ran to some forty pages of typescript).[48] Elsas's summary judgement of his boss is devastating: "Hopefully he will never come into a position in which he must bear responsibility. He is an amazing braggart (*fabelhafter Blender*)."[49]

How to square the portrait of Mulert's vision and influence with Elsas's contemptuous dismissal of both his presidency and person? The record, if anything, bears out the consensus view. Mulert's imprint on DST business in the years 1926–1933 is palpably evident in the extensive records of the DST in the Berlin state archive. It is hard to see him as anything but extraordinarily energetic, focused and productive. The answer may be that the two men, different in bearing and manner, also had different purviews and responsibilities. Mulert, coming from an upper-level career in the Prussian state civil service, looked outward to larger state forms for lasting answers to the cities' problems. Elsas, grounded in city administration and inclined to the detail of the local, may have found Mulert's loftier perspective to be annoyingly irrelevant. Certainly Elsas, as Mulert's subordinate, would have had to bear the weight of differences and friction between them.

Mulert moved quickly after being confirmed in office to streamline the DST's organization and focus its energies. In the first months of his presidency, he pushed for the appointment of a new press representative to help raise public awareness of "the extent and importance of the work of the cities and of the Städtetag," and insisted that the DST intensify its efforts to bring city problems before the public through closer relations with the press. The cost of the increase in DST business, since it was in the interest of all member-cities, could be covered by a contribution of one or two pfennigs per inhabitant from each. Mulert also emphasized the importance of strengthening the DST's connections with state ministries. In late April 1926, the mayoral members of the Prussian State Council assured the DST that legislation affecting the municipalities would be discussed first with a DST representative, most likely Mulert. In the interest of raising municipal issues in the Reich and state parliaments, he also promoted DST representation in each Reichstag party fraction by lobbying for deputies formerly active in communal administrations.[50]

With able and dynamic new directors, a press office for publicity and a clear objective to more closely integrate municipal governments with the new structures of Reich and state administration after the war, the DST by December 1926 was poised for a major reorientation and intensification of its energies. The new program, "The Protection of City Interests," was launched at the Council meeting of 10 December 1926 and marked a watershed in the organization's history.[51] The program first detailed exhaustively the weaknesses of cities continually forced to do more with less. Their overall circumstances were growing more precarious in political, administrative, and economic environments that were increasingly hostile. The Reich's power, rather than being shaped purposefully and rationally, was evolving haphazardly, leaving local governments in a constitutional grey area between the jurisdictions of nation and state. With the Reich now interfering in areas of finance and administration previously under the states' jurisdiction, cities had no institutional means of making their needs known at the critical levels of decision-making. The result, they claimed, was that the Reich laid ever greater burdens on city finances without considering where the necessary funds might come from, and left the problem of balancing communal budgets to the Länder. The states, for their part, paid scant attention to the cities' overall national burden, instead individually passing legislation that made it harder for municipalities to meet their obligations. The problems were not just structural, but also personal: the Städtetag claimed that it systematically encountered widespread "completely anti-communal" attitudes in government officials and business leaders. The latter were especially significant as the private sector experienced recovery in mid-decade and business resumed a prominent role in Germany's economy and policy making.[52]

The cities' new initiatives, formulated in the sixteen-month period from the beginning of Mulert's presidency to the all-member congress of 1927 in Magdeburg, show new scope and ambition. On the surface, it would appear that the reorganization of the business office and the publicity campaign were the most successful. The DST's staff of sixty-eight in 1927 experienced a significant jump in incoming and outgoing business, due mainly to an increase in in-house publishing activity.[53] The Executive Committee reported the 1928 budget of RM 767,000 had grown by one-third over that of the previous year.

In order to combat anti-urban prejudice and the public's "astounding ignorance" of communal issues, the DST also set up a new press liaison office early in 1927.[54] The office published press releases, set up conferences for DST special events, arranged press interviews—firstly with the new president—and collaborated with sympathetic public commentators to raise public awareness of communal issues. The DST Council recommended that high school and academy teachers be encouraged to use Städtetag publications in seminars about local government and urban problems, and that DST committee members, many of them experts in their respective fields, write articles regularly for the daily and specialized presses to ensure that communal issues remained in the public eye. The DST's new Press Committee met for the first time in January 1928. With Mulert as chair, the committee stressed the importance of cooperation and openness with local news organizations.[55] Over the next year or so, special press offices were created in Kassel, Frankfurt am Main, Mainz, and Saarbrücken.[56] The DST began publicizing the Council's business by holding large press conferences immediately after meetings. The press, for its part, found useful color in the cities' struggles with higher administration. One Ruhr newspaper went so far as to suggest that the timing of a Council meeting in Duisburg coincided intentionally with the local performance of Mozart's opera *Abduction from the Seraglio* so that metaphorical parallels would be drawn with the plight of the cities. Thus the hero, "an ill-fated, poor, but brave man" (an Oberbürgermeister), seeks to rescue his love (communal self-government) from the hands of a Pasha (Schacht), though she is watched over by an "unusual" Argus-like guard (the press).[57]

Creating press offices, reorganizing the statistics section, and expanding the DST's official newsletter into a full-blown journal, *Der Städtetag*, were expensive but, the Executive Committee argued, worth it. Press coverage of communal financial difficulties improved in quality and quantity, and journal subscriptions were on the rise.[58] Over the next half-decade, *Der Städtetag* expanded from its beginnings as a parochial and somewhat stuffy reporter of DST internal affairs to become a full-fledged review of local government and urban culture, a "reflected image of communal life." Although it retained its focus on political economy, a wider perspective and more sophisticated format soon made it "a leading organ of German communal policy."[59] Articles ranged from local policing to state and county administrative reform, from building codes to cinema and luxury taxes, from municipal art patronage to comparative commentaries by foreign experts and historians.

The cities' most intensive press activity undoubtedly was occasioned by their spirited defence of municipal spending policies and practices against public attacks by the German banks and the private sector. A pamphlet published in 1926 by the Reichsverband der deutschen Industrie condemned tax policies that favored municipal enterprise.[60] The DST in October 1926 responded with a booklet entitled, "Cities, State, Economy"; within one month, an estimated five thousand copies had been distributed to members of national and state parliaments, ministerial staffs, economic interest groups, Städtetag members, and the other communal associations.[61] In some eighty pages, the DST contrasted the municipalities' heyday before 1914 with their postwar social burdens, increased expenses and reduced financial resources. According to the cities, the great majority (at least 80 percent) of items in their budgets were mandatory, either dictated by the state and federal governments or inescapable requirements of their new social responsibilities. Since local self-sufficiency and accountability were necessary to sustain "living" democracy in the republic, the DST argued, it would be both more efficient and a better fit with republican principles to give the cities the financial discretion necessary to make their own taxing and spending decisions. Simple common sense indicated that local tasks could be carried out in the most sensible and economical fashion by local authorities. Additional savings could be had by scaling down Reich and state supervision of local governments.[62]

The DST's conflict with the private sector intensified in late 1927. Reichsbank president Hjalmar Schacht's speech at Bochum in November, followed by Mulert's numerous replies, received extensive press coverage both at home and abroad—particularly in the United States, where most German municipal loans originated and where Schacht was well known in banking circles.[63] Many news reports, not surprisingly, agreed with the uncontroversial anti-Versailles "correct core" of Schacht's argument. A full recovery for the German economy, heavily burdened by reparations, required strict restraint in borrowing and spending. But agreement with the principles of Schacht's criticism stopped short of endorsing his attack on cities and their "luxury" spending.[64] Not surprisingly, public parks, swimming pools, exhibition halls and the like probably had broad support as visible signs of a return to normalcy and prosperity after ten wrenching years of uncertainty and austerity. Moreover, virtually all accounts lamented Schacht's tactless combativeness in attacking the cities and his blanket condemnations of communal finance throughout Germany: "no one is served by such public disputes, not even the Reichsbank president."[65] The foreign press, too, supported the cities.[66] The *Manchester Guardian* ventured that Schacht's recklessness had hurt his reputation and perhaps jeopardized Germany's international credit. The conclusion that "the majority of the German people... is on the cities' side" suggests that the cities' publicity efforts were paying off.[67] The "completely anti-communal attitude" and "widespread ignorance about communal affairs" lamented by the DST may indeed have been on the wane.[68] But lack of support for Schacht did not have to translate directly into support for the cities. Germans with little interest in the finer points of municipal finance may simply have approved reflexively of the material results of social spending, and the press followed their lead.

The overall structure and principles of the Reich's economy and distribution of revenue were contentious issues that remained unresolved before 1933. Although by the DST's own reckoning the breakthrough for public sympathy and official recognition only came after the Depression started, the cities seem to have had considerable success in making their case heard.[69] Schacht's attacks were parried to good effect, and challenges facing municipal governments appear to have attracted increasing amounts of sympathetic public attention. The same trend can be seen in the wide press coverage accorded the Städtetag's program for extensive constitutional and administrative reform at the end of the 1920s, an indication that the DST had become a noted and familiar institution of German public life.[70]

INTERNAL TENSIONS

Other aspects of the cities' campaign, however, met with mixed results. The DST's attempt to consolidate control over the regional town associations encountered stiff resistance. They resented efforts to enforce organizational discipline and limit their freedom of movement, and so continued to approach ministers and parliaments directly if they thought the problem sufficiently important.[71] Moreover, cities' needs and demands shifted with changes in the postwar economic and political landscape. They were restless within the Städtetag itself, and that restlessness erupted sporadically into open discontent. Small and middling towns continued to resent the domination of the large metropoles; and a number of cases show members decidedly dissatisfied with DST representation. These tensions stemmed in part from the Städtetag's dogged insistence that since it represented the general interests of all cities, it could not honor requests from individual cities for help.[72] Threats of withdrawal frequently followed.

The most striking example of member discontent occurred in 1927, when the city of Berlin itself appeared on the verge of quitting. Berlin Oberbürgermeister Gustav Böss, in addition to being one of the republic's most prominent political figures, was also formally the chair of both the Prussian and German congresses. As the first German city, Berlin's exit would make the Städtetag's claims that it represented all urban interests ring decidedly hollow. That the capital of both old Prussia and the new Reich, Germany's quintessential metropolis, and the Städtetag's flagship member threatened to pull out was a subject of grave concern.

The principal cause of the problem was the consolidation of Greater Berlin in 1920.[73] The resulting metropolis of four million became overnight a giant among lesser cities: its closest rival, Cologne, was a sixth of its size; the next biggest cities were ten to twenty times smaller.[74] This meant, of course, that in terms of population and tax income, Berlin's wealth in absolute terms was beyond comparison. But relatively speaking, on the other hand, its rate of growth and its income per capita fell more or less in line with those of other cities. In addition, its wealth and size, as Böss was fond of pointing out, were offset by the special problems that came with its status and responsibilities. Tremendous mass transportation projects, welfare support, and housing programs all reached an unparalleled scale in the metropolis.[75]

In order to spread municipal burdens evenly across Prussia, a system of financial leveling (*Finanzausgleich*) was instituted in the early years of the republic that, in essence, took from the rich cities and gave to the poor. The basic principle was one of a "relative guarantee" of income: the cities were guaranteed a per-capita income not lower than that prevailing in the years immediately preceding the war, calculated from a Prussia-wide average per capita income determined each year.[76] This financial give-and-take aimed to protect municipalities that had suffered wartime losses to their tax bases and postwar impoverishment from bankruptcy and fiscal chaos in the private sector. But in Berlin's case the reverse was true: the income of the new metropolis after 1920 was far greater than that of the prewar period. The sum difference between its pre- and postwar income, therefore, was eligible for distribution to the poorer Prussian cities. As a result of the relative guarantee, Berlin claimed it gave up RM 89 million to the other cities between 1925 and 1927.[77]

In 1927, the Finanzausgleich came up for renewal. Böss contended that with the currency stabilized and the growing reliability of financial statistics, the entire concept of a guaranteed income based on prewar figures was nonsense. He argued that it was time to set in place a system of finance distribution that accurately reflected existing conditions.[78] Unfortunately for him, the other cities were profiting comfortably by the present system, and had no wish to change it. His proposals to reduce the percentage of municipal income eligible for redistribution found no support from the Prussian government.[79] On 6 April 1927, the Prussian Landtag set the average per capita income of the relative guarantee at twenty-two pfennigs—three pfennigs lower than Berlin had petitioned for.[80] Böss was incensed. He accused his colleagues in the Prussian Städtetag of not supporting him, and recommended to the Berlin city council that the city leave the Städtetag since it was not protecting the city's interests.[81] The final protest declaration, adopted by the city council on 5 May, read: "The actions of the Städtetag have brought injury to the city of Berlin. Berlin feels itself bound together with the German and Prussian cities in a community of need, but it cannot cooperate further in an association that is able to give it no understanding or justice."[82]

On 9 May, the PST Council met in Koblenz to discuss these charges. Böss was not present. According to a detailed stenographic record of that meeting, the main response of the Council members was astonishment at Böss's behavior.[83] While declaring their willingness to revisit the distribution issue with Berlin, they returned repeatedly to their personal sense of affront that the chairman of their own organization had attacked that organization publicly in a newspaper interview.[84] As one member put it, "Not even a skittles-club puts up with its chairman treating the group unfaithfully."[85] Even those PST Council members hailing from Berlin firmly disavowed Böss's tactics in the dispute, though they admitted that the city council was not especially happy with the Städtetag either.[86] After some confusion about whether to respond to the Berlin municipal government or Böss personally, the Council stated officially that it had always supported Berlin's claims when "justified," in this particular case even adopting a higher figure for the relative guarantee than its members originally supported. The Städtetag could not be blamed for a Landtag vote against Berlin, yet this was exactly what Böss appeared to be doing. The Council disapproved in the strongest terms of Böss's airing his discontent publicly, and concluded by emphasizing that the cities had to pull together; the seriousness of their overall situation required subordinating the interests of single members to those of the whole.[87] A date was set, 20 June, for discussions between the Städtetag and the city of Berlin. The morning was reserved for talks between the Council members and Böss alone, in order that they might work out the personal aspects of the dispute. Once that was settled, representatives from Berlin's administration were scheduled in the afternoon to present and clarify the city's financial claims.

By this time, Böss appears to have realized that his attack had been overly hasty. He had first believed that a resolution of the Berlin Magistrat condemning the Städtetag had been formulated "several days before" his press interview, signaling a clear intent on the part of the city to withdraw. In effect, he thought he had the city's support.[88] Since then, however, he heard forceful arguments from his councillors that although the PST may have slighted the city, Berlin's prestige and influence in the organization were high and its needs that much more likely to be met. It was certainly better off inside the Städtetag than out. Böss now contritely assured the Council that although he had expressed legitimate frustration at what he felt were very real anti-Berlin sentiments in the Städtetag, he had intended no offence or insult to anyone. Putting aside what may have been a still keen sense of grievance at the recent diminution of his DST leadership by Mulert, he suggested that it would be best to concentrate on the problems of revising inter-municipal finance. The members (no doubt with some reluctance) agreed.[89] With the air cleared for the afternoon meeting, the eleven representatives from Berlin made their case. The size and special nature of Berlin's problems meant that the current distribution of municipal revenues was completely unacceptable. If allowed to stand, it would give the impression that Berlin could in fact manage the burden without difficulty, and that the whole arrangement had the Städtetag's unified support. Böss insisted that while "Berlin does not want to be favored over the other municipalities," it rejected any demand "that it alone has to pay for the improvement of other municipalities."[90] These arguments appear to have swayed the Council, which ended by resolving that the PST's Finance Committee would review the evidence for Berlin's "uniqueness."[91] It would then decide whether to press the Landtag for alterations in the *Finanzausgleich*.[92] This accommodation on both sides seemed to calm the situation, and a week later a newspaper remarked that harmony again prevailed between Berlin and the PST.[93] In September, the Finance Committee approved the changes in question, and the PST Council adopted a resolution calling for an increase in 1928 of the sum used to calculate the relative guarantee from twenty-two to twenty-five pfennigs which, in turn, decreased the amount contributed by the wealthy cities to their poorer neighbors.[94]

A USEFUL VASSAL

On balance, the Städtetag's greatest success before 1930 lay in deploying publicity for the cities effectively. Yet in comparison with the later period of economic crisis, the limits of its influence before 1930 are particularly striking. In this "relatively stable" period of its supposed greatest power, the cities remained unrepresented on the Advisory Board for Foreign Credit, which regulated their access to international loan markets; apart from several meetings with Schacht, Städtetag leaders had virtually no official traffic with high-ranking ministerial or political personnel.[95] Despite Mulert's strategy to increase direct connections with the ministries, requests were still submitted in writing to the relevant sections and personnel much as they had been before stabilization. When Mulert sent circulars to Reich ministers protesting Allied Reparations Agent Parker Gilbert's attacks on municipal "luxury spending" in November 1927, none of the addressees—who included Chancellor Wilhelm Marx, Foreign Minister Gustav Stresemann, Interior Minister Walter von Keudell, and Finance Minister Heinrich Köhler—bothered to reply.[96] Even in matters that were obviously urban, even exclusively so, such as the consolidation of the Ruhr in 1929, neither ministerial nor planning personnel turned to experts in the DST. Perhaps the clearest instance of the cities' lack of access to power was their exclusion from the States' Conference (*Länderkonferenz*) on constitutional reform that convened early in 1928, despite the DST's central role in bringing those very reform issues to the fore.[97]

It was only after 1929 as the country slid into economic crisis that the cities gained more direct access to German officials. Städtetag leaders regularly attended meetings of Reich and Land ministerial staffs; one-on-one discussions between Mulert and Reich Finance Minister Hermann Dietrich were not unusual, despite the latter's demonstrated hostility towards local governments. Likewise, Reich and Prussian ministers frequently attended meetings of the DST's Executive Committee.[98] Closer contact was greatly facilitated when, as a result of a request by Mulert in late 1930, Chancellor Brüning agreed to "recommend" to Reich ministries that they inform the Städtetag of all pending measures affecting the municipalities, even if still in the early stages of preparation.[99]

Early in the Depression, the DST showed itself an aggressive formulator of constructive measures designed to meet the crisis on the ground. It called for drastic local spending cuts and conversion of short-term communal debt through municipal savings and loan institutions. Painfully aware that local financial management, if dilatory or irresponsible, could lead quickly to a lack of public confidence and to intervention by nervous state and Reich authorities, the DST directed that "every single city administration conduct its spending policies with even greater economy," and urged its members to cut "all expenses that can in any way be set aside."[100] In February 1932, Mulert estimated with some pride a resulting total savings of some RM 1.2 billion.[101]

Similarly for loans, the DST in the first months of the crisis set in motion a plan to create "Credit Committees" in each of the states and the Prussian provinces. The committees, comprised of members from the communal associations and the German Savings and Loan Association, would assess requests for credit on the basis of local need. In this way, the old complaints about the Advisory Board could be laid to rest: the cities now assumed a decisive role in controlling the access of local authorities to loan markets, and their rigorous criteria, careful assessments, and global perspective were exactly the areas in which, a scant two years previous, Schacht had claimed they were lacking. According to reports over the course of the following year, the committees were an unqualified success: models of cooperation between local and central authorities, a point the DST did not hesitate to stress when dealing with the increasingly inflexible Reich and state governments.[102]

But larger developments ominously offset these improvements. As the most prominent and visible representatives of the modern Weimar social state, the urban centers provided an easy target for the conservative agendas of the Brüning and Papen governments from 1930–32. As the Depression deepened from late 1929, municipal finance and politics became scapegoats for the critical state of the German economy. The municipalities' "self-help" programs to cut spending and restrict loans, though stringent, did not prevent the feared state intervention. The emergency decrees, promulgated under Article 48 of the Weimar constitution, squeezed municipal finance in order to balance Reich and state budgets first. Notwithstanding the cities' efforts to present themselves as responsible and capable partners in fighting the crisis, Prussia installed commissioners in over five hundred municipalities in Prussia and gave them the power to ram through harsh budgets, raise old taxes, and impose new ones. The DST's contact with officials focused increasingly on obtaining funds to cover unemployment and welfare costs, or even simply to pay city employees, alternating with protests against the harshness and unfairness of spending cuts ordered by the Reich and passed on to local governments by the states.[103] In the same vein, although the DST's main personnel now negotiated directly and frequently with the Reich and Land ministries and heads of state, the tone of their reception was unrelentingly indifferent, even hostile, especially in the case of Reich Finance Minister Hermann Dietrich. Dietrich was the only minister to remain outwardly skeptical and hostile towards the DST even after Brüning's conciliatory offer in 1930 of early consultation. Both he and Reichsbank President Hans Luther, the former Oberbürgermeister of Essen, evinced little interest in the fate of the cities, despite the fact that both had begun their careers in municipal politics.[104]

In sum, therefore, the Städtetag was viewed by central authorities in the Depression as a useful but essentially powerless vassal. Returning to its role in the First World War, the DST became a mediator, offering detailed information about local conditions while it kept municipal governments herded helpfully into a semblance of conformity.[105] But the DST's closer relations with decision-makers in the Brüning and Papen governments cannot disguise the fact that the cities suffered severe setbacks as a result of policies of those governments, and were able to do little about it. Even Reich and Prussian officials who were aware of and sympathetic to local problems had pressures on them that limited their ability to help. The emergency decree of 5 August 1931, which barred the municipalities from using the financial resources of their own communal Savings and Loan institutions, was sprung on the DST and other associations with no warning. The next day, Mulert dressed down Prussian ministers of interior and finance Carl Severing and Hermann Höpker-Aschoff "as never before," roundly condemning their lack of good faith. Both pleaded they had been under heavy pressure from the Reichsbank.[106] Whatever progress the cities may have felt they made over the course of the Depression, their fundamental demands—consolidation of their short-term debt, amalgamation of unemployment and crisis relief, greater control over local financial decisions, and more help from the Reich—remained unchanged during the three years of rule by presidential decree.[107]

GLEICHSCHALTUNG: THE GEMEINDETAG

In January 1933, then, the DST was a changed institution. Although still a collective association, neither the big member-congress nor the annual meeting had convened since 1930, ostensibly for reasons of cost. The many sub-committees were also in limbo: the "Culture Committee," for instance, had been out of commission so long that one member wrote in to ask if it still existed.[108] The organization's business for the previous two years had been conducted for the most part by the Executive Committee and, less frequently, the Council. Mulert negotiated with Reich and state officials often on his own. The DST leaders seemed almost to be holding their collective breath.

Three days after Hitler became Chancellor, the Executive Committee convened. The agenda contained nothing out of the ordinary until the end, when a "general discussion" of "the possibility of successfully representing critical city demands and proposals" in the new political climate closed out the meeting. The record contains no further details, perhaps because there was nothing to report. The Städtetag did little in the next month beyond circulate information to its Prussian member-cities concerning the legal and practical ramifications of a decree dissolving town councils. The thrust of its advice to councillors and administrators was to keep doing their jobs until their successors were elected on 12 March.[109] At the regional and state levels, new provincial representatives to the Reichsrat and Prussian Staatsrat were also being elected. Just as he had for the previous seven years, Mulert continued to emphasize the need for representatives with a background in local government in these positions.[110]

Although awareness that it would not be "business as usual" dawned only slowly, below the surface events moved quickly. The municipal elections in Prussia and exclusionary measures elsewhere decimated the personnel of the DST Council. In its place, the Executive Committee on 17

March created a "Working Committee" of four National Socialists familiar with municipal administration to act as a bridging mechanism until a new Council could be constituted.[111] Although difficult to define clearly, it appears the two bodies now ran the Städtetag jointly, more or less as an "Executive Committee expanded with communal leaders from the circles of the governing parties."[112] The Committee affirmed the German cities' readiness to cooperate loyally "in the general interest of the German people," and a small delegation was chosen to visit Nazi Reich ministers Wilhelm Frick, Hermann Göring, and Chancellor Adolf Hitler in order to make known the cities' needs and demands. In this way, declared the Committee, "the Städtetag has carried out its Gleichschaltung with the Reich and Länder."[113]

From this point until the final merging of all the communal associations in late May, the question was not so much when the fusion would take place, but how. The Reichsstädtebund (RSB), representing the towns and middling cities, had been the first of the organizations to profess its loyalty to the National Socialist régime. By late April, Nazi members were in full control of the Bund and pushing hard for a complete unification of all the associations, a strategy approved by Hitler several months before.[114] During April and May, the DST and RSB on several occasions discussed the possibility of a merger. But Mulert, at least, remained wholly skeptical that the interests of the DST's big urban centers and the RSB's smaller towns could be represented effectively through a single organization.[115]

When the merger came, it was not the result of negotiations between the associations, but through the activities of a number of outsiders. Karl Fiehler, a long-time follower of Hitler's and the Nazi Oberbürgermeister of Munich after March 1933, oversaw the fusion process, with a small committee of three experts working under him.[116] On 22 May, Mulert and the other association leaders met with German Labor Front leader Robert Ley. Ley threatened that if they did not cooperate new groups would simply be created to replace them, and forced them to sign declarations agreeing to each group's absorption into a new, single unit, the *Deutsche Gemeindetag.*[117] On 30 May, Mulert was suspended from his post after accusations of corruption were brought against him, and on 17 June he was summarily dismissed. Although the charges were dropped a month later for lack of evidence, the damage was done. His removal had been accomplished with relative ease.[118]

The critical planning and maneuvering may have come from Fiehler's committee and the final *coup de grace* from Ley, but the key strategy in the Nazis' Gleichschaltung of the associations was arguably that of personnel replacement. The loss of most of its members through elections, retirements and suspensions in February and early March crippled the DST Council.[119] The strength of the Executive Committee, too, as Gerhard Schulz pointed out long ago, rested on the long-term continuity of its personnel. The new Working Committee, with a high rate of turnover, had new members arriving continuously.[120] Some came via pressure from highly placed National Socialists, others apparently merely because they wanted in.[121] Many of the newly elected or appointed mayors of the Grossstädte clamored for a seat; for some of them, a connection with the NSDAP was seemingly the only prerequisite.[122] Under such conditions, the orderly conduct of business became impossible, and so did any hope of effective resistance.

Mulert's own perceptions and behavior in these last months remain largely inscrutable. Given his passionate belief in the moral, philosophical, and (not least) administrative rectitude of local democracy, the force of his previous protestations against state interference in municipal affairs, and his importance in the DST, it is of some consequence to determine just what he was thinking and doing in the months from February to June 1933. Schulz has seen him as a far-sighted and perceptive observer, one of the few who was aware even in 1930 of the crippling effects of state incursions into the affairs of local government.[123] A wealth of evidence supports this assumption, and Mulert arguably exceeded his colleagues in perspicacity and ability. Yet when an angry letter came in March from Oskar Thomas, a city councillor in Stettin, castigating the DST leadership for refusing to convene the Council so it might "raise a protest against the many incursions into the law of self-government," Mulert responded first by explaining that no more Council members were to be had at present, and finished by rejecting the accusation that the DST was not doing its duty. "Please rest assured," he wrote phlegmatically, "that the organization's leaders even under current conditions are applying all strength towards maintaining the critical interests of the cities, by unremittingly carrying on their essential work." When Thomas responded that he could no longer stomach belonging to such an organization and submitted his resignation, Mulert answered that since Thomas had not been reelected on 12 March he was no longer a member anyway.[124]

As a former civil servant, Mulert was steeped in the judicial and procedural regulations of German administration. Given the Nazis' inventiveness and lack of scruples, he and his contemporaries were hopelessly outgunned after January 1933, and he appears to have had little chance of withstanding the flurry of legal and personnel changes that unraveled the fabric of his organization. He continued to look out for city interests and the Städtetag first, towards the end even considering the possibility that the situation could be used to the DST's advantage if all the other communal organizations were placed under his leadership.[125] At any rate, the record shows him unwilling to do more than bargain warily with the county and town associations about possible mergers. The Nazis' "unify and conquer" strategy ran roughshod over his negotiations with the RSB and the others. The prize was of considerable value: in taking over and fusing the associations into the Gemeindetag, they gained control of some 117 different organizations in which the leaders had influence or seats on supervisory councils. Few Gleichschaltung measures achieved so much with so little effort.[126]

3 The urban spectrum

The pressures and frictions of urbanization were not limited to cities, but spread to the urban periphery and beyond. Small towns and rural areas faced losing financial resources, manpower and prestige to growing metropolitan centers. Although their overarching aim was to preserve their economic viability, husband their resources, and provide local services, their principal challenge in the 1920s was to survive and, if possible, benefit from reforms that recast old administrative structures to reflect more closely the modern urban region as it evolved. Such reorganizations arose in particular from tensions between counties (*Landkreise*) and the towns within their borders over which level of government met modern challenges more effectively, the local or the regional.[1] In the first case, officials and functionaries in town halls knew intimately the subtleties and complexities of local conditions and were on personal terms with the people. But county councils had at their disposal the collective resources of larger areas, as well as the expertise of civil servants trained in the law whose experience extended beyond the locality. Thus, the issue ran, should the counties' jurisdictions and duties simply be amended so they could continue overseeing welfare, communal planning and so on; or should fundamental reforms reshape administrative boundaries to reflect more closely their modern population and economic bases?

Reform debates grew especially heated in cases of urban consolidation and annexation, known collectively as *Eingemeindung*. Consolidation could take one of several forms: neighboring towns melded together into a central conurbation; a city's borders enlarged to encompass surrounding towns and land tracts; counties divided up, their lands going to the cities and the remaining "rump" pieces then combined to form new counties. In essence, the controversies surrounding these reforms concerned fundamentally different visions of urbanization, modern local government, culture and tradition. The counties and small communes looked back on centuries of unregulated settlement, organically evolved administration, and strong local loyalties to the rural *Heimat*. They mounted strong resistance against measures that would alter radically the status quo. The cities, on the other hand, argued that modern urban transformation required equally modern forms of administration, and they warned of the possible consequences of a continued imbalance between twentieth-century conditions and nineteenth-century administrative structures.

Cities, towns, and counties were acutely affected by and closely involved in many reform initiatives of the 1920s and 1930s. To increase their regional and national influence, they turned with zeal to national associations devoted to protecting and furthering local interests (*kommunale Spitzenverbände*). The Städtetag was only the most prominent of these groups. The counties joined the *Deutsche Landkreistag* (LKT) and the rural townships the *Deutsche Landgemeindetag* (LGT). Middling towns and cities were looked after by the *Reichsstädtebund* (RSB). By 1929, the associations had reached unprecedented levels of internal cohesion, authority, and prestige. In the judgment of both contemporaries and later historians, "they ranked among the most important intermediary groups of the parliamentary state in the Weimar period."[2]

The principal orientations and goals of the communal associations were naturally determined by those of their members.[3] The DST's politics and aims were characterized from the beginning as "big-city interests" by towns put on the defensive by the cities' greater resources, unmatched influence and dynamic style. Towns, rural communities, and counties all evinced an abiding hostility towards the "soul-sapping," corrupt politics and impersonal life of the big city— hostility more than once directed publicly at the DST as the agent of Grossstadt politics. The towns and counties emphasized instead how agrarian production, local tradition and the rural values of the "flache Land" offered reserves of inner strength to Germany as it struggled to recover from military defeat and economic chaos.[4] In sum, the associations expressed values, goals, and interests that reflected their members' level of urbanization, from rural settlement to metropolis. Their strategies and interventions over how best to refit or recast local, state and national governments to fit modern social and economic conditions offer insight into tensions between city and town, town and country, and between the traditional and the modern in the republic.

BULWARKS AGAINST MODERN DISINTEGRATION

Furthest from the cities on the urban spectrum were the counties and small townships. Counties (*Kreise*) ranged in size from fifty square kilometers in Brunswick to well over two thousand in East Prussia (Pomerania), with a typical area of around five hundred. County responsibilities, administrative structures, and even usage of the basic term *Kreis* varied considerably across state and provincial borders.[5] Prior to the First World War, counties were important units of state administration and supervision of local government, particularly in Prussia, with responsibility mainly for the planning, construction, and maintenance of regional transportation networks, and for community planning.[6] By the 1920s, these duties had expanded in some cases to include administration of higher education (especially in agriculture), libraries, theaters, cinema halls, hospitals, orphanages, and regional light rail transit systems, as well as local utilities such as water, gas and electric works, and the coordination of welfare and poor relief.[7]

Like the other associations, the Congress of Counties, or *Landkreistag* spent the first half of the Weimar period expanding and consolidating. The parent Prussian Association of Counties (*Verband der preussischen Landkreise*; after 1924 *Preussischer Landkreistag*), founded in 1916, provided the basis on which the national congress was built in 1923. But consolidation was slow, hampered by variations between counties across the Reich, as well as by regional pride and fears that Prussia would dominate a national congress.[8] It was not until 1926 that all counties, representing 37.3 million Germans, were finally affiliated—either indirectly through regional associations or, in the few cases where these did not exist, directly as individual members. The Landkreistag in 1931 counted 773 counties as members.[9]

As county interests were largely rural and traditional, the LKT consistently supported the conservation of existing administrative structures with only limited and necessary reforms. This caution stemmed in part from the lesser impact of urban development on the Kreise during the nineteenth century, especially in East Prussia, where the owners of large rural estates wielded considerable power over their agricultural holdings and tenants. Moreover, many estate owners were also prefects (*Landräte*), the most powerful officials in the county. The Landrat occupied a complicated position, in that he was simultaneously a local functionary, supervising the affairs of the towns under his jurisdiction, while also a servant of the state, appointed before the war by the crown. In Weimar, Landräte could be nominated by county parliaments, the *Kreistage*, with final confirmation by the Prussian Ministry of the Interior. Despite concerted efforts by Prussian central authorities to institute personnel changes after 1918, over half of the Landräte from the prewar period were still in their old posts in 1926; nor did a similar turnover in personnel take place in the other Länder.[10] The tradition of state service, combined with the aristocratic background of many Landräte, inclined them to views more conservative than those of city officials, especially concerning issues of local autonomy versus state power.[11] They saw the Kreise as bastions of traditional, rural values, still untainted by the social tensions and materialism of the urban environment, which they associated with the rise of working-class politics and an alleged politicization of administration after 1918. They stubbornly refused to accept volunteer or lay Kreis representatives in the congress long after it had become common practice in the Städtetage, fearing that an infusion of nonprofessionals would "politicize" the LKT.[12] In sum, the Landräte perceived themselves as "the bulwark of old Prussia against the flood of modern, disintegrating trends," and the Landkreistag as a "coming together of all productive social classes as a balance against elements of decomposition and disorder that have lost connection with the soil."[13]

The association of rural townships, the Deutsche Landgemeindetag (LGT) experienced the most complicated and troubled internal history of the communal organizations prior to 1933. Forged from several groups in 1922, it was divided during most of the Weimar period by tensions between the two main Prussian regional associations, known colloquially as *Westverband* and *Ostverband*, that is, between towns in the industrial West and those in the agrarian East.[14] In its first phase, from 1922 to 1927, the LGT was dominated by the West: its business affairs were handled through the Westverband's Berlin office and overseen by its managing director. During the inflation years it was largely the resources and efforts of the Westverband that kept the new national association "above water";[15] although it survived, tensions between East and West remained strong. In April 1926, the various associations of eastern townships united under the aegis of the Ostverband, so increasing its weight in the national association.[16] Two years later, after reportedly "violent internal struggles," it took control of the national Landgemeindetag.[17] The office of president was now assumed by Ostverband president Günter Gereke, a former Landrat from East Prussia and, after 1928, a conservative (DNVP) delegate in the Reichstag. In the judgment of Kurt Jeserich, one of his most astute contemporaries, Gereke used his new position to further his own high political ambitions, leaving the daily business of the Congress to his vice president, Heinrich Schellen. His rather fantastic career ended up spanning conservative anti-Weimar politics, persecution under the Nazis, and high office in East Germany after 1945.[18] His rise to prominence in the LGT threatened to push the Western towns to the margins of urban politics, as he tried to exclude their now "regional association" from "negotiations of the national communal associations."[19] However, the western association was well-connected politically and its members largely came from the Ruhr basin. It represented an area too important economically to exclude or willfully ignore.[20] Westverband leaders thus continued to attend inter-association meetings, leaving moot the question of their formal participation.[21]

Large cities on one end of the urban spectrum and rural settlements and townships on the other found that the clarity of their positions relative to the urbanization process lent an equal measure of political clarity to their collective aims and desires. Cities were already urbanized; few rural townships experienced levels of growth that forced them to respond to urbanization's pressures. Not so for the larger towns caught in the middle. In the first months of the Weimar Republic, Alfred Belian, First Bürgermeister of Eilenburg and chairman of the towns' association, the Reichsstädtebund (RSB), warned his compatriots that in the postwar period, middle-sized cities and towns must guard against the danger of "being crushed between big cities and rural areas by modern legislation."[22] His comment points neatly to the peculiar situation of the middling towns in the republic's urban environment. On one hand, they were generally too large to be considered rural communes. Many were approaching or had exceeded the size necessary to qualify for independent legal status as a city. On the other hand, their interests were not yet those of Grossstädte, and they could not hope to rival the cities' economic and political power.[23] This ambiguity was reflected in the positions adopted by the Reichsstädtebund in the various debates over urban modernity in the 1920s. The RSB unwaveringly supported the right of growing, maturing towns to escape the constricting control of the counties by gaining city status, and fought bitterly against the counties' efforts in the latter 1920s to make that independence harder to gain.[24] But when it came to the other half of the reform equation, urban consolidation, experience showed that middling towns were by no means safe from being carved up or absorbed by the cities.[25] The RSB therefore joined the counties and rural communes in resisting large-scale changes, and condemned the reforming enthusiasm of the cities.[26] Reviewing a 1928 Städtetag article praising the pending reform of the Ruhr region, for instance, one RSB leader commented wryly that the author "does not appear to be in danger of being annexed by a Grossstadt, otherwise he could not think so naively that the middling cities, towards whom the giant hands of the big cities are stretching out, would want to trust in the leadership and influence of the Deutsche Städtetag."[27] Yet of all the associations, the DST and RSB were closest in their views and interests. The RSB's lack of power even drove it at several points in the 1920s to consider establishing a formal alliance or even merging with the Städtetag. Dealings between the two were correspondingly more extensive than with the other associations, a fact reflected in the documentary record.[28]

The Reichsstädtebund was founded in Berlin in March 1910 under the original name of *Reichsverband deutscher Städte*, a union of municipalities with populations under twenty-five thousand. Beginning with just forty founding towns, its membership by 1933 had reached 1,559 municipalities, representing 9.5 million people.[29] The RSB's three-tiered organization was similar to that of the DST: a Managing Council chaired by the president; a larger General Committee, to which member towns from each state could collectively send two delegates for every 100,000 inhabitants they represented; and congresses held each year in a different city.[30] Each member town was allocated from two to five votes in the assembly, depending on size. The Bund was strongest in Prussia, which contained over four-fifths of its members, organized in an extensive network of local branches.[31]

The impulse behind the RSB's founding in 1910 originated in the towns' not unfounded conviction that the city associations served the interests of and were controlled by the Grossstädte. In 1907, Swabian towns founded a local association when they realized that a proposed state grant covering two-thirds of continuing education costs would go to big cities exclusively. A year later, small towns were excluded from direct membership in a Städtetag being founded in the Rhine Province at Koblenz. And at the second national Städtetag in 1908 in Munich, a credit proposal formulated by Bavarian towns was defeated by the opposition of Dresden—evidence for the towns that they were victims of *Grossstadtpolitik*.[32] Complaining that the Städtetage, led by big-city mayors, both ignored and were ignorant of their concerns, the towns insisted their new Bund would not pursue "narrow-minded provincial politics."[33] The Grossstädte for their part skeptically attributed the RSB's founding to the personal ambition of small-town mayors who lacked the practical experience necessary to make of the RSB anything more than a distracting annoyance and competition for the Städtetag. In the end, two national urban associations could only work against each other and harm the interests of all German cities.[34] Thus began a long competition between county, town and city for legitimacy, influence, the attention of national and state agencies and, after 1918, public favor.

In Weimar's early years, the social, economic, and ideological divisions between the communal associations were not as clear-cut as they became later. Only the cities entered the postwar period with anything resembling a national congress; the others emerged soon after the war. All of them, the Städtetag included, underwent extensive reorganization and consolidation during the first half of the 1920s. As their internal lines of communication strengthened and central offices expanded, their enterprises and projects focused more sharply. With greater national activity came friction and competition; lobbying strategies, counter-strategies and tactical alliances assumed a corresponding importance. Each association strove mightily to influence government policy and public opinion: they lobbied and negotiated with public officials, sent reams of printed material to deputies in the Reichstag and the state parliaments, and published extensive communal reviews highlighting their members' affairs. Until 1933, a common thread in the associations' rhetoric was an emphasis on a united front of cities, towns, and communes working for the common good of all municipalities in the republic, regardless of size. The Städtetag, claiming to represent not just the big metropoles but all German municipalities, found it especially convenient to resort to this device during disputes with the other groups, or when answering the complaints of its own small-town members, unhappy with Grossstadt domination of the DST.[35] The problem, as the associations' uneasy relations in the latter 1920s clearly showed, was twofold: they had very different visions of what constituted the common good of all German municipalities; and the conviction that they should work together remained an abstract rationale of strength-through-unity.[36]

Their relations in the republican period went through three phases. The first, a period of postwar crisis and adjustment, lasted into the early stages of currency stabilization and was marked by haphazard cooperation. It effectively ended with the Städtetag's rejection in 1924 of a merger proposal from the Reichsstädtebund, and the latter's subsequent refusal to join a much broader coalition of all localities, from rural village to Grossstadt, in which each association would have participated equally. The second phase, beginning with economic stabilization around 1924 and lasting until 1931, saw the associations strike out on their own. Realizing that in many respects their interests were fundamentally at odds, they collaborated instead on isolated issues. At several junctures they disagreed seriously with one another, and reached open confrontation over the Ruhr reform of 1929. The third and final phase began with the Depression. Suffering from an astronomical increase in the financial burden of unemployment and welfare support, smaller towns, especially, could no longer afford the luxury of working alone. The associations joined together informally in order to share resources and present their case more effectively to the Reich and Land governments and to the public.

SUPPLICANTS

The associations negotiated intensively over the possibility of jointly establishing a single co-operative organization during the years from the end of the war until the currency stabilization of 1924. The first occasion for a show of solidarity was to protest a 1921 Reich decree raising the wages and salaries of civil servants. Cities faced instituting pay hikes at their own expense if their employees' salaries were to match those of the Reich and Länder—something they accepted in principle but could not afford. The congress was called specifically at the insistence of the city of Berlin, which in order to pay the higher salaries had decided in summer 1921 to withhold tax revenues ear-marked for the Reich.[37] The Städtetag and Reichsstädtebund met in bicameral session in the Reichstag building on 11 November 1921, along with representatives from the LKT and LGT,[38] as well as numerous representatives of the Reich and Land governments.[39] Both cities and towns framed their case within the larger, unsolved problem of the Reich's financial structure and its effect on municipal revenue. In an exasperated speech, Konrad Adenauer, the prominent lord mayor of Cologne, protested that the current distribution of payments—which secured Reich finances first, followed by those of the states—meant that municipal treasuries were always "fed with the crumbs left over." What, he went on to ask caustically, "will the Reich do when the communes are ruined, when they have sunk into poverty?" Financially sound cities were fundamental to the nation's health: "The interests of the communes are financially the same as the interests of the Reich."[40] In obvious agreement, the assembly adopted Adenauer's demand for an equitable, permanent solution to the problem of financial distribution, one that would ensure the communes' right to self-administration. Citing the increase in their responsibilities and decline in their resources during the previous two years, the assembly demanded unanimously that the Reich provide immediate funds to cover the salary increases.[41]

Although these demands went unanswered, the extraordinary congress marked a high point in the solidarity of the municipalities. The open anger and frustration with which they addressed the Reich and Land governments, many of whose representatives were in the room as observers, was unprecedented in their dealings with official agencies. The extent of their concern showed itself in their unanimity. The final resolution of the assembly had the full support of all participants—both socialist and conservative, from small town and big city.[42]

Over the next several years, the associations made two simultaneous but distinct efforts to pull together into a single organization. One involved only the DST and the RSB; the other was cast more broadly to include them all.[43] Discussions toward the latter end began in January 1923, when Adolf von Achenbach, chairman of the new national county association, approached Gustav Böss, chairman of the DST and lord mayor of Berlin. Achenbach was convinced that only economically productive local governments would survive Weimar's crises intact: hard times would cripple smaller localities whose independence was not supported by strong economic roots. He suggested that if local self-government was to survive, communes of all sizes must forge a cooperative organization, or *Arbeitsgemeinschaft*.[44] Government officials dealing with a sole authority for communal interests would not be swamped with petitions and publications from different quarters, and were more likely to read those they did receive. At the time, Städtetag leaders were also considering an internal proposal for a merger with the RSB.[45] Both sets of negotiations were carried on more or less openly. This is not to say that the other associations were invited to the table. Both the cities and the counties occasionally suggested it might be wise to bring the others into the negotiations in the first half of 1923, but neither pursued it. LKT leaders seemed aware that although it was they who had started the ball rolling, they could be upstaged when others joined the negotiations. The LGT was annoyed to find out about the negotiations from the DST's official newsletter.[46] Plans for the Arbeitsgemeinschaft developed to the point that actual regulations were drawn up specifying the number of members to be allocated to each association. The projected "Cooperative Association of German/Prussian Communal Self-Government" was to consist of members divided into Prussian and non-Prussian sections who would meet once per year. A supervising council and a chairman would meet more frequently and, among other things, set meeting agendas and select special committees.[47]

The DST from the beginning made clear that forming the larger Arbeitsgemeinschaft depended first on the outcome of its bilateral negotiations with the RSB.[48] A Städtetag-Städtebund coalition would dominate the Arbeitsgemeinschaft by nature of its combined strength, representative weight, collective experience, and the collaboration of two professional staffs. The DST may also have simply considered the merger the more likely of the two to occur; its relations with the RSB were always closer than with the other associations, reflecting often overlapping interests and constituencies.

But the negotiations did not go smoothly. The RSB's fundamental concern was to protect the interests of its smaller members, the county towns, from being overshadowed by the economic and political power of the Grossstädte. RSB President Gotthold Haekel demanded that the DST increase the representation of small towns at every level of its management, voting and membership: a town delegate would occupy a seat on the DST's small and powerful Executive Committee; seats would be set aside in the Council of the Prussian Städtetag to allow representation of towns from every Prussian province;[49] a special standing committee would be formed to deal exclusively with small-town affairs; and the towns would be organized separately within the DST's yearly and three-year congresses, either as a "Smaller Cities Group" or else as a distinct entity within the new "Deutsche Städtetag und Reichsstädtebund." The RSB also demanded that the Städtetag's staff be overhauled to give equal weight to the smaller members. This included installing Haekel as co-managing director alongside Paul Mitzlaff.[50]

Though the cities continued negotiating, the DST evinced irritation at the extent of the towns' demands and a growing conviction that the whole scheme was unworkable.[51] Time was also a problem. With inflation reaching extreme levels in late 1923, the cities were preoccupied with more urgent matters. When the special nine-member DST committee created in May 1923 to consider the merger finally met the following March, it overwhelmingly rejected the idea, a decision confirmed by the DST Council a month later. The principal obstacle was the two membership systems and their different voting structures. Towns belonged to the Städtetag indirectly through their provincial and state associations. They did not individually send delegates to the national congress. In the Bund, however, each town had its own representatives and possessed from two to five votes in the main assembly, depending on its size.[52] When Mitzlaff communicated the disappointing verdict to the RSB, he hastened to add that it did not exclude the still-feasible alternative of the all-association Arbeitsgemeinschaft. But now it was the RSB's turn to refuse. Perhaps fearing that, as the weakest member, its voice would go unheard in an association dominated by the Grossstädte on one hand and the counties on the other, Haekel commented that he did not believe such an organization was necessary.[53] He remarked that the communal associations usually cooperated well with one another, and that care should be taken to avoid the creation of new, superfluous groups. He also found problematic the power of veto that each member of the Arbeitsgemeinschaft would possess. Since unanimity was required before taking collective action, he pointed out that "only in seldom, isolated cases could the Arbeitsgemeinschaft have any practical importance." The need for unanimity might also damage relations between the members, as each came under pressure to sacrifice its members' interests for those of the whole.[54]

Just two years later, the RSB was again discussing the whole issue of organizational relations with redoubled intensity, occasioned this time by the DST's choice of Oskar Mulert as its new president. (Interestingly, Haekel was approached about the position, but refused.)[55] Mulert's energy, ability, and dedication to his new post, as well as high prestige and influence through his personal connections in Prussian and Reich government circles, made inter-associational relations again "one of the most important issues for the Bund."[56] In November 1926, Haekel drafted an internal strategy memo weighing the value of formal alliances with the other associations, the effectiveness of the resulting power constellations, how pressure raised by various issues might bring associations into line or, equally, into conflict. In the case of the townships, conflict was bound to arise over the rights of small rural communes versus those of the RSB's larger towns. The counties, on the other hand, remained an uncertain factor. They usually opposed the big cities and urban reforms on principle, but were also fundamentally against one of the RSB's cardinal concerns, the right of growing towns to gain independence from county jurisdiction. Consequently, the Landkreistag might side with the RSB in one instance but not in another. After getting a clear picture—the RSB working with the counties and communes against the cities, working with the cities against the towns and counties, and so forth—Haekel concluded it would be best for the RSB to form a closer association with the Städtetag, which included within its ranks towns and middling cities and could be relied on to support urban over rural interests. Admittedly, the DST historically had looked out for the largest municipalities, but Haekel argued that an alliance with the RSB would increase internal pressure on the Städtetag Council and its central office from its smaller members, many of whom were also Bund members.[57]

Haekel's initiative this time was undermined by his closest co-worker, RSB Chairman Alfred Belian. In a circular to RSB Council members, Belian agreed that the RSB could use allies, but warned against inflexibly following a single strategy. Where Haekel saw growing commonalities with the DST, Belian saw dangerous differences. He concluded that the Bund should be free to pursue whatever tactics best suited a given situation: "In every question we must determine each time: is it a matter of fundamental importance that can best be represented by ourselves alone, and who will help us with it?"[58]

The positions laid out by the two RSB leaders summed up succinctly the difficult choices facing the weaker, "supplicant" town associations of the RSB and LGT in the latter 1920s.[59] Seeking to influence both government and popular opinion during a period of reform, they realized acutely the importance of finding a unified voice to represent their interests, as well as the advantages of combining their representative weight, experience and expertise. However, the magnitude of their tasks also forced them to weigh carefully the dangers of being identified too closely with groups who in the final analysis were competitors. Memories of inter-organization scrapping, combined with fears that working together would hurt their own members' interests, led each association to choose independence over formal collaboration.[60]

TO EACH HIS OWN [61]

Relations between the communal associations entered their second phase around 1926, when the Mulert's appointment as DST executive president set the associations a harder pace. Following suit, they increased the executive powers of their leaders, which sped up decision making, but at the expense of collegiality in the committees and congresses.[62] Concentrated executive power also facilitated municipal representation in many public and semi-public organizations, where the association leaders sat on managing boards and executive councils. Mulert, for example, by 1930 was officially associated with no less than 122 councils and organizations of various types.[63]

Under Mulert, all merger negotiations stopped. In the nervous atmosphere of rivalry and competition in Weimar's stabilization period, inflexible, formal arrangements would restrict the Städtetag's own interests.[64] The unique needs of the Grossstädte could be represented fully only by their own organization.[65] Informal cooperation thus became the strategy of choice. Problems were discussed and disagreements ironed out in private breakfast and dinner meetings in Berlin, which grew increasingly common.[66] The leaders resolved in early 1925 that all proposals, petitions or requests would be circulated amongst themselves before being released to the public or submitted to official agencies, in order for the others to formulate a position and participate if they wished. No one would be caught by surprise or blind-sided.[67] They also agreed to avoid intruding individually in affairs that did not concern them directly and to refrain from bickering publicly and in the press.[68] Communal finance received their particular attention. A number of petitions and memoranda destined for various Reich and Prussian ministries were formulated collectively in their meetings.[69] Requests for municipal financial statistics, especially, were treated with special caution, even when coming from a relatively benign source like the International Association of Cities, headquartered in Brussels. The cities were so careful in this respect that Reichsbank President Hjalmar Schacht, an outspoken critic of their financial practices, agreed that no official statistics detailing German municipal short-term debt would be published unless they agreed with those of the DST.[70]

Undercurrents of tension ran through even the most positive efforts of communal groups to collaborate, however.[71] As the importance of a particular issue increased so too did the stakes, raising suspicions and setting tempers on edge. Although the associations emphasized how much they valued cooperation, the burden of compromise rested invariably with the other party. Correspondence, press releases and discussions between the leaders from 1925 to 1931 show the associations engaged in a continual process of collaboration and realignment. Ability to affect the outcome of a given issue—an impression of advantage, power, an edge—in turn decreased their willingness to compromise with the others or look for common ground. During a period of especially tense bargaining with the DST in 1928 over communal representation on official Reich and Prussian committees, RSB Chairman Belian griped that, within the RSB, it was widely believed that "cooperation" had no meaning for the Städtetag, which showed no flexibility and forced the towns to make all the concessions.[72]

Competition for new member-cities was a special sore point between the two associations before 1933. Although each recognized the general territory of the other, cities with the Städtetag and towns with the Bund, the boundaries were not clearly marked. Medium-sized municipalities of between twenty-five and fifty thousand inhabitants fell within both jurisdictions and were thus regarded by each group as potential recruits. In 1917, the Städtetag, addressing what its director, Hans Luther, believed to be a growing resentment among medium-sized cities at their continuing lack of sufficient representation in the DST, lowered the required minimum size for direct membership from twenty-five thousand to ten thousand inhabitants. At the same time, the RSB extended its membership ceiling upward, from twenty-five thousand to forty thousand.[73] The resulting overlap strained their relations throughout the 1920s. The Bund agreed in 1926 to a proposal from the DST Executive Committee to establish a line clearly dividing the medium-sized cities: the larger ones would belong solely to the Städtetag, the smaller to the Reichsstädtebund.[74] But Mulert's repeated requests to firm up the details met with hedging and evasive replies.[75] One reason may be a theme that runs through the entire history of the RSB: it was able to exert very little real influence on state policy and law-making.

Mid-point in 1926—just when Haekel was advocating his new collaborative strategy—marked the end of a three-year period of intense internal evaluation of the RSB's overall strategy and tactics.[76] Both the Bund and the Städtetag arrived independently at the same conclusion: the old method of trying to get the attention of legislators and central administrators by bombarding them with proposals, petitions, and statistics, had failed. Instead, the RSB embarked on a course of personal, one-on-one meetings and correspondence with officials. The towns called for more candidates with backgrounds in small-town administration and politics to run for seats in federal and state parliaments; a new RSB "Parliamentary Advisory Committee" would consist of Reich and Land parliamentary deputies, in order to involve them directly in small-town concerns. The RSB also made a determined effort to attract press attention by inviting officials and reporters periodically to large gatherings called "parliamentary evenings"—a combined press conference and cocktail party—in order to raise awareness of municipal problems on the part of legislators and the public. Some three hundred guests who attended the first one in May 1925 heard Belian's after-dinner speech:

> In modern life, only mass organizations get noticed. It's not personal ambition or megalomania that's brought the small and middling cities together, but the sincere wish to work for Volk and Fatherland. Efforts are underway to lay more and more responsibilities (*Aufgaben*) on the rural counties. This would be to the detriment of all. It would be unnatural if the foundational cell (*Urzelle*) was eliminated. Governments, parliaments, and all other organizations in civic life (*Staatsleben*) can founder, only the fundamental cell, the commune, remains everlasting. The essential tasks must therefore remain left with it.[77]

In the long run, none of these measures was successful. Reichstag and Landtag deputies declined or ignored the RSB's increasingly forlorn invitations to sit on the advisory committee, even when assured that participation entailed no real work on their part. Candidates with backgrounds in local politics continued to come mainly from the Grossstädte. Press coverage, despite some improvement, remained perfunctory at best.[78] Thus underlying the RSB's 1926 emphasis on tactical freedom of movement and reluctance to make formal alliances was a deeper sense of weakness: little influence in official circles, scant interest from the public and the press, and the comparatively small proportion of the German population it represented.[79] As Haekel pointed out, any formal working agreement with the Städtetag was likely to work to the Bund's disadvantage. Convinced that the cities could afford more flexibility in dealing with officials and the other associations, the Bund leaders concluded that the DST's aims, influence, and contacts would become the determining factors in any cooperative venture.

In sum, underlying the Bund's "reorientation" phase was a realization that it was on its own. In 1927, it began an aggressive campaign to increase its size and influence that lasted into the Depression. Tension quickly arose with the DST over the allocation of municipal seats on various official committees and councils, including the Reichstag Inter-Party Committee on Communal Politics, the administrative councils of the Reichsanstalt für Arbeitsvermittlung und Arbeitslosenversicherung, and in the Prussian Welfare Ministry.[80] The most heated of these exchanges concerned the Reich Economic Council (*Reichswirtschaftsrat*, RWR). Created as a constitutionally independent body in May 1920, the Council brought together representatives from trade unions, employers, the public sector and other "representatives of economic life," to advise the government on economic policy.[81] However, dissatisfaction with its unwieldy and semi-official character led the Reich government, in a 1925 bill, to propose drastic changes. Of the 326 members of the council, sixteen were designated communal representatives, eight belonging to the DST. The reform proposed reducing the number of members by over half, to 151; six would go to the communal associations: two each to the DST and LKT, one each to the RSB and LGT. For the next five years, until the defeat of the bill in July 1930, the communal associations debated the proper shape and constitution of the Council and maneuvered for more seats on it.[82] The proposed decrease in the cities' share meant a corresponding increase for the counties and towns, a "formal equalization of city and country" which, the DST protested, did not correspond to economic reality. Representation in the RWR was above all a matter of "valuing urban life," Mulert declared in his speech to the DST tri-annual congress at Magdeburg in 1927. "The focal point of economic life lies in the German cities. The dominant majority of industrial, business and trade concerns, nine-tenths of the most important communal economic undertakings, are concentrated in the cities."[83] Perhaps more significantly, the RWR provided the only official connection through which the cities could make their voices heard in federal legislation and policy making. Mulert considered sufficient representation on the council as a key strategic point if the cities wanted any part in the debates over the much more important national reforms being bruited in the late 1920s.[84]

In the competition for more seats on the RWR, the Städtetag consistently came out on top. Mulert's influence in Prussian and Reich government circles played an important role here. In June 1927, the DST secured a promise of help from his old office, the section for communal affairs in the Prussian Ministry of the Interior. The negotiations suggest much about the Prussian ministry's attitude towards cities. The director of the section for communal affairs, Victor von Leyden, at first protested that it was a matter of indifference to the ministry how the associations divided up the communal seats. DST vice president Fritz Elsas, however, reminded him how strongly the ministry had supported the cities in the past, and insisted that this was a similar instance. Von Leyden finally agreed to one more DST seat on the council.[85] The new total of five was satisfactory, and in December, the Städtetag and Landkreistag, the most powerful associations, submitted a joint letter to the Reichstag recommending passage of the bill as it currently stood.[86]

The loser in this arrangement was the RSB. Chairman Belian wrote to Mulert in early 1928 that the RSB was "greatly embittered" over the fact that the new communal seat, rather than being awarded to the towns, had been finagled into a fifth seat by the DST, while the RSB had to be satisfied with just one.[87] Mulert unsympathetically fired back that the cities had merely fought for and won back a seat unfairly transferred from the cities to the counties; the DST's gain simply marked a return to the status quo—which, he reminded Belian, the RSB had originally approved.[88]

"CLOSER TO THEIR HEARTS"—THE SMALL TOWNS REVOLT

The sharpness of Mulert's response may have been due in part to the fact that around this time the Reichsstädtebund began poaching openly among DST membership, quietly approaching officials of small- and medium-sized cities in the DST, denigrating its "Grossstadt" politics and pointing out the advantages of membership in the Bund.[89] The record leaves no doubt that these tactics both irritated and worried Mulert. In response to his increasingly exasperated demands for an explanation, the RSB refused to explain its intentions or admit any wrongdoing.[90] Belian instead countered that it was the DST who had broken the peace first. Back in 1918, when it lowered its membership limit to ten thousand without consulting the Bund, the RSB merely defended itself by raising its own limit to forty thousand. Since then, Belian claimed, middling cities had approached the RSB repeatedly with requests that they be allowed to join up, complaining that the DST routinely ignored them in favor of the Grossstädte.[91] Even the Städtetag's own members reported that the towns considered the RSB "closer to their hearts."[92]

Whether or not the RSB's campaign for new members was successful, there can be no doubt that its criticism of big-city politics found special resonance among smaller Städtetag members, whose increasing restlessness caused headaches for DST leaders in the later 1920s and early 1930s. The Congress could not of course please everyone, especially when its deliberations and decisions touched, as they often did, on issues of fundamental importance to all municipalities. As part of its internal consolidation in the mid-1920s, the concerted effort of the Berlin office to coordinate and control communication between the cities and government authorities meant curtailing the independence of the provincial and state sub-organizations. All requests, petitions, and proposals from individual cities to their state governments were to be channeled through the state associations; similarly, materials submitted to Reich ministries and parliaments were to be routed solely through the central office in the DST Städtehaus in Berlin. In the case of Prussia, the PST reasoned, "In order to achieve a unified advance of the cities, it appears indispensable to reserve the representation of the cities' interests in parliaments and the government solely to the Prussian Städtetag." Under no circumstances were the state and provincial associations to approach the Prussian or Reich governments directly on matters that exceeded the limits of their own local affairs.[93]

Government policy in Weimar similarly limited communication between the central and local governments. Prominent in state-local relations after the turn of the century were efforts by the cities to get more direct access to central authorities. Even before the war, Prussian municipalities complained that district representatives, the *Regierungspräsidenten*, refused to pass along local appeals for central adjudication to higher administrative channels.[94] The cities' frustration with bureaucratic bottlenecks continued after 1918, though many managed to circumvent the problem through the influence of a powerful mayor.[95] But the Reich and states also desired to strengthen their control over local governments, most of whose personnel, practices and ambitions pre-dated Weimar. In the early years of the republic, they decreed that municipalities could not go over the heads of local supervisory authorities; communications between local and central had to follow prescribed channels.[96] In their efforts to avoid getting enswamped in the details of local affairs, governments found the communal associations to be convenient intermediaries. By the end of the Weimar period, the Prussian Minister of the Interior thought not only that the associations had the right to act as screening authorities, but were in fact obligated to do so.[97] This suited the DST central office, which worked hard to improve its communications with regional Städtetage, requesting details of organizational setups, personnel, and specifically local problems.[98] The value of information exchange showed clearly in late 1930, when Prussia installed state commissars in over five hundred cities and towns. The DST used its branch associations in other states to survey municipal conditions and determine whether the other Länder were contemplating similar measures.[99] As late as March 1933, Mulert was insisting on more complete information from the state associations, in order "to obtain a unified line of communal policy in keeping with the goals of the national government."[100] In sum, through their control of the DST's Executive Committee and its Council, the tight focus of DST policy on large urban issues, and aided by the explicit preferences of Reich and state officials, the Grossstädte consolidated their hold on the organization. This in turn facilitated their representation of the Städtetag as a "united front" of all German cities.[101]

But middling cities and small towns constituted a significant presence within the Städtetag's own membership. In 1924, exactly two-thirds of municipalities holding direct membership were mid-sized towns with fewer than 50,000 inhabitants. Many more too small to be direct members belonged indirectly through their regional and state organizations. Even allowing for an overlap in membership, approximately three times as many small towns belonged to the Städtetag as did cities with populations over 50,000.[102] Yet their representation on the DST's important directing bodies, the Council and the Executive Committee, showed the reverse: slightly over 60 percent of Council seats went to the cities over 250,000, with Berlin alone occupying 13 percent of them.[103] With the Grossstadt leaders concentrating Städtetag energies on large-scale urban issues, the towns' frustration came through in a litany of discontent, rebelliousness, and threats to abandon the association for a more sympathetic venue.[104] Not unnaturally, they were doubly incensed by DST efforts to clamp down on their activities. The branch association in Schleswig-Holstein objected to one "such thoroughly annoying resolution of the Prussian Städtetag," protesting that it "ignores [the fact] that the provincial Städtetage are not sub-organizations of the Prussian Städtetag, because belonging to them along with the larger cities that belong to the Prussian Städtetag [are] the smaller cities organized in the Reichsstädtebund."[105]

Although the DST's towns were restive throughout the 1920s, the arrival of the Depression and new restrictions on local finance and self-government after 1930 drove them to push harder for better representation. In mid-1932, the Schleswig-Holstein municipalities again rebelled, claiming that the PST in Berlin neither knew nor cared about small-town problems in the provinces. In July, Mulert received a letter warning that the Verein had splintered into groups of large, middling, and small cities; the latter had voted unanimously to leave the Städtetag, claiming that the Reichsstädtebund's fuller representation of their interests made it much more "their organization."[106] Alarmed, Mulert traveled to Kiel in late November, accompanied by Reichsstädtebund president Haekel. There, at the association's council meeting, the two visitors heard the Schleswig-Holstein towns declare categorically that "the Prussian Städtetag must represent the larger cities and the Reichsstädtebund the smaller towns. The small towns no longer wish to belong indirectly against their will to an organization that does not view them as necessary." Political battles between the Nazis and Communists were especially sharp in the area, and municipal administrations were suffering exceptionally hard times: "There is no more time to be lost. Things are completely falling apart. The Berlin offices have had enough time for reflection, we must have help, and that immediately." Their desperation was forcing them to exert pressure openly, and they finished by threatening to leave the provincial Verein altogether if it did not resign from the Städtetag.

Mulert then addressed the town representatives. He admitted that the Städtetage looked after big-city interests primarily, and conceded that the small towns sometimes had difficulty making themselves heard. But he stood firm by his claim that both the Prussian and the national associations looked after all city interests, and emphasized the importance of solidarity between cities and towns of every size.[107] He reminded them that the cities had recently fought against Prussian emergency decrees that would have put the small towns under the direct supervision of their county prefects—something the towns greatly feared.[108] Mulert warned that the towns could count on stiff bureaucratic opposition when they tried to secure their share of Reich funds for unemployment support, and that it could be overcome only with the help of the influential Prussian Städtetag.

Haekel took the side of the towns. He noted that many of them were paying dues to as many as five different city associations and their subbranches, an unaffordable luxury in hard times.[109] This called forth a hubbub of small-town voices, each with differing opinions: that all the associations, whether city, town or county, should unify and then deal with the provincial organizations; that, contrarily, the towns should reject all umbrella groups and work only with local and provincial organizations; and, more pessimistically, that the real winner in scraps between cities and towns would always be the state. The meeting broke up temporarily to let tempers cool and give the towns a chance to consult with Haekel. Upon returning, the Council resolved that although the Verein would not quit the PST, it would also join the RSB, which would receive 25 percent of the towns' fee payments.[110]

Three days later, eight small-town mayors from the state sub-organizations arrived at the Städtehaus for a meeting with Mulert and Haekel. They again made their case: they might not be large metropoles, but they were nonetheless municipalities possessing savings banks, water- and electric-works, slaughter-houses, professional, middle and high schools, public libraries, and so forth. They therefore claimed the right to be represented just as energetically as the big cities.[111] Mulert agreed. Over the next month, both the Executive Committee and the Council discussed the problem of misunderstanding and tension between center and periphery, and how to work more closely with the smaller cities and the Reichsstädtebund.[112] In the first days of 1933, the DST set up a new "Information Service" expressly to prepare reports clarifying for the provincial towns exactly what the Städtetag was doing for them.[113]

The Depression made closer cooperation between the DST and the other associations increasingly urgent, but no easier. In 1931, beleaguered city, town, and county organizations came together in an "informal" cooperative to negotiate with the Reich and states.[114] Yet old patterns continued. Mulert and the Städtetag, unbidden, took the lead in speaking for all the associations, a liberty much resented by the others. From their perspective, the programs that now emanated from the "collective" were again geared solely towards easing the burdens of the Grossstädte. The towns, in particular, broke ranks to complain publicly about the big-city favoritism in the DST's "Savings Program" of August 1931.[115] The Landkreistag, Landgemeindetag, and Reichsstädtebund all wrote to the Reich Minister of the Interior to protest the DST's high-handedness and reassert the essential differences between big urban centers, small towns, and purely rural areas: "Grossstädte and 'German municipalities' are not one and the same!" Spending cuts proposed for the cities were "practically meaningless" for other local governments. They requested that before implementing any local savings measures, the Reich should hear from all the associations, not just one.[116]

The weakest town associations, the RSB and LGT, were especially frustrated with the arrangement. A conservative East Prussian newspaper in Stettin noted with some satisfaction that open confrontation between the RSB and the Städtetag promised a new alignment. The towns would finally leave the DST's orbit and move closer to "their natural ally," the Landkreistag.[117] When the Nazi *Machtergreifung* offered the towns new paths to patronage and power after January 1933, they followed eagerly. The West Prussian townships wrote to Hitler's Interior Minister, Wilhelm Frick, to extol the bucolic virtues of rural life, and referred pointedly to the key roles they expected to play in the new Reich.[118] The Reichsstädtebund was first in line to express its delight at the Nazi "national awakening" and declare its "unreserved" support for Hitler's government. Only three days after Hitler became chancellor, Haekel wrote both Hitler and Göring congratulatory letters; later in February, Frick delivered the keynote address to the RSB's 1933 congress.[119] Perhaps more significantly, the RSB's belief that the Nazi solution to the political and economic crisis would bring added power and prestige to the towns led it to pursue enthusiastically the internal personnel changes that most undermined the associations in April and May 1933. National Socialist members of the RSB's new "Working Committee" exerted considerable pressure on Mulert and the DST to join them in unifying the communal associations—significant steps towards the eventual Gleichschaltung of the associations that took place in June.[120]

The associations' respective approaches to the challenges they faced, and the effectiveness with which they could express their views, were determined largely by the sum total of their social power—in other words, by what sorts of claims could be based on their members' economic, financial and population resources. As the Reich's principal sources of tax revenue, for instance, the Grossstädte had more to say about welfare policy than the towns and rural communes did. The new electoral franchise after 1919 gave the cities a political weight unmatched by the towns and counties; it was thanks to the SPD's strength in urban centers such as Berlin and Hamburg that Prussia was the republic's "rock of democracy."[121] Whether on the Reichswirtschaftsrat, in the Reich and Land parliaments, on various administrative boards, or dealing personally with government ministers and their staffs, the Städtetag exerted far more influence on its environment.

Of equal importance were the associations' organizations and personnel, especially in making good personal contact with government officials. The DST's two leaders, Mulert and Vice President Fritz Elsas, were widely respected experts on municipal affairs with access to officials within both the Prussian and the Reich governments. DST staff analyzed data collected from the members, wrote up press releases and articles, prepared material for committee meetings and member-congresses, followed legislation from initial submission through the various committee stages to the final reading, and kept an eye on their own realms of expertise.[122] Judging by sheer output and media attention, the Städtetag's Berlin office in "the Städtehaus" at Alsenstrasse 7 outperformed the other associations.[123]

Toward the end of the 1920s, Haekel commented that he had never seen such open strife between the associations. Although repeating the old truism that they would have to cooperate if they were going to achieve any real success, he confessed that at present they were further apart than ever.[124] The actual source of these difficulties is likely the smaller municipalities' failure generally to make themselves heard. The pressing need for local administrative reforms—in particular, for standard national municipal charters and for rationalization of the postwar patchwork of administrations, procedures, and jurisdictions—had met with little success in the first ten years of the republic, despite considerable effort by local governments and their associations and despite attention from the government and the press. Most critically, financial reform remained stonewalled, with the municipalities futilely demanding better access to revenue and more control over their own spending. With the Reich government unable to equitably share out postwar Germany's scant financial resources—aptly described by Richard Bessel as "distributing poverty"[125]—the much-bruited distribution of finance remained, like the Reichswirtschaftsrat, infamously "provisional" in the Weimar years.

4 Experiment

Urban modernity and the "Great Reform" of 1929

This chapter looks beyond the simple urban/anti-urban dichotomy so familiar to historians of the period to the collective interests and activities of urban and quasi-urban localities. Multivalent tension, the "free-for-all" for land, prestige, and authority between villages and townships, middling and larger towns, provincial metropoles, and Berlin, describes a virtually Darwinian competition for resources. If the crude urban-rural, metropolis-province polarity found in so much of Weimar historiography can be more subtly differentiated, it should illuminate much about the republic for whom cities posed such pressing economic, social, and cultural questions, and whose final verdict on the metropolis in 1933 was so devastatingly negative.

Inter-urban struggles were particularly fierce in the Ruhr. By the turn of the twentieth century, the Ruhr district (*Ruhrgebiet*) in western Prussia had become one of the world's foremost industrial regions, ranking second and third in global production of iron and coal, respectively. Large numbers of migrant laborers from Germany's eastern provinces, as well as Austria, Hungary and especially Poland settled in the area, quickly transforming rural and satellite towns into urban centers in their own right. In the north where development was especially heavy between the Ruhr and Emscher rivers, some towns swelled with such speed that, though statistically metropoles (*Grossstädte* with over 100,000 inhabitants), they still retained their legal designation as villages.[1] The high rate of urbanization continued into the 1920s. Overall population density in the rhenish province of Westphalia, for example, jumped by 171 percent between 1871 and 1925, compared to an increase of only 75 percent for the rest of Germany. Robert Schmidt, the high-profile director of the Ruhr Coal District Housing Association (*Siedlungsverband Ruhrkohlenbezirk*), estimated that in the period 1898–1928 one Ruhr town had reached city size on average every two years, and a city metropolis size every four.[2] New cities "shot up out of the earth" in such numbers that the Ruhr conurbation by 1900 had become a decentralized "city of cities, or an urban realm."[3]

Paralleling regional planning trends elsewhere in Europe and in North America, Prussian state planners by the mid-1920s aimed to shape and regulate haphazard urbanization through overarching, long-term restructuring of the area that would promote regional, state, and national economic health.[4] The Prussian Interior Ministry's foremost expert on urban affairs concluded with some complacency in 1926,

> Basic alterations of communal borders between urban and rural districts, when limited to the purely local solution, will always have the disadvantage that one party will be left mutilated, while with an organic redrawing of the territory this concern is completely eliminated.[5]

On 6 December 1927, the Prussian Minister of the Interior, Social Democrat Albert Grzesinski, announced his ministry's intention to begin immediate preparations for an extensive reorganization of administrative districts in the Rhineland. Eighteen months later, the reformers' efforts resulted in the "Law for Communal Reorganization of the Rhenish-Westphalian Industrial Region" of 1929, which reorganized over three thousand square miles or about 3 percent of Prussia's entire territory, and affected over 16 percent of the Prussian population, some 6.4 million people.[6] Cities absorbed neighboring towns and lands. Communities and counties were broken up into new administrative units.

Urban consolidation (in Germany *Umgemeindung* or *Eingemeindung*)—the integration or annexation of small and satellite communities into larger units—is a commonplace of urban history as expanding cities continuously both shape and adapt to their environments over time. The now considerable historical literature on consolidations starts from the premise that they are far more than mere geographical and legal sleight-of-hand, redrawing borders for obscure administrative purposes. Rather, they illuminate the relationships of peripheral communities with the urban core. As suburbs in the nineteenth and twentieth centuries defined themselves both in relation to the urban center and to their suburban neighbors, the tensions between their pro- and anti-urban interests—expressed variously as commercial competition, ethnic ties both real and perceived (especially in North America), religious affinities, or the protection of communal morals—emerge in the hurly-burly of annexation and consolidation campaigns as local populations react to proposals to join with (or exclude) their neighbors. In short, consolidations offer opportunities to hear what people in the past thought about their cities and urban life.[7]

Studies of consolidations in Germany have tended, on the other hand, to treat them more as mechanical processes of politics, planning and administration than sites of negotiated social and cultural meaning.[8] Larger contexts and questions can get lost as historians follow "consolidation battles" (*Eingemeindungskämpfe*) through to their ends, whose apparent inevitability can obscure their many turning-points and contingent, historical openness. Yet materials for less linear histories are not lacking. In the case of the 1929 reform, dozens of legal, economic, political, and philosophical publications and newspaper articles addressed such fundamental questions as how to define a "city," how best to offset the provision of local services with more balanced regional tax burdens, and how to find equitable ways to ensure democratic participation in newly-shaped political districts. Rhenish mayors and their administrations flooded Prussia's ministries and the state parliament in Berlin with pamphlets and analyses pressing for terms most advantageous for their own cities. Such issues, profound and mundane, manifested widely differing perspectives on the nature of modern urban life: from the management of traffic flows to the procurement and distribution of resources undergirding community welfare; from the proper height of a building to the cultural affinities and social bonds of groups and persons living in proximity to one another.

THE PREVAILING WIND

Germany experienced over four hundred urban consolidations between 1850 and 1930. The largest and most significant of these are clustered in the decade before the First World War, while roughly one-sixth occurred in the 1920s. Some cities required repeated adjustment of their borders: Chemnitz twelve times, Dresden eleven, and Leipzig and Munich ten times each.[9] By far the most spectacular of these consolidations was the 1920 amalgamation of seven towns, fifty-nine counties, and twenty-seven manorial estates into the twenty new administrative districts of Greater Berlin. The new conurbation became overnight the world's third-largest metropolis, with a population of over four million (behind London and New York), and an area of 878 square kilometers (second to Los Angeles).[10]

Towns and suburban areas most often joined with nearby cities when their populations paid taxes commensurate with those in the city yet lacked the benefits of urban services. Growing satellites required more comprehensive welfare provisions, more schools, better sanitation and policing, and a more efficient, rationalized infrastructure. Towns also frequently secured promises from the city for future large-scale works projects, such as construction of roads and streetcar lines, greater representation in city hall, the installation of special metropolitan administrative offices in the area, and remapped electoral districts. Cities, for their part, gained more territory and taxpayers, as well as enhanced control over regional policing, waste and water treatment, transportation lines and the roads extending outside their borders.[11] Consolidation negotiations on these and other issues culminated in a detailed contractual agreement (*Eingemeindungsvertrag*) between the urban center and its surrounding communities.[12] Successful negotiations generally ensured state approval and, though not legally binding, in practice usually became the working basis of the ensuing law or decree.[13]

Of course, consolidations did not always proceed smoothly. The most powerful and consistent opponents of consolidation were the *Kreise*.

Administered simultaneously by both state and local authorities, Kreis areas could be altered only by a legislative act of the Prussian lower house of parliament (*Landtag*). The counties' notorious anti-urbanism, coupled with their traditionally strong influence in parliament, could also complicate consolidation projects. But cities often got around such difficulties by offering to compensate a county for the loss of its town and attendant revenue. A city might take over a county's administration and funding of local services, assume part of its debt, or make a direct compensation payment.[14] Towns too, if already financially secure or possessing a strong sense of communal identity, could resist annexation and the loss of their independence to what they condemned as the naked greed and "imperialism of the metropolis."[15] The wealthy Berlin suburbs of Wannsee and Charlottenburg, for instance, convinced that the consolidation of metropolitan Berlin would force them to hand over tax revenue in order to support socialist big-city welfare programs, fought fiercely but futilely to escape amalgamation in 1920.[16] Finally, opinion concerning consolidation was often divided within the urban core itself. City councils, for instance, could reject plans to stretch their already thin municipal finances to cover new districts.[17] City dwellers with special economic and social interests also on occasion mounted effective resistance. Middle-class shopkeepers and small-business owners in the Ruhr town of Barmen, for instance, fearful of losing trade once their competition from neighboring Elberfeld was inside the same metropolitan tax borders, three times in the course of a century defeated their city's plans to expand.[18]

Before 1918, the Prussian government's involvement in such reform projects was limited to that of disinterested overseer, largely rubber-stamping agreements drawn up by local authorities. After the war and upheaval of revolution in 1918–19, however, idealistic principles of social engineering and modern rationalization inspired ministerial personnel in Berlin to adopt a more assertive role for the state in such a critical area of economic and social management.[19] Over the next decade, the state and its provincial agents became active participants in the municipalities' and counties' long-standing free-for-all— *"ein Kampf aller gegen alle"* —for land.[20] This new role was affirmed by the passage in December 1927 of Prussian legislation "Regulating Various Points of Communal Law," which specified that a proposal to alter communal borders was to be judged ultimately on whether it was in the greater public interest to do so. If the proposed changes indeed furthered the "general welfare" (*Gemeinwohl*), the law empowered the state to institute them, if necessary, against the wishes of local authorities.[21]

The bill for reform of the Ruhrgebiet was worked up in the Prussian Interior Ministry, which then shepherded it through parliament. The ministry's avowed planning strategy was to promote "growth centers"—nodes of settlement and economic activity that, given an otherwise optimal environment, would ensure maximum productivity throughout the region.[22]

The Interior Minister, social democrat Albert Grzesinski, went to repeated pains to reassure the counties and towns that his reform would settle equitably and fairly their rivalry with the cities for land and resources.[23] He insisted that he intended to remain neutral and to maintain "parity between *Stadt* and *Land*." Unfortunately, both the underlying reality of the counties' increasingly defensive position in the urban landscape, as well as the complex politics of the reform suggest otherwise. Though his disclaimers may not have been strictly dishonest, they were misleading. In the first place, regional reorganization was and is fundamentally propelled by urban growth and designed in the first instance to respond to the changing needs of cities. Rural areas were, in a sense, "the problem" to be solved, and thus at a disadvantage from the beginning. Second, as a social democrat, Grzesinski's primary political allegiance was to urban workers, and his political vision was urban-centered. Third, the reform was politically divisive across party lines, particularly for members of the Catholic Center Party, which contained a strong rural component. Grzesinski had to manage his votes with care. His emphasis on the scientific bases of the ministry's economic and planning criteria was thus part of an elaborate and complicated political strategy to defuse criticism and make the reform more attractive to deputies, as well as protect them from highly reactive local pressure groups. It is naive to write, as have the historians of the counties' association, that Grzesinski regrettably "could not sail against the prevailing wind," when in fact he had little personal or political interest in doing so.[24]

The "prevailing wind," that of progress and its referents, equated modernity with technology, industry, urban growth, and the attendant transition to mass production and consumption and an urban way of life. The weight of the evidence here points to a strong undercurrent of popular agreement on the value and inevitability of an urban-based—as distinct from metropolitan—modernity in Germany at this time. Streamlining communal borders fit in with the general Weimar fascination with modern rationalization and productivity.[25] Regional restructuring was simply rationalization lifted to a higher plane, bringing balance and equilibrium to the urban environment. It was thus a natural strategy for the cities to stress economic fitness as the basis for reorganization.[26] Proponents of the reform, often comparing it directly with rationalization in the private sector, presented it as a "step forward," of such sweeping and authoritative extent as to obviate other alternatives for the foreseeable future, including the many piece-meal solutions proposed by individual cities.[27]

After meeting with city leaders to discuss the pending reform, one ministry official reported that "in general, each one judges the problem solely on the basis of conditions in his own city."[28] Certainly, focused on making their own case as strongly as possible, each city had priorities and perspectives every bit as parochial and locally self-interested as those of small towns desperately fighting off a "hungry Grossstadt." Despite the variety of their interests, however, the cities' views did have a meeting-point. The larger cities were the primary engines of consolidation in the first place;[29] as their primary representative, the Städtetag was a powerful and consistent supporter of urban-based territorial reform.[30] Not only were many of them slated to receive new tracts of land and communities of untapped taxpayers, but more generally all cities stood to benefit ultimately from what was after all ***urban*** reform. As a precedent, the reorganization of an entire region to accommodate urbanization suggested that greater attention, both official and lay, would be given to the cities' needs in the future.

Recognizing that urbanization in Germany as elsewhere was characterized by an increasingly dense network of interdependencies between cities and towns of all sizes, a "net of collectivity," the DST by late 1927 had distilled the cities' many local approaches to consolidation into a coherent program. Given that Germany was no longer a predominantly rural nation, the DST argued that dynamically growing cities were hemmed in by obsolete, inflexible borders that restricted "life, economy and administration."[31] Growing cities needed room and resources, "light and air." It was therefore of primary importance "to bring economic relationships into agreement with communal borders, to improve the productivity of the communes, and to effect a streamlining of administration." "Organic" appears regularly as a metaphor for modernity in these descriptions. So urban growth was not a matter merely of borders, offices or jurisdictions, but of the expanding and contracting settlement patterns of a living and growing people—a process not unlike breathing. Artificially restricting these growth patterns hampered the natural adaptation of local economies to new conditions, to the detriment of all.[32] The DST praised Grzesinski's reform as natural and "organic"—and thus inevitable—while at the same time placing it within a larger vision of industrial, economic, and national progress.[33]

LIVING ORGANISMS

With "the wind" at their backs, the cities could watch the reform debate with a measure of confidence the other associations could not afford. The cities could anticipate "objectivity" in the Prussian parliament, knowing that it would in fact work to their advantage. But the towns saw in Grzesinski's rhetoric of balance and fairness "an openly acknowledged [issue of] political power."[34] Prussian counties (*Landkreise*) had a long history of implacable enmity towards urban-based territorial reforms that supported the cities' claims to large portions of their tax-paying and laboring populations. In the years 1905–10, the counties of Cologne, Düsseldorf and Königsberg all lost around one third of their populations to their central metropoles.[35] When the reform agenda accelerated after the war, county resistance intensified.[36] Deploying the rhetoric of local tradition, organicism, and loyalty to *Heimat* (homeland), the counties and rural towns charged that the proposed reorganization would establish the metropolis as the predominant urban form in the republic, at a stroke creating a modern Germany of big cities.

The Landkreistag's own program, "Regional Reform and County Constitution," appeared as a pamphlet in September 1928. It focused on protecting the counties' territorial integrity and economic viability against threats both from without and within.[37] This meant, on one hand, strengthening the legal foundations of county borders so as to hinder future annexations by cities. On the other, county authorities needed greater internal control to keep their growing county towns from gaining independence and taking valuable sources of revenue with them. Towns should not be allowed to leave, nor should "weak" and "unproductive" counties be broken into parts or annexed—only maintaining the counties' territory would ensure their economic health. In sum, the counties aimed to preserve what they had, and to tighten their control over it.[38]

Viewed from a strategic perspective, administrative reforms determined by "modern" criteria such as economy, production, and rationalization put the counties on the defensive with little room to maneuver. Their first aim was thus to redefine the terms of the debate in their favor. They insisted that the real basis of territorial restructuring should be the living needs of people, their (again) "organic" social bonds, and the protection and nurturing of their "social life." In this vein, the LKT quoted with approval Robert Schmidt's warning that "the disparity between economic and political borders cannot be solved with the simple formula that economic borders and political borders must match."[39] Complaining that even highly urbanized countries like Britain had not experienced similar pressures to consolidate, the counties argued that, contrary to the pervasive conviction that consolidations increased efficiency, the evidence in fact pointed the other way. Authorities in centralized metropoles had greater responsibilities over larger areas, less contact with their constituents and needed too many field personnel. To the objection that its arguments ignored the *fact* that modern Germany was predominantly urban, the LKT retorted that the "high percentage" of the German population that the cities cited as being already "urban" in actuality lived predominantly in small towns, and was thus more closely tied to the traditions of communal life, the countryside and the Kreis. The LKT also objected that the Städtetag's rosy portrayal of past consolidations as benefiting all participants ignored the lively protests of the many losers in a process that "in the course of time has more and more taken the form of a purely urban-oriented annexation of the most extreme sort."[40]

Second, the counties claimed they could be as industrially productive and modern as cities while preserving communal ties to the past that would not otherwise survive the melting pot of urban life. They played up their potential for industrial production, administrative and tax advantages, but without the alienation, crime, corruption and crowded living conditions associated with urbanization. As alternatives to the metropolis they proposed "Greater counties" (*Grosskreise*) or "City-area counties" (*Stadtlandkreise*), which would be similar to cities only in the efficiency and quality of their administrative services.[41]

Although debate was spirited between the Städtetag and the Landkreistag, it should be remembered that the big cities, in firm control of DST policy, had little to fear from increased county internal powers and everything to gain from territorial reorganization. From the counties' side, although some did indeed face dismemberment and extinction in 1929, compensatory enhancement of their administrative powers offered the survivors greater security and increased power over their internal affairs. Both sides stood to gain from the cluster of reforms being proposed.

The towns and rural communes, on the other hand, faced the choice of losing their independence to more powerful counties or of being annexed by cities. The *Reichsstädtebund* and *Landgemeindetag* attacked with ferocity the entire reform enterprise.[42] If heavy social burdens or costly construction projects exceeded an individual community's resources, they should be taken over by county authorities only with the agreement and cooperation of the town concerned. The towns also argued that, since larger administrations would in fact need more field representatives, centralization would increase costs, not savings. Expensive tasks set by counties would unfairly burden small, poor towns that could ill-afford them, and increase the periphery's resentment against the center. The worst possible abuse of power, of course, would be the counties' outright confiscation of town property, such as a gas- or waterworks.[43]

The towns also condemned the political distance in the metropolis between urbanites and their "local" government, maintaining that after some consolidations, twenty or thirty local representatives had been replaced by one or two city councilmen for the entire district. Small-town life, with its close communal ties, encouraged greater levels of public involvement, political participation and voluntarism, so making towns the ideal environment for independent, responsible, and enlightened self-administration. The towns followed the counties in viewing the entire project of "rationalization" based on planning and "economic borders" as materialistic and soulless. The essence of community—tradition, communal awareness and feeling for the local homeland—were intangibles not subject to administrative calculus. "Towns are not machines," they argued, "or 'geographic areas and map elements' that can be cobbled together, but living organisms whose essence is beyond fabrication."[44] In the metropolis, wrote LGT President Günther Gereke, "one has the feeling not of having one's own communal self-administration, but rather a form of strictly legal self-administration that is bureaucratic and alien."[45] Large cities suffered from "a decrease in popular political participation in local government," and a decline of communal involvement and voluntarism. The West Prussian townships took up these arguments with some force:

> Even if, viewed from a material standpoint, the transfer of an area of [communal] responsibility to the Kreis were more economical, the advantage would be outweighed by the destruction of imponderables, leading to the end of love for the homeland and the exclusion of the townsperson from participation in determining his community's fate.[46]

The towns' principal disadvantage was a lack of political power. Both the Reichsstädtebund and the Western townships association lamented continually that very few deputies in the Prussian Landtag had roots in small-town politics or were familiar with local concerns. Neither of the town associations had the press attention or access to ministry and planning officials enjoyed by the Städtetag and Landkreistag.[47] Many of the big cities had special offices in Berlin for on-the-spot lobbying, an expense small towns could not afford. With little political clout, insufficient publicity, and no compelling solution for the urban growth problem in the Ruhr, the towns could not go it alone. Choosing the lesser of the two evils, they ranged themselves with the counties, the traditional rural administration they knew, and against the cities.[48]

From the towns' awareness of futility and helplessness came an unyielding antagonism towards the Grossstadt and all things urban. Lacking other resources, only public pressure could help the towns stave off reform in 1928–29. They launched a furious offensive against the cities, "direct[ing] an appeal to all German people, in the interest of the general welfare, to protect the self-administration of the small and middling cities" and highlighting in inflammatory terms the most unpopular and problematic aspects of urban modernity.[49] The towns charged that the 1929 reform would "create metropoles at any price" to feed the "insatiable evil six," the Ruhr's biggest metropoles, who would "overshadow everything around them" and turn living, flourishing communities into dead satellites.[50] The year 1929 was one of "consolidation sickness... when many communes fell sacrifice to the interests of the Grossstädte, to their greed for power and their party-political omnipotence."[51]

THE EINGEMEINDUNG

On 10 July 1929, the Prussian parliament passed the reform legislation by a majority of 210 to 167; seventy-three members did not vote. On 1 August, the region's thirty independent cities (*Stadtkreise*) decreased to twenty-six; the number of counties sank from twenty-two to twelve, with fifteen dissolved and five new ones formed from the unattached scraps and remainders. In broad terms, the reform transferred land, taxpayers, and labor from the rural areas and towns to the cities.[52] The counties lost 418 square kilometers of territory, or 18 percent of their total area in the region. More significantly, they gave up over half (56 percent) of their population to the cities. The number of centers technically categorized as metropoles rose only slightly, from thirteen to fourteen, but they grew considerably in size. The percentage of Ruhr population categorized as living in a large city rose from less than half to over two-thirds. Overall, the region's urban population increased greatly, from 2.9 million to 4.1 million.[53]

The towns' protests had little real effect: "God once again sided with the big guns."[54] The town of Hamborn, slated to be melded against its will with larger Duisburg, registered its defiance with sirens and a five-minute shut-down of the entire city. Shops closed, traffic stopped, and black flags flew over the factories.[55] The small town of Lennep, due to be absorbed by Remscheid, flew flags at half-mast on the day the law passed the Landtag. A week later, the Bürgermeister made a fiery speech to an angry crowd, invoking local resistance to French occupation forces during the Napoleonic Wars, and exhorting his listeners to resist "annexation by an alien city."[56]

If the Berlin press is any indication, Berliners were inclined to look down on such passionate demonstrations as humorously provincial. One article pedantically reminded the Lennepers that "foreign soil does not begin in Remscheid," while another admonished "mourning" Hamborn that when "Lokalpatriotismus" went "over the top" the results were comical.[57] Yet other cases of consolidation in the period show the same rhetorical excess on the part of opponents of reform, particularly by those hostile to the metropolis and its "socialist" politics. Anthony McElligott's close examination of a local consolidation battle in Altona in the mid-1920s vividly depicts mobilized Germans from the suburbs declaring "war" against the city, whose annexation plan—a "rape of the communities" —they likened to the "Strangulation Treaty of Versailles."[58] Similarly, the right viewed the "artificial" expansion of Breslau's borders in 1928 as opening the gates to Bolshevism in the East.[59]

In the Ruhr, protests had no effect and the reform process marched on. During the last days of July, the Rhenish dailies reported somberly on the final, farewell meetings of dissolving local councils.[60] Seeing that protests got them nothing but colorful press notices, twenty-two towns and cities sued the Prussian state, challenging the constitutionality of the reform in Germany's highest court, the *Staatsgerichtshof*. Their case asserted that forced consolidation was a direct infringement of their right of self-administration as guaranteed by Articles 127 of the Reich and 70 of the Prussian constitution. A verdict in their favor would have had considerable import, nullifying not only the 1929 law specifically, but its 1927 legal underpinnings as well. But their hopes proved vain. In December, the court refused to consider the case, citing the longstanding constitutional practice of leaving communal affairs firmly in the hands of the states. The 1929 reform was a Prussian affair.[61] The towns could do little but acquiesce to the inevitable.

In addition to new borders, the legal relationship between counties and towns changed. County demands for increased powers and greater restrictions on town independence were finally granted.[62] After 1929, large

Prussian towns could escape county control only by special law. The key criterion was not the interests of the town in question but, again, the "general welfare" of the entire Kreis.[63] Admittedly, restrictions on these powers as well as the towns' right of appeal kept them from being both the effective tool the counties had fought for and the direct danger to communal independence the towns had feared.[64] But inarguably, the towns' essential rights of self-government had suffered damage. Before 1929, towns and counties had been equal legal entities. The counties' new power to interfere in local affairs, particularly in cases where they shared responsibility for certain tasks with local governments, brought corresponding deterioration in the towns' constitutional right of self-administration.[65]

What might have come of this remains a matter of speculation. Germany's swift succession of economic and political crises after 1929 limited the counties' use of their new powers to just once prior to November 1931.[66] The Nazis notoriously wrought far more damage in German local administration after 1933, but their restructuring measures were not "reforms" in any reasonable sense of the word. For example, Weimar-era municipal leaders fought long and hard for a national municipal code (*Städteordung*), yet it was only in 1935 that communal affairs came under the jurisdiction of a new national Communal Code (*Gemeindeordnung*). Consolidations were still justified nominally by the legal criterion of "public welfare," but emptied of all democratic content. Outside Prussia, all agreements and contracts between consolidating communes were subject to supervision and approval by state governors (*Reichsstatthalter*); within Prussia, control of the entire process of urban restructuring was centralized in the hands of Reich authorities.[67]

There are nonetheless intriguing continuities between the communal reorganizations of the Weimar and National Socialist periods.[68] Both manifest a reforming zeal to solve large, often urgent problems decisively with little or no patience for a protracted process of democratic consultation. Nazi administrators and legalists found in the annexations of the Weimar era helpful precedents for consolidating the régime's control over the communes. From the forced Eingemeindung of unwilling towns and counties in 1929, to the installation in many cities in early 1931 of state commissioners empowered to compel the passage of communal budgets, to the decree of 14 February 1933 dissolving local representative councils, Nazi leaders detected a useful erosion of the legal inviolability of communal self-administration.[69]

Although mountains of statistical materials were mustered at the time to support both pro- and anti-consolidation arguments, assessing the 1929 reform after the fact is difficult.[70] This is partly the result of insufficient data: to date, only one monograph has researched the reform in detail. Equally limiting are exigencies specific to interwar Germany. At the time, the reformers presented as given that rationalizing city and county administrations meant fewer administrative personnel, decreased expenditure, and reduced taxes—claims that still provide virtually automatic justifications for consolidations. But lower costs after 1929 were just as likely the result of drastic cuts in local spending in the midst of economic crisis as they were of prior administrative reforms. According to at least one historian, the reform resulted in *higher* taxes for the urban centers involved.[71] Even voter radicalization and support for the Nazis cannot be traced with any certainty back to the mobilization of anti-urban forces in the reform. Research shows a clear "overrepresentation" in the growth of rural and small-town support for the Nazis from 1930 to 1933, suggesting a correlation between the mobilization of anti-urban sentiment in consolidation battles and the Nazis' mobilization of anti-Weimar votes.[72] But until we know more about *specifically* political reactions to urban modernity in Weimar, these results can be no more than tantalizingly suggestive.[73] The cascade of crises and recoveries over the next decade and a half—the rise of National Socialism; rearmament and economic recovery in the mid-thirties; war-time bombing and devastation (particularly heavy in the Ruhr); occupation and reconstruction after 1945—leaves the question open as to whether the reform may be judged a success. Most commentators have restricted themselves to the remark that the most telling sign of its necessity, usefulness and effectiveness is that it lasted so long, almost forty years in a region of continuing economic and urban change.[74]

Interestingly, the spirited debate over the 1929 reform appears to have captured the attention of German officials and the public in ways suggestively absent, for instance, in the similarly tremendous "Regional Plan of New York and Its Environs" of the same year.[75] All of the participants in the reform were aware that the cities retained the greatest ability to shape the outcome. Despite many Germans' deep misgivings about the proliferation of the metropolis, the great cities benefited directly from their close association with popular assumptions about the inevitability (and desirability) of a modernity that was specifically urban. Germans' apparent interest in a raft of reform measures proposed by cities in the late twenties points to the need to balance the well-known negative emphasis on Weimar's weaknesses and early demise with what appears to be public awareness of a need for experiment and change. This chapter shows, at least for the short period between stabilization of the currency in 1924 and the arrival of economic depression in 1930, that many Germans were finding accommodation, however uneasily, with their "urban republic."

5 A nation of city republics

The urban bases of Reichsreform

Germany after the First World War was covered by a patchwork of nineteenth-century local and state jurisdictions of such byzantine intricacy that even official experts were pessimistic about achieving "a really objective overview of the whole administration."[1] They had no doubts about the resulting inefficiency and waste, however. Frustration and a desire for reform were evident at all levels of government. One deputy in the Saxon parliament, for instance, complained that the array of authorities involved in opening a simple railway trunk line—including officials of the Reich and two state governments, as well as the local *Kreishauptmann*, *Amtshauptmann*, *Regierungspräsident*, and *Landrat*—made it easier to travel from Berlin to Siberia than the thirty kilometers from Merseburg to Leipzig.[2] Police officials, to take another example, argued that centralizing state and municipal criminal records would aid greatly their efforts to control crime.[3] Debates about the republic's viability thus often turned on the thorny problems of constitutional and territorial reform. By the late twenties, Germans encountered almost daily an extraordinary variety of proposals, committees and panels, speeches, pamphlets, books and position papers of considerable technical complexity, all proposing to reshape the Reich's administration, constitution and territory.[4] One prominent commentator concluded it was impossible to survey them all, another that if the task could have been accomplished simply by producing reports, the Reich would have been reformed long since.[5]

Of the handful of historical works that have addressed specifically the issue of constitutional reform, the majority have treated the reform problem largely as a matter of high politics between the Reich and states, whose primary aims were to overcome the duality of the Reich government on one side and the powerful Prussian state on the other, and to establish standards of administrative practice (especially tax collection and distribution) uniformly across the country.[6] Very few studies have expanded the focus to include the campaign of German cities to shape a constitutional and financial environment better suited to their needs.[7] The lack of attention has historical roots. Prior to the mid-1920s, German municipalities played little part in high politics, and evinced little desire to do so; their interests did not extend far beyond their own bailiwicks, and the municipal associations had little to say about state or federal matters.[8] In the early Weimar years, the newness and uncertainty of many postwar governmental improvisations, in addition to unrelenting fiscal chaos and high levels of unemployment, kept municipal authorities scrambling to secure sufficient funds for municipal welfare, unemployment relief, and emergency works.[9] Too preoccupied to enter systematically into Reich affairs, the cities continued to understand local self-administration in its traditional sense and saw no need to redefine its rights and responsibilities on a larger scale.[10] But by mid-decade, the cumulative effects of economic chaos, political uncertainty, and the hard constraints of new financial practice had forced urban leaders and technocrats to recognize that old bureaucratic and financial structures needed to be brought into balance with the cities' rapidly changing roles and growing burdens. Although local authorities remained nominally subordinate to the Länder, the Reich now imposed many onerous new social responsibilities directly on them, and interfered increasingly in communal finance, welfare provision, and the regulation of local taxation. The new financial and administrative environment made them acutely aware that the decisive power governing their future lay in Berlin, not the state capitals. Adenauer summed up the problem succinctly: "The cities belong to the Länder, while the Reich has the money."[11]

TOWARDS A NEW ORDER

From the mid-1920s, the disadvantages of the cities' position increasingly found expression as a constitutional problem. Mulert's formulations of the cities' problems and the solutions he proposed set the agenda for their reform campaigns. His insight into the changed relations between local, state, and federal governments led him to focus immediately on creating connections for the cities at the Reich level as the best way to redress their lack of influence. The DST's December 1926 manifesto, "The Protection of City Interests," aimed ultimately to create institutional connections between municipalities and central authorities.[12] This issue dominated the cities' deliberations over the next three years at the Städtetag's annual congresses in Magdeburg (1927), Breslau (1928), and Frankfurt am Main (1929). The all-member Magdeburg congress was undoubtedly the most visible and widely publicized demonstration of the cities' collective power during the Weimar period. Over one thousand delegates from DST member-cities and organizations from all over the Reich attended, along with a great many key figures in politics and administration, including for the first time a Reich Chancellor, Wilhelm Marx, and Finance Minister, Heinrich Köhler.[13] Mulert's keynote address announced clearly the DST's intention to expand the cities' role in national and state policy making. His central demands were for enhanced municipal participation on the Reich

Economic Council (RWR), the establishment of a communal policy office in the Reich Ministry of the Interior, and the creation of an inter-party committee for communal affairs in the Reichstag. He also proposed that cities be given seats on the Reichsrat, the upper chamber of state and federal representatives responsible for passing national legislation, so that their practical expertise and knowledge of specific conditions would balance federal power with local needs and perspectives.[14]

The sum effect of these proposals formed what Mulert termed "a unified whole": a thoroughgoing reform of German administration based on the modern need for tighter links between a strengthened central government, on the one hand, and urban authorities with increased social burdens, on the other. The new section of the Interior Ministry, the committee in the Reichstag, and seats on the Reichsrat would together establish an "organic," binding relationship between the cities and the center, thereby integrating them fully into the Reich.[15] Once law-makers and parliamentary deputies began working more closely with municipal experts and administrators, they would gain precise and accurate knowledge of local needs and conditions. The cities, for their part, would be able to ensure that central legislation reflected more realistically their immediate requirements and long-term plans, especially in tax matters.

The full scope of the cities' Magdeburg proposals was considerable. Forging direct links between center and locality would perforce have altered the Reich's constitutional structure, and had far-reaching implications for the authorities in the middle, the Länder. If the states yielded to the Reich their jurisdiction over local affairs and lost seats on the Reichsrat to the communes, they stood to suffer a significant diminution of their power. The danger of a defensive counter-campaign by the states was thus very real, and Mulert trod carefully. He avoided referring directly in his speeches and articles to the sensitive issue of Reichsreform, downplayed those sections of the program most threatening to state power, and stressed the "interdependence" of Land and commune: "Obviously the communes are not contemplating... limiting the competencies of the Länder."[16]

Response both from official circles and the press was encouraging. Open support came in 1928 from Prussian Interior Minister Albert Grzesinski, whose government at that moment was itself engaged in preparing the reform of the Ruhrgebiet. The Reich also responded positively, with Minister of the Interior Carl Severing promising DST delegates a communal affairs bureau by April 1929.[17] Press observers sympathetically underlined the cities' financial difficulties and lack of influence in Reich legislation, and argued that reform was necessary in a modern state.[18] Negative notices, principally in the conservative, agrarian, and regionally-oriented press (particularly in Bavaria), were in the minority. They denounced the cities' "dangerous" plans and condemned the Städtetag for leaving "the banal paths of communal politics and raising itself proudly to the higher spheres of Reich and state policy."[19] But whether observers approved or condemned, all seemed aware of the larger significance of the proceedings, of the increasing tempo of the reform movement, and of the cities' central role in it. Berlin city councillor Paul Michaelis (DDP) wrote that "connections between the Reich and communes propel [us] towards a new order."[20] With the public blessing and active support of the Reich's two most powerful administrators, Severing and Grzesinski, the cities appeared well on their way to transforming their constitutional position in the republic.

TO REFORM THE REICH

By mid-1928, reform had been in the air for some time. The Prussian government had ten major projects pending. Ex-Chancellor Hans Luther's high-profile reform association, the *Bund zur Erneuerung des Reichs* ("Association for the Renewal of the Reich" or "Luther-Bund"), had recently published its own reform manifesto, *Reich und Länder* (1928).[21] Outspoken criticism of Germany's tangled administration had also appeared the previous October in the form of an influential memorandum submitted to the German government by the Allied agent for reparations, S. Parker Gilbert. According to Gilbert, administrative inefficiency was hurting the national economy and—the main reason for his assessment—endangering Germany's ability to fulfil its postwar reparations obligations.[22] One month later, in a much-noted speech in Bochum, Reichsbank President Hjalmar Schacht sharply criticized the cities' irresponsible spending on "luxuries" —construction and development projects such as sports stadiums, swimming pools and parks, libraries, exhibition halls, office buildings, hotels, museums, and airports. Although Schacht admitted that he did not have complete figures on these expenditures, he claimed that what he did have justified his conclusion that they amounted to almost all of the municipal foreign debt.[23]

Taken together, the cities' Magdeburg proposals and the two public attacks by Gilbert and Schacht brought a new immediacy to the reform issue. Prominent personalities from across the spectrum of Weimar political parties took up the problem, falling into a general pattern of support for a unified state on the left and for a loose federal association of the traditional Länder on the right. Only the nationalist DNVP established a firm official position, calling for the maintenance of the federated state as part of its demand for reinstitution of the monarchy. There appears also to have been considerable variety of opinion within the parties. Social Democrats in the south, for example, supported a federal solution that would preserve Bavaria's favored status amongst the other states.[24]

From October to December, the Reich government worked up plans to convene a conference to discuss reform, most particularly of the national tax structure (*Steuerrahmengesetz*).[25] In January 1928, national and state delegates convened in Berlin for a *Länderkonferenz* to hammer out reasonable and practicable plans for a comprehensive *Reichsreform.* Over the next two years, experts and representatives came together periodically to prepare reports on administrative, territorial, and financial issues.[26] In his opening speech on 18 January, Reich Chancellor Wilhelm Marx declared that as the purpose of the conference was to discuss relations between the Reich and states, no other authorities would participate.[27] The cities immediately protested with some force: "Communal interests must receive due consideration in its preparation if the decisions of the Länderkonferenz are to be moulded into a positive outcome."[28] But as long as the Länder were suspicious of the Städtetag and of Mulert, whom they viewed as an "impassioned unitarian" and enemy of state power, the cities were forced to watch the proceedings as "outside petitioners."[29] Several full members of the conference had close connections with the DST, including former wartime mayor of Kassel and prominent Reich politician Erich Koch-Weser, as well as Hamburg Senate President Carl Petersen. But none of them represented city interests per se. The DST had no alternative but to submit its proposals and demands in writing—a strategy that held little promise of success with over ninety different Reichsreform reports and programs competing for the conference's consideration.[30]

The DST's final Reichsreform proposal, submitted to the conference in June 1929, summarizes succinctly the cities' reform program, presenting it as a simple and—as Mulert claimed at Magdeburg—"unified whole."[31] Local affairs must remain the business of local governments exclusively. Reich legislation should set principles and guidelines, while practical implementation of federal laws reverts to local authorities. Future territorial reforms and urban consolidations were to be undertaken solely to ensure the continued health, productivity and efficiency of local communities. Moreover, if Reich lawmakers were to make informed decisions about local legislation, they needed information about local conditions and experience that could come only from firm institutional contact with local authorities. The regulation of communal affairs, often showing considerable variation between the states, would be standardized across the country.[32] At the Land level, too, supervision of communal affairs would be unified under a single authority, a proposition stemming from the contemporary debate over the problem of overlapping supervisory powers of the *Regierungspräsidenten* and *Oberpräsidenten* in Prussia.[33]

Since implementation of these reforms would have to be equal and uniform across the country, the cities also demanded a national municipal charter, or *Reichsstädteordnung* (RSO). A standardized charter had been high on their list of priorities ever since the founding of the republic; in the late 1920s, twenty-five different charters were in place nationally. The most common form of communal government was the *Magistratsverfassung*, a two-chamber system unique to Germany. Appointed by the elected city assembly, the *Magistrat* was a council of professional and lay deputies that supervised the various branches of city administration. The

Bürgermeisterverfassung, an innovation of the Rhenish provinces dating back to Napoleon, made do with a single council. As its name suggests, it concentrated decision-making power, political responsibility, and administrative control in the office of the mayor. A third regional variation, the *Stadtratsverfassung* in the southern states, left municipal administration in the hands of the city council, with the mayor merely presiding.[34]

The cities' previous charter proposals had been marked by a pluralist willingness to accommodate these and other forms of communal government within the new charter.[35] But in 1929, opinion within the DST had shifted to a firm preference for a unicameral system with strong mayoral powers. The vociferous campaigns of the banking and private sectors against public spending in the municipalities contained implicit accusations of irresponsibility and corruption. The Sklarek scandal of 1929 brought accusations of corruption and bribery against long-standing Berlin lord mayor (and Städtetag chairman) Gustav Böss, casting a pall of distrust and suspicion over big-city politics and administration.[36] As a result, "self-responsibility" (*Selbstverantwortung*) became a watchword for local administrators and politicians, demanding of them extra diligence, care, and sobriety in conducting their affairs and those of their cities.[37] Of equal concern, crises in municipal finance and the increasing unruliness of extreme political groups in municipal councils combined to paralyse local governments, raising the danger that the states would intervene in the cities' affairs in order to reestablish financial and political stability.[38] Once this happened, warned the DST executive, the damage to local self-government would be permanent. Extending and strengthening mayoral powers was thus a step toward obviating this threat, since streamlining and simplifying municipal authority would bring a stronger public awareness of governmental responsibility. Both power and accountability would be vested in a central figure, the Bürgermeister, who would have the power to cut through political and bureaucratic entanglements and get things done.[39]

The charter proposal found a broad basis of support among the cities and the press, and by early May 1930 it had been sponsored in the Reichstag by the Democratic (DDP) and People's parties (DVP).[40] Objections came mainly from the agrarian and traditional right, which prophesied that any federal interference in the Länder's regulation of communal law would set a constitutional precedent leading to further erosion of the states' power.[41] The towns, through the Reichsstädtebund, complained that the proposed charter made no distinction between the metropolis and the middling or smaller city. A "unified" charter would lump together all cities and towns regardless of size and character, thereby failing to allow for regional variation and specific circumstance.[42] Naturally, these objections were aimed to some extent at the cities and the DST itself, who came under attack from writers hostile to the idea of dictatorial Bürgermeister dominating the cities. The "Oberbürgermeister-Städtetag," critics claimed in a telling phrase, would be the principal beneficiary of the law, which would create a Germany of "city republics with presidents elected to long terms, whom no one, but no one, would be able to gainsay."[43]

The DST's program, finalized in late June and submitted to the conference sub-committee in early July 1929, arrived too late to be included in the all-important preliminary reports.[44] Based on the latter's recommendations, the conference's Constitution Committee drew up a "differentiated general solution" (*differenzierende Gesamtlösung*) proposing the establishment of two different kinds of Länder, "old" and "new." The "old" southern states would remain largely unchanged. "New" states would be built in the north around the former Prussian provinces.[45] The lesser of these would be enlarged by absorbing small neighboring Länder that had become patently unable to support themselves. According to a 1928 survey by the Reich Ministry of the Interior, many of Prussia's smaller neighbors (e.g., Lippe, Lübeck, Schaumburg-Lippe, and Mecklenburg-Strelitz) had been forced to conclude agreements whereby Prussia either supported or took over their administration of justice, commerce, police and welfare.[46] The plan's final preparation by the Reich Ministry of the Interior took an additional year. By the time it reached the Cabinet in 1931, the German economy was in a dire state and the government of Chancellor Heinrich Brüning was too preoccupied with domestic emergencies and foreign policy issues to give the bill consideration; the attention of officials and the public was directed elsewhere. Prussian delegate Arnold Brecht, the staunchest and most optimistic advocate of reform, remembered: "During the tumultuous events of those days, Germany's reorganization was considered of secondary importance."[47]

THE REICHSRAT PROPOSAL

Of the various fronts fought by of the cities in their failed campaign to address the republic's urban deficit, Mulert's proposal for city representation on the Reichsrat heralded the clearest and most radical relocation of power down to the local level. If the regulation of matters relating to the communes was to be centralized with the Reich authorities, it followed logically that the communes required closer connections with the center. The Städtetag and its cities, Mulert insisted, were precisely the proper agents of such reform. While he recognized that as a tradition-bound "anachronism" in a modern state of powerful and dynamic metropoles, the Reichsrat offered an imperfect solution to the problem of equitable distribution of power and resources, but it was the only option available. "The Reichsrat," he argued, "is the key."[48]

Interestingly, it was also a reform plan on which the cities themselves could not agree. The day before the proposal was to be ratified at the Magdeburg congress, the DST Council met to hammer out its position on the issue. Members from the center and left agreed with Mulert. Magdeburg

Oberbürgermeister Hermann Beims, who spoke for the SPD, said "nothing could be more natural" than for the cities to take their place on the Reichsrat. Ludwig Landmann, lord mayor of Frankfurt am Main, stated bluntly that the real anachronisms were the Länder themselves, who had become too weak to justify their current levels of power and influence. Although the cities wished to support the Reich and Länder equally, "politically, the division of strength is such that the communes [will] sink helplessly into insignificance if they don't have the opportunity to make their wishes known in the Reich's central agencies."[49]

But cities could get the power they needed only at the expense of regional diversity and healthy state governments; in essence, demanding Reichsrat representation meant demanding a unified state. While many on the left considered such an innovation "progressive," it was here that some Städtetag members parted ways with Mulert's grand vision.[50] Especially uneasy with the idea and its complex politics were the southern Oberbürgermeister, Karl Scharnagl (Munich) and Hermann Luppe (Nuremberg), who feared that the carefully phrased subtleties of the Reichsrat proposal would escape the German public, who would believe simply that the cities were demanding a unified state. Several other members, Duisburg mayor Karl Jarres (DVP) most prominently, were also opposed to such a drastic shift in the cities' roles in the republic. Clearly holding to the traditional view that the state should be both apolitical and above interest politics, Jarres protested that the cities and their associations represented "other interests" that had no business mixing in the high politics of statecraft. The Reichsrat was a forum for the states, he argued; the cities did not belong there.[51]

The majority of Magdeburg delegates, including southern members of the SPD, apparently agreed with Jarres. The resolution was dropped from the list of proposals to be ratified by the congress.[52] Even so, Mulert went ahead and mentioned it in his speech. In the end, the objections of his conservative colleagues were justified to an extent: press reporters and even Congress delegates came away with the general impression that Magdeburg had been a clear "demonstration in favor of a unified state." His speech, in particular, made such a strong impact on his audience that although the Reichsrat proposal never became part of the DST's official platform, it was widely viewed as such by the public and even by Städtetag members.[53] This fact speaks eloquently for the entire program's unity of conception, and indicates something of the cities' understanding of their own roles and interests in modern urban Germany. Mulert's listeners were clearly predisposed to make the connection between the proposal's specific aim to strengthen the cities' collective voice in German administration and law-making, which they were long familiar with by now, and its more general implications, whether formally included or not. While historians of urban Weimar have undoubtedly been correct to view Mulert as a formative influence on the cities' sense of collective identity as agents of modernity within the Reich, they risk underestimating the extent to which municipal leaders themselves were already sensitized to the economic and political realities of the cities' situation.[54] Others like Brecht, as well as observers in the press, were sensitive to the problem of urban power at the core of Reichsreform. It was no accident "that the cities push ever more strongly from the idea of self-government toward the concept of the German unified state."[55]

With the arrival of economic depression and renewed political crisis in 1929–30, the cities lost any hope of effecting a negotiated reform. Early in 1930, the Reich informed the DST in no uncertain terms that no reform plans would be considered or undertaken in the foreseeable future.[56] As the Depression settled in, the cities' efforts to situate themselves more favorably within the Reich's constitutional and financial structure ran out of steam or—as in the case of their earlier exclusion from the Länderkonferenz—encountered stiff resistance from conservatives convinced that "Reich institutions are becoming representatives of interests, and all of these interests want to become independent holders of power."[57] The Depression did bring marked improvement in one important respect. Scrambling desperately for funds to cover skyrocketing unemployment and welfare relief costs, Mulert and his staff were wholly absorbed with trying to stabilize municipal finances, even for a short while, and with trying to repair the political and administrative damage wrought by the Brüning government's emergency decrees. Ironically, it was here, negotiating with ministries, bank presidents, and upper-level officials that Mulert's personal influence—and that of the Städtetag—reached its peak. He met frequently during this period with the highest Reich and state officials to explore ways of alleviating the crisis in the cities or, more often, to protest against the latest emergency decree. In 1932, he noted that two years of authoritarian rule had set a premium on the informal cooperation of the Städtetag and the other communal associations, and that as a result some improvement was noticeable in the cities' relations with the Reich and states.[58] But he was equally conscious of the formal weakness of the cities' new position, pointing out that whatever benefits they enjoyed now were more than offset by the self-serving fiscal policies of federal and state authorities who balanced their own budgets with little regard for the municipalities' heavy load of unemployment and crisis relief payments.[59] State intervention, Mulert warned, posed "a great danger for the communes" that would undercut local self-government catastrophically and permanently.[60]

In the final analysis, the cities failed to reshape their constitutional and administrative environment in ways that appeared to them both urgent and practicable in the late 1920s. In the early thirties the rules changed. Reform was now effected from above, driven both by economic emergency and by the centralizing agendas of the conservative officials who held the purse-strings.[61] The fortunes of the municipalities in this period lay especially in the hands of Hans Luther (Reichsbank President, 1930–33) and Hermann Dietrich (Reich Finance Minister, 1930–32), both of whom hoped to realize "a reform born out of catastrophe" by consolidating control of finance in Berlin and further undermining the autonomy of the states and municipalities alike. Luther, for one, "did not believe it right always to start from the premise that cities should not be allowed to go bankrupt," and thought "it would be most beneficial for the cities if some of them should go to the wall," since "it was dangerous if communes always had the feeling that they would be helped."[62] As for Dietrich, Mulert in 1933 looked back with unwonted venom on the finance minister's poor record of working with the cities, concluding that he "had fully [and] intentionally put the interests of the communes behind all other interests."[63] Luther's and Dietrich's obvious lack of sympathy for the communes is all the more remarkable when it is remembered that both men began their public careers in municipal administration, Luther as Oberbürgermeister of Essen from 1918–24 and Dietrich of Konstanz during the war.[64]

Too often, the cities' failure is taken as evidence that their objectives were never reasonable or realistic. In this view, powerful conservative forces and structural constraints from the outset seriously undermined whatever chances for reform existed; once the Depression started, all opportunity for negotiated reform disappeared. Yet negative judgements after the fact leave unexplained the intensity of reform activity across Germany at every level of government and politics from late 1927. Even more, they are not reflected in the memories of those most intimately connected with it. Arnold Brecht, for one, continued to affirm even in retrospect the determination of Prussia's Minister-President, Otto Braun, to follow through with a meaningful reform once one was available.[65]

The deeper significance of the Städtetag's efforts lies in the cities' central role in creating new potentials for constructive change that prevailed before economic depression and emergency decrees ended all tolerance for negotiated experiments. Even more than the wide public swath cut by the Städtetag's active campaigns, the cities were more fundamentally responsible for the debate simply by the fact of their existence or, to put it more exactly, by the continued systemic disruption of Germany's economic and administrative structures wrought by sustained urban growth. In closed Städtetag strategy sessions, mayors and city councillors expressed their conviction that urbanization, combined with foreign demands that Germany restructure in order to meet its reparation obligations, posed an "unanswerable argument" that the days of the Länder and federalism were numbered; and that cities were uniquely positioned to help bring the unified state into existence.[66] Experienced civil servants at all levels of government agreed that the relations of the Reich and Länder could not return to those of the Kaiserreich; nor could they be maintained in their present state.[67] There was "only one way to go ... forward!"—a much-quoted phrase of Mulert's reflecting two deep-seated convictions in the minds of both the experts and the lay public: that cities were defining features of modern life; and that a modern state should be based on principles of scientific planning and rational management.[68] The main issues of reform—the need to cut away the impenetrable layers of old administrative jurisdictions, form more direct connections between localities and the center, and distribute more equitably and efficiently the republic's scarce resources—were driven by, and spoke to, the problem of structural urban change. That the reforms failed should not obscure the equally important point that they were widely perceived in postwar Germany as appropriate, even inevitable, or that the details of the various proposals, though technically arcane and difficult to understand, appeared frequently in the popular press. From this perspective, the republican "experiment" exhibited a healthy interest in acknowledging and adapting to a new environment. Fundamentally at issue in these reform proposals was the place and role of large, powerful urban centers within a central modern state, a problem yet to be resolved. Although Weimar's cities ultimately failed, the remarkable experimental energies they exerted to create a republic that would sustain, economically and politically, its increasingly urban environment—that is, towards finding feasible ways to assimilate a specifically urban modernity into the constitutional and economic fabric of the Reich after 1918—describe with special force the multiple ambiguities of their place in Weimar, and the crises and opportunities of the short-lived republic.

Conclusion
Germany's vulnerable cities

Harold James has described German local administration as "the most obvious and the most disliked form of government intervention" during the Weimar years, and has linked that popular rejection of local power with its very real erosion in the Depression.[1] As authorities whose day-to-day business most intimately affected local inhabitants and whose workings were most easily observable, local governments provided the closest and easiest targets of social and political discontent. When new taxes such as the *Bürgersteuer* (head tax) were imposed via the emergency decrees, taxpayers naturally directed their resentment first at the local messengers. Municipal councils, tied into knots by local representatives scrapping for financial leverage and political power, were undermined just when they needed most to appear responsible and decisive. Although municipal politics in Germany were relatively sober compared to those in the United States during the prohibition era, several city scandals that came to light tarred all local governments with the same brush.[2] With central government riding roughshod over local administration, and warring Nazis and Communists paralyzing the councils, it is little wonder that local government, always undervalued, was undercut and discredited.

But this judgment misses deeper and more significant conclusions to be made about the nature of local power in the republic and the special vulnerability of the cities after the First World War. Bounded by two major financial crises and fractured by political instability, the republican era was one of tremendous technological and social change. Channeling and shaping urban growth, formulating principles of communal government, managing local politics, implementing strategies for the provision and regulation of municipal finance, determining more effective ways for local administrations to answer the physical needs and cultural desires of local inhabitants—virtually every area of municipal endeavor during the republican period was open to question, negotiation, redefinition, and revision. The social and economic roots of these changes lay before the war, but it was only in the interwar period that administrators, politicians, and planners began to come to grips with them outside the local site of change. This was the particular challenge of urban modernity for the ramshackle republic:

how to integrate productively, control efficiently, and govern democratically an urban whole whose parts formed a patchwork of unique local administrative environments, laws, and regulations.

The task was hampered at the most fundamental level by the cities' deeply ambiguous position in Weimar. Constitutionally and financially, there was little guarantee of their local power or of their access to necessary revenue. The cities also occupied an equally uncertain place in German social and cultural consciousness. On one hand, they symbolized engines of modernity: economic growth, national technological achievement, progress and productivity, icons of national power and places of artistic vitality; and on the other, they seemed to foreshadow the end of old rural Germany, embodied industry against agriculture and tradition, and provided foci of new cosmopolitan and—in the extremes of *völkisch* thought—Jewish milieux.

The widespread criticism directed at the cities and municipal governments, therefore, should be seen within a larger context of ambiguity towards urban modernity in general. As Ben Lieberman has convincingly demonstrated, the "relative stability" of mid-1920s Germany afforded its urban polity flexibility for judgments about the city.[3] Pride in municipal achievements and active, creative participation in local government appear to have waned after 1930, as crisis pressures increasingly pushed out the positive, as there was a very real weakening of the characteristics and abilities that most recommended local governments as the fundamental building blocks of modern administration. Given the cities' traditional roles as the primary caretakers of the German populace, their expertise in managing resources, and their intimate knowledge of local conditions, it was logical they should assume the most sensitive of Weimar's new caretaking and social responsibilities. Their new role in the republic—defined by administrative jurisdictions and described by the flows of financial supply and distribution—was reflected most clearly in the assumption of their duties as modern urban centers.

But now the power to solve their most intransigent problems—easing unemployment and financing reconstruction—lay for the first time with the Reich. The logical consequence of amplified roles for the local and federal governments in the postwar era should have been a closer, more organic relationship between municipal and Reich administrations, which the cities urged with considerable force from the mid-1920s onward. In this context, the communal associations, and above all the Städtetag, assume their signal importance in the later Weimar years. It is no coincidence that the two greatest areas of Städtetag endeavor were, respectively, revising the Finanzausgleich to provide more adequately for the cities, and securing institutional guarantees of local government input in Reich policy making. The DST's struggle to integrate the municipalities more effectively points clearly to structural weaknesses in the republic whose most common symptoms were an inadequate distribution of financial resources and an overly centralized administration. Within such an environment, there appears to have been little chance of the cities escaping their political and financial vulnerability. In other words, the DST's campaigns, programs, and underlying rationales as recounted and analyzed here point to exactly the kind of social, cultural, and structural modern tensions Peukert was looking for.[4] In Weimar's good times, "the local" remained isolated and taken for granted; in bad it was ghettoized, controlled, restricted, and attacked. As this worst-case scenario shows, at stake for the municipalities was not merely their fiscal well-being. They were quite justified in seeing municipal finance as only the most urgent symptom of a greater malady, the slow but sure starvation of communal self-government.

Given more time, the cities might have managed to integrate themselves more fully into the Reich. Municipal finance could have been shored up with the distribution-and-supply structure necessary to fulfill their new obligations; self-government might have found a distinct and protected constitutional niche in the network of relations between local and center, Land and Reich.[5] It could have been the cities' moment—evidence that the Reich was evolving into a more specifically modern, urban republic. Unfortunately, as the emergency decrees showed, the resistance of the Länder to such extensive reform could only be broken from above and by force; the cities alone could not escape the particularist tutelage of the state governments, and the Reich appeared at first too weak and, later, unwilling to help.[6]

Notes

INTRODUCTION

1. Basic surveys are Peter Gay, *Weimar Culture: The Outsider as Insider* (New York: Harper & Row, 1968); Walter Laqueur, *Weimar: A Cultural History, 1918–1933* (London: Weidenfeld & Nicolson, 1974); Jost Hermand and Frank Trommler, *Die Kultur in der Weimarer Republik* (Munich: Nymphenburger Verlagshandlung, 1978); and John Willett, *Art and Politics in the Weimar Period: The New Sobriety, 1917–1933* (New York: Pantheon, 1978).
2. David W. Sabean, *Power in the Blood: Popular Culture and Village Discourse in Early Modern Germany* (Cambridge: Cambridge University Press, 1984), 95.
3. Andrew Lees, "Berlin and Modern Urbanity in German Discourse, 1845–1945," *Journal of Urban History* 17 (1991): 174.
4. An explicit focus of Anthony McElligott's document collection, *The German Urban Experience: Modernity and Crisis* (London and New York: Routledge, 2001). Examples include Katherina von Ankum, ed., *Women in the Metropolis: Gender and Modernity in Weimar Culture* (Berkeley and Los Angeles: University of California, 1997); Anke Gleber, *The Art of Taking a Walk: Flanerie, Literature, and Film in Weimar Culture* (Princeton, N.J,: Princeton University Press, 1999); and Janet Ward, *Weimar Surfaces: Urban Visual Culture in 1920s Germany* (Berkeley and Los Angeles: University of California, 2001). A fundamental starting point of such studies remains Detlev J.K. Peukert, *The Weimar Republic: The Crisis of Classical Modernity* (New York: Hill and Wang, 1989).
5. Lees, "Berlin and Modern Urbanity," 170.
6. The history of anti-urbanism in Germany is limited to a surprising extent to the intellectual aspects, leaving the cultural, social, and political ramifications unexplored. See e.g.: Klaus Bergmann, *Agrarromantik und Grossstadtfeindschaft* (Meisenheim am Glan: Hain, 1971); Andrew Lees, *Cities Perceived: Urban Society in European and American Thought, 1820–1940* (New York: Columbia University Press, 1985), esp. 142–48, 158–64, 171–74, 181–86; Dirk Schubert, "Grossstadtfeindschaft und Stadtplanung: Neue Anmerkungen zu einer alten Diskussion," *Die alte Stadt* 13 (1986): 22–41; essays by Jeffrey Herf and Ulrich Linse in *Im Banne der Metropolen: Berlin und London in den zwanziger Jahren*, ed. Peter Alter (Göttingen and Zürich: Vandenhoeck & Ruprecht, 1993), 237–58 and 314–44.
7. Jost Dülffer, Jochen Thies and Josef Henke, *Hitlers Städte: Baupolitik im Dritten Reich, eine Dokumentation* (Cologne and Vienna: Böhlau, 1978);

Paul Jaskot, *The Architecture of Oppression: The SS, Forced Labor and the Nazi Monumental Building Economy* (London: Routledge, 2000); Barbara Miller Lane, *Architecture and Politics in Germany, 1918–1945* (Cambridge, Mass.: Harvard University Press, 1985), 185–216.

8. Marshall Berman, *All That is Solid Melts into Air: The Experience of Modernity* (New York: Simon and Schuster, 1988), 14 and passim.
9. Peukert, *Weimar Republic*; see also David F. Crew, "The Pathologies of Modernity: Detlev Peukert on Germany's Twentieth Century," *Social History* 17 (1992): 319–28. Wolfgang Sauer earlier explored many motifs and ideas similar to Peukert's in "Weimar Culture: Experiments in Modernism," *Social Research* 39 (1972): 254–84.
10. Peukert, *Weimar Republic*, 81–85. Also Jeffrey Herf, *Reactionary Modernism: Technology, Culture, and Politics in Weimar and the Third Reich* (Cambridge: Cambridge University Press, 1984). The problem of modernization in Germany is usefully summarized in Geoff Eley, "German History and the Contradictions of Modernity: The Bourgeoisie, the State, and the Mastery of Reform," in *Society, Culture, and the State in Germany, 1870–1930*, ed. Eley (Ann Arbor: University of Michigan Press, 1996), 67–103.
11. David F. Crew, *Germans on Welfare: From Weimar to Hitler* (New York and Oxford: Oxford University Press, 1998), 6–7; Young-Sun Hong, *Welfare, Modernity, and the Weimar State, 1919–1933* (Princeton, N.J.: Princeton University Press, 1998), 4–7. For wide-ranging discussions of Peukert's influential legacy: Frank Bajohr et al., eds., *Zivilisation und Barbarei: Die widersprüchlichen Potentiale der Moderne: Detlev Peukert zum Gedenken* (Hamburg: Christians, 1991); and Moritz Föllmer and Rüdiger Graf, eds., *Die "Krise" der Weimarer Republik: Zur Kritik eines Deutungsmusters* (Frankfurt and New York: Campus Verlag, 2005).
12. This problem is explicitly discussed in Ben Lieberman, "Testing Peukert's Paradigm: The 'Crisis of Classical Modernity' in the 'New Frankfurt,' 1925–1930," *German Studies Review* 17 (1994): 287–303.
13. See Lieberman's discussion of this literature, "Peukert's Paradigm," 289; and idem, *From Recovery to Catastrophe: Municipal Stabilization and Political Crisis in Weimar Germany* (New York and Oxford: Berghahn), 1998.
14. Otto Ziebill, *Geschichte des Deutschen Städtetages: Fünfzig Jahre deutsche Kommunalpolitik* (Stuttgart: W. Kohlhammer, 1956), 246.
15. Prussian Ministerial Presidium, meeting of 24 Aug. 1931, Landesarchiv Berlin (LAB) 142-01, St.B 3612.

CHAPTER 1

1. The definition of "city" here follows statistical practice in interwar Germany, designating an urban area with more than 2000 inhabitants. See Statistisches Reichsamt, *Wirtschaft und Statistik* 6 (1926), Sonderheft 3: *Die Gemeinden mit 2000 und mehr Einwohnern*: 5–11. Also Jürgen Reulecke, *Geschichte der Urbanisierung in Deutschland* (Frankfurt am Main: Suhrkamp, 1985), 68–78, 203; Wolfgang Köllmann, "The Process of Urbanization in Germany at the Height of the Industrialization Period," in *The Urbanization of European Society in the Nineteenth Century*, ed. Andrew Lees and Lynn Lees (Lexington, Mass.: Heath, 1976), 28–44; and Clive Trebilcock, *The Industrialization of the Continental Powers, 1780–1914* (London and New York: Longman, 1981), 165–66.

2. Reulecke, *Geschichte der Urbanisierung*, 86–131; Peter Merkl, "Urban Challenge under the Empire," in *Another Germany: A Reconsideration of the Imperial Era*, ed. Joachim Remak and Jack R. Dukes (Boulder, Colo., and London: Westview Press, 1988), 61–72.
3. Wolfgang Hofmann, "Die Entwickung der kommunalen Selbstverwaltung von 1848 bis 1918," in *Handbuch der kommunalen Wissenschaft und Praxis*, vol. 1: *Grundlagen*, ed. G. Püttner (Berlin: Springer, 1981), 83–84.
4. A good example is William Harbutt Dawson, *Municipal Life and Government in Germany* (London: Longmans, 1914), esp. 189–207; also Lees, *Cities Perceived*, 239.
5. Jürgen Reulecke, "Zur städtischen Finanzlage in den Anfangsjahren der Weimarer Republik," *Archiv für Kommunalwissenschaften* 21 (1982): 202–3, 206; idem, "Wirtschaft und Bevölkerung ausgewählter Städte im Ersten Weltkrieg (Barmen, Düsseldorf, Essen, Krefeld)," in *Die Deutsche Stadt im Industriezeitalter: Beiträge zur modernen deutschen Stadtgeschichte*, ed. Jürgen Reulecke (Wuppertal: Peter Hammer, 1978), 114–15; idem, *Geschichte der Urbanisierung*, 215; Hartmut Pogge von Strandmann, "The Liberal Power Monopoly in the Cities of Imperial Germany," in *Elections, Mass Politics, and Social Change in Modern Germany: New Perspectives*, ed. Larry Eugene Jones and James Retallack (Cambridge: Cambridge University Press, 1992), 100.
6. Figures are for cities with a population of over 50,000 in 1911. George Steinmetz, *Regulating the Social: The Welfare State and Local Politics in Imperial Germany* (Princeton, N.J.: Princeton University Press, 1993), 154. See James J. Sheehan, "Liberalism and the City in Nineteenth-Century Germany," *Past & Present* no. 51 (1971): 116–37; Richard J. Evans, *Death in Hamburg: Society and Politics in the Cholera Years, 1830–1910* (Harmondsworth: Penguin, 1987), 47–48; Pogge, "Power Monopoly," 105; Merkl, "Urban Challenge," 61–62.
7. Pogge, "Power Monopoly," 103–4. Also Stanley Suval, *Electoral Politics in Wilhelmine Germany* (Chapel Hill: University of North Carolina Press, 1985), 232–41; Hofmann, "Entwicklung," 82–83.
8. Steinmetz, *Regulating the Social*, 194–97; Pogge, "Power Monopoly," 108.
9. See Hermann Beckstein, *Städtische Interessenpolitik: Organisation und Politik der Städtetage in Bayern, Preussen und im Deutschen Reich, 1896–1923* (Düsseldorf: Droste, 1991), 194–298; and Belinda J. Davis, *Home Fires Burning: Food, Politics, and Everyday Life in World War I Berlin* (Chapel Hill: University of North Carolina Press, 2000). A comparative perspective is offered in Jay Winter and Jean-Louis Robert, eds., *Capital Cities at War: Paris, London, Berlin, 1914–1919* (Cambridge: Cambridge University Press, 1997).
10. Gerald D. Feldman, *The Great Disorder: Politics, Economics, and Society in the German Inflation, 1914–1924* (New York and Oxford: Oxford University Press, 1993), 49.
11. The constitution and extensive commentary are in F.F. Blachly and M.E. Oatman, *The Government and Administration of Germany* (Baltimore: Johns Hopkins University Press, 1928), see here 216–17; also Harold James, *The German Slump: Politics and Economics, 1924–1931* (New York: Oxford University Press, 1986), 40.
12. Surveyed in Herbert Jacob, *German Administration since Bismarck: Central Authority versus Local Autonomy* (New Haven and London: Yale University Press, 1963), 73–78.

13. On the Landessteuergesetz, see Josef Wysocki, "Die Kommunalfinanzen in Erzbergers Reformkonzept: Finanzzuweisungen statt eigener Steuern," in *Kommunale Finanzpolitik in der Weimarer Republik*, ed. Karl-Heinrich Hansmeyer (Stuttgart: W. Kohlhammer, 1973), 35–59; and Reulecke, "Zur städtische Finanzlage," 201–02.
14. Blachly and Oatman, *Government*, 216.
15. Christian Engeli, *Gustav Böss: Oberbürgermeister von Berlin, 1921–1930* (Stuttgart: W. Kohlhammer, 1971), 187–206; and materials in LAB Rep. 142-01, St.A 501.
16. Deutscher Städtetag, *25 Jahre Gemeinschaftsarbeit Deutscher Städte* (Berlin: Selbstverlag des Deutschen Städtetages, 1930), 11.
17. Quotations from Reulecke, "Zur städtische Finanzlage," 209 (paraphrasing Thomas Nipperdey); and Feldman, *Great Disorder*, 161.
18. Feldman, ibid.
19. Konrad Adenauer, quoted in Ziebill, *Geschichte*, 231.
20. See the invaluable work of Timothy Moss, "Cities in the Inflation: Municipal Government in Berlin, Cologne, and Frankfurt am Main during the Early Years of the Weimar Republic" (Ph.D. diss., Oxford University, 1992), here 84–89.
21. Albert Hensel, *Kommunalrecht und Kommunalpolitik in Deutschland* (Breslau: Ferdinand Hirt, 1928); *Quellen zum modernen Gemeindeverfassungsrecht in Deutschland*, ed. Christian Engeli and Wolfgang Haus (Stuttgart: W. Kohlhammer, 1975), 660–62.
22. Hofmann, "Entwicklung," 71–79; a useful survey is in Arthur Gunlicks, *Local Government in the German Federal System* (Durham, N.C.: Duke University Press, 1986), 5–23.
23. Siegfried Grassmann, *Hugo Preuss und die deutsche Selbstverwaltung* (Lübeck and Hamburg: Matthiesen Verlag, 1965), 16–17. On the widespread use of biological metaphors to describe the state, see Paul Weindling, "Theories of the Cell State in Imperial Germany," in *Biology, Medicine, and Society, 1840–1940*, ed. Charles Webster (Cambridge: Cambridge University Press, 1981), 99–155, esp. 135–43.
24. Celia Applegate, "Democracy or Reaction? The Political Implications of Localist Ideas in Wilhelmine and Weimar Germany," in Jones and Retallack, eds., *Elections, Mass Politics, and Social Change*, 262; and Grassmann, *Hugo Preuss*, 39 and 110.
25. Grassmann, *Hugo Preuss*, 94–103. Map and summary in Arnold Brecht, *Federalism and Regionalism in Germany: The Division of Prussia* (Oxford: Oxford University Press, 1945), 94–95; Applegate, "Democracy or Reaction?," 259–60 (quotation).
26. Grassmann, *Hugo Preuss*, 111; Applegate, "Democracy or Reaction?," 260; Jacob, *Administration*, 87–92.
27. Translated in Blachly and Oatman, *Government*, 667.
28. Grassmann, *Hugo Preuss*, 121; Christian Engeli, "Städte und Staat in der Weimarer Republik: Hans Herzfeld zum Gedenken," in *Kommunale Selbstverwaltung—Idee und Wirklichkeit*, ed. Bernhard Kirchgässner and Jörg Schadt (Sigmaringen: Jan Thorbecke, 1983), 166–67; Rebentisch, "Die Selbstverwaltung in der Weimarer Zeit," 1:87–89; and Moss, "Cities in the Inflation," 62–63, 66.
29. Gisela Upmeier, "Die Entwicklung der kommunalen Ausgaben und Einnahmen im Verlauf des Währungszerfalls," in *Kommunale Finanzpolitik*, 64.
30. Municipal responsibilities are listed in *Mitteilungen des Deutschen Städtetages (Mitt. DST)* 9 (1922): cols. 49–50; see also the survey in Jürgen

Reulecke, "Die Auswirkungen der Inflation auf die städtischen Finanzen," in *Die Nachwirkungen der Inflation auf die deutsche Geschichte, 1924–1933*, ed. Gerald D. Feldman (Munich: Oldenbourg, 1985), 105–7.
31. Feldman, *Great Disorder*, 562; also 119–20, 232–34, 557.
32. Feldman, *Great Disorder*, 235; Moss, "Cities in the Inflation," 225; survey in *Mitt. DST* 10 (1923): cols. 210–14.
33. Moss, "Cities in the Inflation, 217; Feldman, *Great Disorder*, 232–33, 766, 784.
34. Paul Mitzlaff, "German Cities since the Revolution of 1918," *National Municipal Review* 15, no. 11 (1926), supplement, 683.
35. Reulecke, "Auswirkungen," 97, 112; also Upmeier, "Entwicklung," 67; and Ziebill, *Geschichte*, 234–35.
36. DST Council resolution of 30 July 1919, quoted in Wysocki, "Erzbergers Reformkonzept," 41.
37. *Mitt. DST* 10 (1923): col. 172; Moss, "Cities in the Inflation," 345; Feldman, *Great Disorder*, 562.
38. Gisela Upmeier, "Neue Auswahlkriterien für Gemeindesteuern," in *Kommunale Finanzpolitik*, 71–76; Reulecke, "Auswirkungen," 109–12.
39. For example, Moss, "Cities in the Inflation," 288–92 (quotation, 292); Ziebill, *Geschichte*, 236; Reulecke, "Auswirkungen," 110; Anthony McElligott, *Contested City: Municipal Politics and the Rise of Nazism in Altona, 1917–1937* (Ann Arbor: University of Michigan Press, 1998), 125–61.
40. Moss, "Cities in the Inflation," 69; Karl-Heinrich Hansmeyer, "Der kommunale Kredit als 'ordentliches Deckungsmittel,'" in *Kommunale Finanzpolitik*, 82–83; Reulecke, "Auswirkungen," 111–12; Feldman, *Great Disorder*, 562.
41. See *Mitt. DST* 10 (1923): cols. 144–45; Hansmeyer, "Deckungsmittel," 78–86; Moss, "Cities in the Inflation," 371–73; Feldman, *Great Disorder*, 590–91, 706; Reulecke, "Auswirkungen," 102–03; Steven B. Webb, *Hyperinflation and Stabilization in Weimar Germany* (New York and Oxford: Oxford University Press, 1989), 14–15.
42. DST Council meeting of 19 Oct. 1923, *Mitt. DST* 10 (1923): col. 203. Also DST Council, 16 Sep. 1922, *Mitt. DST* 9 (1922): col. 322; and DST Finance Committee, 31 Aug. 1923, *Mitt. DST* 10 (1923): col. 172.
43. *StatJbDSt* 22 (1927), 5.
44. *Mitt. DST* 10 (1923): col. 144.
45. See, e.g., meetings for 1922–23 of the Finanz-Dezernenten grösseren westdeutschen Städte, in Düsseldorf Stadtarchiv (DüssStA), III 9980; *Mitt. DST* 7 (1920): cols. 417–18; and ibid., 9 (1922): cols. 328–29. Also Moss, "Cities in the Inflation," 386–87; Feldman, *Great Disorder*, 521–22; Hansmeyer, "Deckungsmittel," 76–78.
46. Moss, "Cities in the Inflation," 374–75.
47. See Reulecke's comments, "Auswirkungen," 97, 112.
48. See Moss's assessment, "Cities in the Inflation," 354–59.
49. Hansmeyer, "Deckungsmittel," 78; see also Reulecke's quotation of Prussian Finance Minister Ernst von Richter in "Auswirkungen," 108.
50. Upmeier, "Entwicklung," 68–71.
51. See esp. Moss, "Cities in the Inflation," 339, 397, 406–08; and Hansmeyer, "Deckungsmittel," in idem, ed., *Kommunale Finanazpolitik*, 87–88.
52. Municipal authorities took the importance of such perceptions very seriously, and resolved to disseminate correct information in the press. See 15 Nov. 1924 meeting of the Finanz-Dezernenten grösseren westdeutschen Städte, DüssStA, III 9980. Also Reulecke, "Auswirkungen," 112–13.
53. See pp. 25–27, 46–47.

54. Lieberman, *From Recovery to Catastrophe*, 87–91.
55. Wilhelm Ribhegge, "Die Systemfunktion der Gemeinden: Zur deutschen Kommunalgeschichte seit 1918," in *Kommunale Demokratie: Beiträge für die Praxis der kommunalen Selbstverwaltung*, ed. Rainer Frey (Bonn-Bad Godesberg: Neue Gesellschaft, 1976), 33.
56. Ribhegge, "Systemfunktion," 32–34; Engeli, "Städte und Staat," 164–65; Moss, "Cities in the Inflation," 39, 48–51; quotation from James, *German Slump*, 87.
57. Ribhegge, "Systemfunktion," 34.
58. Party affiliations of city council-members for 1920 are detailed in *Mitt. DST* 7 (1920): cols. 447–52; and after the 1924 communal elections in Prussia, *Mitt. DST* 11 (1924): cols. 123–32. See also Detlef Lehnert, *Kommunale Politik, Parteiensystem und Interessenkonflikte in Berlin und Wien, 1919–1932* (Berlin: Haude & Spener, 1991), 51; Ribhegge, "Systemfunktion," 35–36; Engeli, "Städte und Staat," 165; Moss, "Cities in the Inflation," 54–55.
59. These included the nationally prominent mayors Bernhard Blüher (Dresden), Karl Jarres (Duisburg), Richard Robert Rive (Nuremberg), and Konrad Adenauer (Cologne). See Wolfgang Hofmann, *Zwischen Rathaus und Reichskanzlei: Die Oberbürgermeister in der Kommunal- und Staatspolitik des Deutschen Reiches von 1890 bis 1933* (Stuttgart: W. Kohlhammer, 1974), 67 and passim.
60. Quoted in Jeremy Noakes, "Oberbürgermeister and Gauleiter: City Government between Party and State," in *Der "Führerstaat"—Mythos und Realität: Studien zur Struktur und Politik des Dritten Reiches*, ed. Gerhard Hirschfeld and Lothar Kettenacker (Stuttgart: Ernst Klett, 1981), 194.
61. Useful summaries of these careers and others are in *Persönlichkeiten der Verwaltung: Biographien zur deutschen Verwaltungsgeschichte, 1648–1945*, ed. Kurt G.A. Jeserich and Helmut Neuhaus (Stuttgart: W. Kohlhammer, 1991).
62. Richard Bessel, *Germany after the First World War* (Oxford: Clarendon Press, 1993), 283.
63. Karl Kautsky, quoted in Steinmetz, *Regulating the Social*, 195.
64. Steinmetz, *Regulating the Social*, 194–97; Moss, "Cities in the Inflation," 34; and David McKibben, "Who Were the German Independent Socialists? The Leipzig City Council Election of 6 December 1917," *Central European History* 25 (1992): 425–43. For the Weimar period, Dieter Rebentisch, "Programmatik und Praxis sozialdemokratischer Kommunalpolitik in der Weimarer Republik," *Die alte Stadt: Zeitschrift für Stadtgeschichte, Stadtsoziologie, und Denkmalpflege* 12 (1985): 33–56.
65. Mitzlaff, "German Cities," 682.
66. Lieberman, *From Recovery to Catastrophe*, 184, 191.
67. Hans Herzfeld characterized the cities' postwar lack of room to maneuver as a "pressure on many fronts" (*Mehrfrontendruck*), a metaphor suggesting multiple continuities with the wartime *Heimatsfront*. See his *Demokratie und Selbstverwaltung in der Weimarer Epoche* (Stuttgart: W. Kohlhammer, 1957), 20.
68. These included Erich Koch-Weser (long-time OB of Kassel, then Reich Minister of the Interior), Hans Luther (wartime OB of Essen, and eventual holder of virtually every important federal office in the republic), Robert Schmidt (Luther's second in Essen, and after 1920 director of the Ruhr Housing Association), Robert Lehr (in 1924 elected OB Düsseldorf), Fritz Elsas (vice president of the Städtetag 1926–31 and then BM of Berlin), and Gotthold Haekel (president of the Reichsstädtebund).

69. *Die Zukunftsaufgaben der deutschen Städte*, ed. Hans Luther et al. (Berlin-Friedenau: Deutscher Kommunal-Verlag, 1922), 15.
70. Peukert, *Weimar Republic*, 207 (quotation). Also Eberhard Kolb, *The Weimar Republic* (London: Unwin Hyman, 1988), 66.
71. See below, chap. 4.
72. *Stenographische Verhandlungsberichte der Stadtverordneten-Versammlung zu Düsseldorf* (1925), council meeting of 8 May 1925, p. 220.
73. Harold James, "Municipal Finance in the Weimar Republic," in *The State and Social Change in Germany, 1880–1980*, ed. W.R. Lee and Eve Rosenhaft (New York, Oxford and Munich: Berg, 1990), 233–35; Ekkehard Mai, "Gesolei und Pressa: Zu Programm und Architektur rheinischen Ausstellungswesens in den zwanziger Jahren," in *Rheinland und Westfalen im Industriezeitalter*, vol. 4: *Zur Geschichte von Wissenschaft, Kunst und Bildung an Rhein und Ruhr,* ed. Kurt Düwell and Wolfgang Köllmann (Wuppertal: Peter Hammer, 1985), 271–87.
74. Of 233 streetcar companies in Germany, 120 were operated directly by the communes, who also held a controlling interest in an additional sixty-seven of mixed capital. Städtetag president Oskar Mulert in 1929 presented an extensive report on the economic activities of German cities to the International Congress of Local Authorities (Union international des villes) at Seville, "L'Activité économique des Communes en Allemagne," *L'Administration Locale,* no. 49 (Jan.–Mar. 1929): 653–700. The report was published simultaneously in German, "Die wirtschaftliche Betätigung der Gemeinden," *Mitt. DST* 23 (1929): cols. 249–58; and expanded in English, "Economic Activities of German Municipalities," *Annals of Collective Economy* 5 (1929): 209–70 (here 236); and generally Lieberman, *From Recovery to Catastrophe*, 27–56.
75. James, "Municipal Finance," 233.
76. Specifically, 94.2 percent water, 82.9 percent gas, and over 80 percent electricity. Mulert, "Economic Activities," 224–34.
77. Theo Balderston, *The Origins and Course of the German Economic Crisis, November 1923 to May 1932* (Berlin: Haude & Spener, 1993), 344–46.
78. Balderston, *Origins*, 351. For a general discussion of the housing problem, see Dan P. Silverman, "A Pledge Unredeemed: The Housing Crisis in Weimar Germany," *Central European History* 3 (1970), 112–39 (shortage figures, 119).
79. In Prussia, it was known as the *Hauszinssteuer*, Balderston, *Origins*, 221, 352–53; and Silverman, "Pledge Unredeemed," 122–23. For the negotiations between Reich and Länder concerning passage of the tax, and the disadvantageous outcome for the municipalities, see Feldman, *Great Disorder*, 819–20.
80. Balderston, *Origins*, 351, table 9.16.
81. Balderston, *Origins*, 354; Ben Lieberman, "Luxury or Public Investment? Productivity and Planning for Weimar Recovery," *Central European History* 26 (1993): 203.
82. Gisela Upmeier, "Die Kommerzialisierung der Kommunalwirtschaft," in Hansmeyer, ed., *Kommunale Finanzpolitik*, 90–99; Gerold Ambrosius, "Öffentliche Unternehmen in der Inflation 1918 bis 1923: Der Konflikt zwischen der betrieblichen Finanzwirtschaft der städtischen Werke und den fiskalpolitischen Ansprüchen der Kommunen," in *Die Anpassung an die Inflation/The Adaptation to Inflation*, ed. Gerald D. Feldman et al. (Berlin: Walter de Gruyter, 1986), 357–91.

83. Several categories of utilities were exempt from corporate and sales taxes. See Gisela Upmeier, "Auseinandersetzungen um die Besteuerung der Kommunalbetriebe," in Hansmeyer, ed., *Kommunale Finanzpolitik*, 143–44.
84. Lieberman, "Testing Peukert's Paradigm," 287–303; Lane, *Architecture and Politics*, 87–145.
85. Engeli, "Städte und Staat," 170 (quotation). Bismarck had similarly called the old Reich the "Kostgänger" of the states. See Carl-Ludwig Holtfrerich, "The Modernisation of the Tax System in the First World War and the Great Inflation, 1914–1923," in *Wealth and Taxation in Central Europe: The History and Sociology of Public Finance*, ed. Peter-Christian Witt (Leamington Spa, 1987), 126.
86. The quickest path through the dense thicket of Finanzausgleich legislation and commentaries is in Statistisches Reichsamt, ed., *Verwaltungsaufbau, Steuerverteilung, und Lastenverteilung im Deutschen Reich* (Einzelschrift zur Statistik des Deutschen Reichs, no. 6; Berlin, 1929), 124–27, 144–45, and 246–47.
87. For details, see *Verwaltungsaufbau*, 140; also Josef Wysocki, "Der permanent vorläufige Finanzausgleich," in *Kommunale Finanzpolitik*, 125–28.
88. For example, the cities' position as laid out at the key DST Council meeting of 10 Dec. 1926: "Finanzlage der Städte und Gesetzentwurf über den Finanzausgleich," LAB, Rep. 142–01, St.A 315 (published in shortened form in *Mitt. DST* 21 [1927]: cols. 3–4).
89. Wysocki, "Erzbergers Reformkonzept," in Hansmeyer, ed., *Kommunale Finanzpolitik*, 42. The specifics of the temporary laws are in *Verwaltungsaufbau*, 136–39.
90. The resulting fiscal imbalances for 1925–30 are therefore deceptive, in that they far exceed those for the post-1930 years. See Balderston, *Origins*, 226, table 7.2, col. 7.
91. Calculated from *StatJbDSt* 22 (1927), 18.
92. On the importance of the *Zuschuss-* or *Finanzbedarf*, see *StatJbDSt* 22 (1927), 5; and Josef Wysocki, "Die finanzwirtschaftliche Ausgangslage," in Hansmeyer, ed., *Kommunale Finanzpolitik*, 31, n.30.
93. Lieberman, *From Recovery to Catastrophe*, 93.
94. *Verwaltungsaufbau*, 418–34.
95. *Mitt. DST* 26 (1932): 117.
96. Ziebill, *Geschichte*, 246.
97. Hansmeyer, "Deckungsmittel," in idem, ed., *Kommunale Finanazpolitik*, 77–78.
98. Refers to cities with populations above 10,000. See Balderston, *Origins*, 255, table 7.11; James, *German Slump*, 96–97; and William C. McNeil, *American Money and the Weimar Republic: Economics and Politics on the Eve of the Great Depression* (New York: Columbia University Press, 1986), 240–41. The smaller towns probably also accumulated considerable debt not included in these figures, ibid., 243.
99. McNeil, *American Money*, 240–41, and Balderston, *Origins*, 253–54. Balderston points out that greater German municipal borrowing in the decade prior to the First World War fits with other aspects of Germany's economic acceleration in the imperial period.
100. Press release of the central associations for industry, business, agriculture, and banking, dated 10 Nov. 1926 (in materials for DST Council meeting of 10 Dec. 1926, LAB, Rep. 142-01 St.A 315); also Ribhegge, "Systemfunktion," 41–42. For a comparable statement from the cities' viewpoint, see the record of the DST Council meeting on 23 Jan. 1928, in LAB, Rep. 142-01, St.A 751.

101. "Local authorities" included the Länder. Although not bound by the board's recommendations as the cities were, they agreed among themselves to follow them anyway—a decision doubtless eased by the board's virtual rubber-stamping of all Land loan proposals, no matter how transparently "unproductive." Hermann Dietrich-Troeltsch, "Die Errichtung der Beratungsstelle für Auslandskredite und ihre Funktionsweise," in *Kommunale Finanzpolitik*, 174–86; McNeil, *American Money*, 63–65, 251–55.
102. As the Reich Finance Ministry admitted in a 1926 memo to the Reichstag. McNeil, *American Money*, 67.
103. James, *German Slump*, 94.
104. Lieberman, "Luxury or Public Investment?," 198–201 (quotation, 201); McNeil, *American Money*, 52, 64, 94.
105. McNeil, *American Money*, 27–30.
106. The *Report of the Agent-General for Reparation Payments*, published in London, appeared three times: 30 May and 30 Nov. 1925, and 15 June 1926. On Gilbert's influence, see "Parker Gilbert und die Gemienden," *Gemeinde und Wirtschaft* no. 44 (Jan. 1929): 4; and McNeil, *American Money*, 206.
107. DST Council, 12 Oct. 1927, LAB, Rep. 142-01, St.A 177; and Oskar Mulert, "Der deutsche Reichsbankpräsident gegen die deutschen Städte," *Mitt. DST* 21 (1927): col. 386.
108. Gisela Upmeier, "Schachts Kampf gegen die kommunalen Auslandsanleihen," in *Kommunale Finanzpolitik*, 160–71; McNeil, *American Money*, 15–17, 112–13.
109. Hjalmar Schacht, *Eigene oder geborgte Währung* (speech in Bochum of 18 Nov. 1927) (Leipzig: Quelle & Meyer, 1927), 22–23. This section of Schacht's speech, along with a vigorous rebuttal by Reichstag SPD deputy Aufhäuser, is excerpted in *Quellen zur deutschen Wirtschafts- und Sozialgeschichte vom ersten Weltkrieg bis zum Ende der Weimarer Republik*, ed. Walter Steitz (Darmstadt: Wissenschaftliche Buchgesellschaft, 1993), 315–27.
110. Schacht, *Eigene oder geborgte Währung*, 22.
111. Paraphrased from *Mitt. DST* 21 (1927): cols. 538–39.
112. "Grossstädte" encompassed municipalities with over 100,000 residents, excluding the Hansa cities. Mulert, "Reichsbankpräsident," cols. 387–88.
113. Mulert contended that the cities had "repeatedly and urgently requested" that these projects be housing construction, but to no avail. Mulert, "Reichsbankpräsident," col. 390.
114. Mulert, "Reichsbankpräsident," cols. 389–90; also Lieberman, "Luxury or Public Investment?," 203–11.
115. Mulert, "Reichsbankpräsident," cols. 391–92.
116. Mitzlaff, "German Cities," 685–86.
117. McNeil, *American Money*, 14–17, 55–56, 112; Harold James, *The Reichsbank and Public Finance in Germany, 1924–1933: A Study of the Politics of Economics during the Great Depression* (Frankfurt am Main: Fritz Knapp, 1985), 22.
118. Roland Brauweiler, "Artikel 127: Selbstverwaltung," in *Die Grundrechte und Grundpflichten der Reichsverfassung: Kommentar zum zweiten Teil der Reichsverfassung*, ed. Hans Carl Nipperdey (Berlin: Reimar Hobbing, 1930), 2: 200, 208–9. This issue had special significance when it came to defining in which areas the cities should have direct access to central authorities. They could approach Reich ministries about matters of self-government but not those delegated to them. DST 1930 memo summarizing the regulations and describing variations in local practice, LAB, Rep. 142-01, St.B 4214.
119. Ernst Forsthoff, *Die Krise der Gemeindeverwaltung im heutigen Staat* (Berlin: Junker & Dünnhaupt, 1932); Arnold Köttgen, *Die Krise der kommunalen*

Selbstverwaltung (Tübingen: J.C.B. Mohr, 1931); Carl Schmitt, *Der Hüter der Verfassung* (Tübingen: J.C.B. Mohr, 1931); Hans Peters, *Grenzen der Selbstverwaltung in Preussen: Ein Beitrag zur Lehre vom Verhältnis der Gemeinden zu Staat und Reich* (Berlin: Julius Springer, 1926).

120. See the thoughtful discussion in Wolfgang Hofmann, "Plebiszitäre Demokratie und kommunale Selbstverwaltung in der Weimarer Republik," *Archiv für Kommunalwissenschaften* 4 (1965): 264–81.
121. *Mitt. DST* 26 (1932): 117; ibid., 27 (1933): 123; and Rebentisch, "Selbstverwaltung," 100.
122. Ribhegge, "Systemfunktion," 44.
123. See Mulert's comments to Reich Finance Minister Hermann Dietrich on 29 Aug. 1931, recounted in his circular to DST member-cities of same date, LAB, Rep. 142-01, St.B 3692; also published in *Politik und Wirtschaft in der Krise, 1930–1932: Quellen zur Ära Brüning*, ed. Ilse Maurer and Udo Wengst (Düsseldorf: Droste, 1980), 2:926–29, doc. 298.
124. Mulert's circular on "Kommunalkredit" to DST member-cities of 5 Nov. 1929, LAB, Rep. 142-01, St.A 163; and Mulert, "Verantwortung!," *Mitt. DST* 24 (1930): 1–5.
125. Reich Chancellory discussion of 10 Oct. 1931, memo of same date in St.B 3765; also in *Quellen zur Ära Brüning*, 2:873-81, doc. 284.
126. *Mitt. DST* 27 (1933): 123.
127. James, *German Slump*, 105.
128. Otto Büsch and Wolfgang Haus, *Berliner Demokratie, 1919–1985*, vol. 1: *Berlin als Hauptstadt der Weimarer Republik, 1919–1933* (Berlin and New York: Walter de Gruyter, 1987), 228–31.
129. In 1930, on 26 July and 1 Dec.; in 1931, on 5 June, 24 Aug., 6 Oct., and 8 Dec.; and in 1932, under Papen, on 4–5 Sept. See Walter Delius, "Die Notverordnungen und ihre Auswirkungen auf die Gemeinden," *Zeitschrift für Kommunalwirtschaft* 21 (Nov. 1931): cols. 1257–77; and the survey in Fritz Terhalle, "Geschichte der deutschen öffentlichen Finanzwirtschaft vom Beginn des 19. Jahrhunderts bis zum Schlusse des Zweiten Weltkriegs," in *Handbuch der Finanzwissenschaft*, ed. Wilhelm Gerloff and Fritz Neumark (Tübingen: J.C.B. Mohr, 1952), 1:310–11.
130. James, *German Slump*, 67–69, 77.
131. Mulert's discussion with Prussian Ministers of Interior and Finance Severing and Höpker-Aschoff, 6 Aug. 1931, LAB, Rep. 142-01, St.B 3612; and Mulert's protest to the Reich Chancellor and Ministers of Finance and Economy, also 6 Aug. 1931, St.B 3613.
132. See especially Gerhard Schulz, *Zwischen Demokratie und Diktatur*, vol. 3: *Von Brüning zu Hitler—Der Wandel des politischen Systems in Deutschland, 1930–1933* (Berlin: Walter de Gruyter, 1992), 487–92.
133. For example, Delius, "Notverordnungen," col. 1260.
134. "Das Problem der Staatskommissare," *Mitt. DST* 25 (1931): 126–27; W. Zeck, "Staatsaufsicht in Angelegenheiten des Gemeindehaushalts," *Staats- und Selbstverwaltung* 12 (1931): 65–67; and Johannes Seidel, *Die Haushaltspläne der deutschen Gemeinden* (Jena: Gustav Fischer, 1933), 64–66. Considering the attention given them at the time, the Staatskommissare have been surprisingly neglected by historians. See Wolfgang Haus, "Staatskommissare und Selbstverwaltung, 1930–1933," *Der Städtetag* 9 (New series, 1956): 96–97; Engeli, "Städte und Staat," 176, Rebentisch, "Selbstverwaltung," 99.
135. Viktor von Leyden, director of communal affairs for the Prussian Interior Ministry, to PST, 14 Jan. 1931, LAB, Rep. 142-01, St.B 435.

136. For a contemprorary discussion of "Gemeinwohl," see Zeck, "Staatsaufsicht," 65–67 (quotation, 66). Also James, *Reichsbank*, 261–82; and idem, *German Slump*, 88–92.
137. Engeli, "Städte und Staat," 176; Rebentisch, "Selbstverwaltung," 99.
138. Büsch and Haus, *Berlin als Hauptstadt*, 228–30; Lehnert, *Kommunale Politik*, 179–206.
139. Haus, "Staatskommissare," 96–97; Büsch and Haus, *Berlin als Hauptstadt*, 243.
140. Haus, "Staatskommissare," 97.
141. Rebentisch, "Selbstverwaltung," 99.
142. Ibid., 92–93.
143. On Nazi approaches to communal politics and government, see Horst Matzerath, *Nationalsozialismus und kommunale Selbstverwaltung* (Stuttgart: W. Kohlhammer, 1970), 33–60; and Albert von Mutius, "Kommunalverwaltung und Kommunalpolitik," in *Deutsche Verwaltungsgeschichte*, ed. Kurt G.A. Jeserich et al. (Stuttgart: Deutsche Verlags-Anstalt, 1980–85), 4:1060–62.
144. See esp. Matzerath, *Nationalsozialismus*, 61–98; also Noakes, "Oberbürgermeister," 197–98; and Ribhegge, "Systemfunktion," 47. The most well-known local study of the Nazi rise to power remains William Sheridan Allen's *The Nazi Seizure of Power: The Experience of a Single German Town, 1922–1945* (New York, 1984). A survey of more recent literature is in Jeremy Noakes, "Regional and Local Perspectives on Nazism," *German History* 13 (1995): 388–97.
145. Noakes, "Oberbürgermeister," 197–98; Matzerath, *Nationalsozialismus*, 79–80.
146. Matzerath, *Nationalsozialismus*, 121–26.
147. The DGO is printed with commentary in *Quellen zum modernen Gemeindeverfassungsrecht*, 673–98. On the DGO, see first Matzerath, *Nationalsozialismus*, 132–64; also Noakes, "Oberbürgermeister," 203–5.
148. Voluminous correspondence often developed over seemingly trivial issues of proper communication channels. Correspondence in LAB, Rep. 142-01, St.B 3613. See especially the "Vermerk: Amtlicher Verkehr mit den Provinzial- und Lokalbehörden" of February 1930, in St.B 4214; and more generally Jürgen Bertram, *Staats- und Kommunalpolitik: Notwendigkeit und Grenzen ihre Koordinierung* (Stuttgart: W. Kohlhammer, 1967), 73–80.
149. Karl M. Hettlage, "Die Finanzverwaltung," in *Deutsche Verwaltungsgeschichte*, 4:195.
150. See the comments of Noakes, "Oberbürgermeister," 202, 221–22. The DST's 1925 Reichsstädteordnung bill proposed that the two forms of municipal government, the Magistratsverfassung and the Bürgermeisterverfassung, be allowed to coexist side by side. The 1930 bill favored only the latter. See *Quellen zum modernen Gemeindeverfassungsrecht*, 660–61; and Wolfgang R. Krabbe, "Die Tendenz zur autoritären Kommunalverfassung: Preussen, Deutschland und das Rheinland 1920–1935," in *Preussen und die rheinischen Städte*, ed. Margret Wensky (Cologne: Rheinland-Verlag, 1994), 75–94.
151. *Mitt. DST* 27 (1933): 148.

CHAPTER 2

1. DST, *25 Jahre*, 24.
2. For example, Karl Dietrich Bracher, Wolfgang Sauer, and Gerhard Schulz, *Die nationalsozialistische Machtergreifung: Studien zur Errichtung*

des totalitären Herrschaftssystems in Deutschland 1933/34 (Cologne and Opladen: Westdeutscher Verlag, 1960), 450; Christian Engeli, "Zur Geschichte der regionalen Städtetage," *Archiv für Kommunalwissenschaften* 19 (1980): 197.

3. For samples at various points during the 1920s, see the following items in *Mitt. DST*: DST Finance Committee, 14 Jan. 1922 (9 [1922], cols. 33–38); DST Council, 10 Dec. 1926 (21 [1927], cols. 1–4); "Notjahr und Gemeinden" (23 [1929], col. 445).
4. Matzerath, *Nationalsozialismus*, 61–104; Noakes, "Regional and Local Perspectives," 388–97.
5. In Silesia (1863), Hanover (1866), Saxony (1867), Thuringia (1869), Brandenburg and Schleswig-Holstein (1873), Pomerania (1875), and Westphalia (1876). Beckstein, *Städtische Interessenpolitik*, 36–37; Engeli, "Zur Geschichte," 177.
6. Beckstein, *Städtische Interessenpolitik*, 84–87; Engeli, "Zur Geschichte," 181–82.
7. Engeli, "Zur Geschichte," 180.
8. Ziebill, *Geschichte*, 10–11; quotation from Engeli, "Zur Geschichte," 177. On Ziebill's directorship, see Wolfgang Hofmann, *Städtetag und Verfassungsordnung: Position und Politik der Hauptgeschäftsführer eines kommunalen Spitzenverbandes* (Stuttgart, 1966), 152–61.
9. "Hand in Hand mit dem Staat und seiner Verwaltung" was the title of a volume published in 1902 celebrating the twenty-five-year founding of the Westphalian Städtetag. Engeli, "Zur Geschichte," 179; and Beckstein, *Städtische Interessenpolitik*, 31.
10. Engeli, "Zur Geschichte," 179.
11. Beckstein, *Städtische Interessenpolitik*, 72–83.
12. Quotations from DST, *25 Jahre*, 6–7. See also Oskar Böttcher, *Die kommunalen Reichsspitzenverbände* (Berlin-Friedenau: Deutscher Kommunal-Verlag, 1932), 5.
13. Steinmetz, *Regulating the Social*, 194–97.
14. There is still remarkably little research on the important subject of the cities' wartime activities. Beckstein's *Städtische Interessenpolitik* supercedes all others, see esp. 194–324. Food distribution is discussed in George Yaney, *The World of the Manager: Food Administration in Berlin during World War I* (New York: Peter Lang, 1996), esp. 45–51, 80–98; cf. Davis, *Home Fires Burning*.
15. DST, *25 Jahre*, 10.
16. Ziebill, *Geschichte*, 51.
17. The interests of small and middling cities are discussed in "Die Deutschen Mittel- und Kleinstädte," *Zeitschrift für Kommunalwirtschaft* 19, Nr. 16 (25 Aug. 1929 [special issue]). On the smaller townships, Günther Gereke, "Die Landgemeinde," in *Volk und Reich der Deutschen: Vorlesungen gehalten in der Deutschen Vereinigung für Staatswissenschaftliche Fortbildung*, ed. Bernhard Harms (Berlin: Reimar Hobbing, 1929), 2:397–425.
18. Beckstein, *Städtische Interessenpolitik*, 317–19; Hans Luther, *Im Dienste des Städtetages* (Berlin: Schriftenreihe des Vereins zur Pflege kommunalwirtschaftlicher Aufgaben, 1959).
19. Differences between the Prussian and national organizations were negligible by this point. Although meetings of both continued to be held separately until 1930, this served largely to facilitate the transaction of business specific to Prussia. Beckstein, *Städtische Interessenpolitik*, 323; Ziebill, *Geschichte*, 51, 56; Böttcher, *Die kommunalen Reichsspitzenverbände*, 18. Committee

personnel are listed in "Jetzige Zusammensetzung der engeren Vorstände," 1 Oct. 1928, LAB, Rep. 142-01, St.A 156.

20. Ziebill, *Geschichte*, 55. For a survey of personnel in the Executive Committee, see memo of December 1932, LAB, Rep. 142-01, St.A 156.
21. See esp. correspondence in LAB, Rep. 142-01, St.A 156 from Goerdeler (Leipzig), Lehr (Düsseldorf), Menge (Hanover), and Wagner (Breslau).
22. Surveyed in detail in "Zusammensetzung der Gemeindevertretung deutscher Städte," *Mitt. DST* 7 (1920): cols. 447–52.
23. Engeli, "Zur Geschichte," 190–95.
24. A proposal by the SPD to increase the percentage to half was rejected. "Neunter Preussischer Städtetag in Goslar," *Mitt. DST* 9 (1922): col. 204. See "Satzung des Preussischen Städtetages," §10, in LAB, Rep. 142-01, St.A 527.
25. DST Council, 5 Feb. 1925, LAB, Rep. 142-01, St.A 527. See DST regulations, § 7, in *25 Jahre*, 59. Comparison of the number of city council members on the DST and PST Councils is in preliminary report to Exec. Committee meeting of 13 Sep. 1929, LAB, Rep. 142-01, St.A 370.
26. Any of the larger meetings' proceedings amply documents their overtly political character, e.g., *Siebenter Deutscher Städtetag: Magdeburg, 23. September 1927* (hereafter *DST Magdeburg, 1927*) (Berlin: Selbstverlag des Deutschen Städtetages, n.d. [1927]).
27. Chap. 5.
28. *Stenographische Verhandlungsberichte der Stadtverordneten-Versammlung zu Düsseldorf* (1924), 138–40. Mulert, circular to member cities of 18 Dec. 1929, LAB, Rep. 142-01, St.B Nr. 243.
29. See DST, *25 Jahre*, 16; Engeli, "Zur Geschichte," 195.
30. Deutscher Städtetag, *Verhandlungen des Sechsten Deutschen Städtetages am 25. und 26. September 1924 in Hannover* (Berlin: Selbstverlag der Geschäftsstelle des Deutschen Städtetages, 1924), 77–78, 115–16.
31. See for example, the debate over constitutional reform in *DST Magdeburg, 1927*; and DST, *Jahresversammlung des Deutschen Städtetages: Breslau, den 25. September 1928* (hereafter *DST Breslau, 1928*) (Berlin: Selbstverlag des Deutschen Städtetages, 1928).
32. Among the candidates were Carl Goerdeler (OB Leipzig), Leo Lippmann (a Hamburg city councillor), and Gotthold Haekel (president, Reichsstädtebund). See Haekel to Mitzlaff, 13 Nov. 1925, NRWHSTA, Bes. 50, Nr. 775; also Hofmann, *Städtetag und Verfassungsordnung*, 41 and n.131.
33. On Mulert's (1881–1951) early years prior to 1919, see his personnel files in BA-Lichterfelde,R 1501 PA /9278-81. Also the biographical sketch in LAB, Findbuch to Bes. E, Rep. 200-34 (vol. 6). Mulert's "erstaunlicher Aufstieg" was noted by his old colleague, Königsberg OB Hans Lohmeyer, in a tribute after his death, "Dem Andenken Oskar Mulerts," *Der Städtetag* 4, New series (Dec. 1951): 374–75; and Kurt G.A. Jeserich, "Oskar Mulert (1881–1951)," in Jeserich, ed., *Persönlichkeiten der Verwaltung*, 391. The best personal portrait is in Hofmann, *Städtetag und Verfassungsordnung*, 41–50.
34. It was the chairman of the latter Verein, OB Lueken of Kiel, who initially proposed Mulert as president. Hofmann, *Städtetag und Verfassungsordnung*, 40; and Jeserich, "Oskar Mulert," 392–93.
35. Mulert to Reichsstädtebund (RSB) President Haekel, 18 Feb. 1926, LAB, Rep. 142–03, RSB 302. Severing to Mulert (draft), 5 Mar. 1926, BA-Lichterfelde, R 1501 PA/9281.
36. Mulert to RSB Chairman Alfred Belian, 6 Mar. 1926, LAB, Rep. 142-03, RSB 302. The DST Council voted Mulert in as president on 4 Dec. 1925,

LAB, Rep. 142-01, St.A 654; and Hofmann *Städtetag und Verfassungsordnung*, 48. The most detailed account of the tense negotiations between Böss and Mulert is in Engeli, *Gustav Böss*, 187–206.

37. Bronisch, "Erinnerungen an den Deutschen Städtetag," typescript memoir, LAB, Bes. E, Rep. 200-34 (Mulert Nachlass), 3.
38. Von Leyden was Mulert's own choice as his successor, Hofmann, *Städtetag und Verfassungsordnung*, 50.
39. Chap. 5.
40. RSB leaders Belian and Haekel to RSB Managing Council, 5 Dec. 1925 (?), NRWHSTA Bes. 50, Nr. 775; Belian to Mulert, 10 Dec. 1925, and Haekel to Belian, 8 Nov. 1926, both in LAB, Rep. 142-03, RSB 302.
41. Compare the minutes of Mulert's first meeting with the Exec. Committee, 19 Mar. 1926, LAB, Rep. 142-01, St.A 315, with any of those preceding. Also Bronisch, "Erinnerungen", 9.
42. Elsas (1890–1945) directed the municipal Food Office of Stuttgart in the war years from 1915–18, and in 1919 became a city councillor. On his early years, see Fritz Elsas, *Auf dem Stuttgarter Rathaus, 1915–1922: Erinnerungen von Fritz Elsas (1890–1945)* (Stuttgart: Klett-Cotta, 1990). On his appointment as DST Vice-President in Sept. 1926 (over high-profile communal figures Carl Goerdeler and Friedrich Surén), see meetings of DST Exec. Committee, 28 June 1926, LAB, Rep. 142-01, St.A 315 and DST Council, 17–18 Sep. 1926, St.A 136; Hofmann, *Städtetag und Verfassungsordnung*, 52; and Ziebill, *Geschichte*, 54. A short biographical sketch is in Jeserich, ed., *Persönlichkeiten der Verwaltung*, 506. Due to his suspected involvement in the July 1944 plot to assassinate Hitler, Elsas was imprisoned in late 1944 and murdered by the SS in early 1945.
43. Elsas memo to Mulert, 24 Apr. 1931, LAB, Rep. 142-01, St.B 3764; and DST Exec. Committee meeting, 29 Apr. 1931, St.A 165.
44. For example, his conversations with the director of the Prussian Interior Ministry's communal affairs section, Victor von Leyden, of 15 June 1927, LAB, Rep. 142-01, St.B 3763; and 17 Feb. 1928, St.B 3964h.
45. For example, Fritz Elsas, "Vergnügungssteuer, Filmindustrie und Gemeinden," *Neue Frankfurter Zeitung*, 9 Sep. 1927 (morning ed.); idem, "Um die Kinosteuer," *Zeitschrift für Kommunalwirtschaft*, Nr. 19 (10 Oct. 1927), in *Mitt. DST* 21 (1927): press clippings, cols. 356–57.
46. Bronisch, "Erinnerungen."
47. Diary entries of 12 Nov. 1927 and 8 Nov. 1928, in *Fritz Elsas, Ein Demokrat im Widerstand: Zeugnisse eines Liberalen in der Weimarer Republik,* ed. Manfred Schmid (Gerlingen: Bleicher, 1999), 29.
48. Meeting of 2 Feb. 1933, LAB, Rep. 142-01, St.A 340.
49. Diary entry of 8 Nov. 1928, in Schmid, ed., *Fritz Elsas*, 29.
50. DST Exec. Committee meetings of 19 Mar., 9 and 26 Apr. 1926, all in LAB, Rep. 142-01, St.A 315.
51. The following paragraphs are taken from the two most extensive versions of the minutes, in LAB, Rep. 142-01, St.B 3764b, and St.A 315. A shortened version was published in *Mitt. DST* 21 (1927): cols. 1–4
52. Preliminary report, DST Council, 10 Dec. 1926, LAB, Rep. 142-01, St.A 315.
53. In January 1928, the DST set up its own publishing company, the "Selbstverlag des Deutschen Städtetages GmbH." Exec. Committee, 13 Jan. 1928, LAB, Rep. 142-01, St.A 195.
54. Achim Bonte, *Werbung für Weimar? Öffentlichkeitsarbeit von Grossstadtverwaltungen in der Weimarer Republik* (Mannheim: Palatium Verlag, 1997), 56–62.

55. DST Exec. Committee meetings of 17 Sep. (LAB, Rep. 142-01, St.A 315) and 24 Nov. 1927 (St.A 177); DST Council, 25 Nov. 1927, St.A 541/II (also in *Mitt. DST* 21 [1927]: cols. 514–17); and meeting of DST Presseausschuss, 12 Jan. 1928, reported in *Mitt. DST* 22 (1928): col. 139. See also Mulert's speech to the Berlin branch of the Reichsverband der Deutschen Presse on 17 Jan. 1928, in *Mitt. DST* 22 (1928): cols. 51–58.
56. *Mitt. DST* 21 (1927), cols. 158–60 and 547–48; and ibid., 22 (1928): cols. 56–58. Also the survey in Gerhard Bader, "Die Nachrichten- und Presseämter deutscher Städte: Ihre Verteilung und Organisation," *Schwartzsche Vakanzenzeitung-Kommunales Echo*, Nr. 49 (5 Dec. 1928), reported in *Mitt. DST* 22 (1928): press clippings, cols. 1491–92.
57. For example, at Duisburg, 25 Nov. 1927, *Mitt. DST* 21 (1927): cols. 511–14, 577–83; and Leipzig, 10 Dec. 1928, ibid., 22 (1928): cols. 1393–94, 1485–88. *Ruhrwacht*, 27 Nov. 1927, in *Mitt. DST* 21 (1927): press clippings, cols. 581–82.
58. The first issue of the revamped bulletin appeared the same month of the Magdeburg congress. See also DST budget of 1928/29, LAB, Rep. 142-01, St.A 195, and Exec. Committee, 23–24 March 1928, St.A 3.
59. Quotations from Ziebill, *Geschichte*, 278; see also "Der Städtetag," *Mitt. DST* 24 (1930): 62.
60. Carl Böhret, *Aktionen gegen die "kalte Sozialisierung," 1926–1930: Ein Beitrag zum Wirken ökonomischer Einflussverbände in der Weimarer Republik* (Berlin: Duncker & Humblot, 1966), 172–86; Upmeier, "Auseinandersetzungen," in Hansmeyer, ed., *Kommunale Finanzpolitik*, esp. 148.
61. Deutscher Städtetag, *Städte, Staat, Wirtschaft: Denkschrift des Deutschen Städtetages* (Berlin: n.p., 1926). On Mulert's involvement and preparation of the pamphlet, see: Böss correspondence with Landmann and Mitzlaff, 19 and 26 Feb. 1926; DST Exec. Committee, 9 Apr. 1926; and "Denkschrift 'Städte, Staat, Wirtschaft' und deren Weiterbehandlung in den Ländern," DST Council, 10 Dec. 1926, all in LAB, Rep. 142–01, St.A 315.
62. DST, *Städte, Staat, Wirtschaft*, esp. 80–82 (quotation, 82).
63. Positions in the controversy are explored in Böhret, *"Kalte Sozialisierung,"* 172–86.
64. *Rheinische-Westfälische Zeitung*, 27 Nov. 1927, in *Mitt. DST* 21 (1927): press clippings, col. 581. Also reports in *Frankfurter Zeitung*, 19 Nov. 1927 (morning ed.), and *Berliner Montagspost*, 21 Nov. 1927; both excerpted in ibid., cols. 460 and 464. Press excerpts published by the DST concerning this issue are quite extensive. See ibid., cols. 363–71, 439–65, and 553–77.
65. "Schachts Verteidigung und Angriff," *Magazin der Wirtschaft* 5 (1927), 1781–84.
66. See stories from the *New York Herald*, *Herald Tribune*, and *Evening Post* of 24–28 Nov., and especially the summary and analysis in the *Manchester Guardian* of 3 Dec. 1927. All are translated and excerpted in *Mitt. DST* 21 (1927): press clippings, cols. 573–77.
67. Ibid., col. 577.
68. Preliminary report for DST Council, 10 Dec. 1926, LAB, Rep. 142-01, St.A 315, and St.B 3964b.
69. Assessments prepared by DST section heads in 1931–32 in the file "Erfolge der Städtetagsarbeit," LAB, Rep. 142-01, St.B 525.
70. Chap. 5.
71. See Exec. Committee meetings of 14 May 1926, LAB, Rep. 142-01, St.A 315, and 24 Nov. 1927, St.A 177; and relevant materials in St.B 1143.
72. Correspondence between the Reichsstädtebund, Prussian Städtetag, Prussian Landkreistag, Association of Prussian Provinces, and the Prussian

Landgemeindetag West of 27–29 March, and 2 and 10 April 1928, all in LAB, Rep. 142-01, St.B 1144. At a meeting on 18 Oct. 1928, leaders of the associations declared that no representation would be made of individual members' interests to the Prussian or Reich governments, ibid.
73. Chap. 4.
74. Engeli, *Gustav Böss*, 178.
75. Berlin's case for its uniqueness is detailed in "Warum muss die Stadt Berlin auf einer Änderung der preussischen Finanzausgleichs bestehen?," report dated 22 Sep. 1927, LAB, Rep. 142-01, St.A 186/II; and Engeli, *Gustav Böss*, 178–79.
76. Set at 80 percent of the prewar sum in 1923, it was increased to 100 percent in 1925. Engeli, *Gustav Böss*, 181.
77. For details, see Engeli, *Gustav Böss*, 179–81.
78. See Böss's speech to the Berlin city council, 28 April 1927, in *Stenographische Berichte über die öffentlichen Sitzungen der Stadtverordnetenversammlung der Stadt Berlin* (*Berlin SVV*) (1927), 331.
79. In hope of swaying the Landtag's decision, Böss on the preceding day gave a controversial interview to the *Berliner Tageblatt* in which he criticized the PST's lack of support and mentioned the possibility of Berlin's leaving the organization. Clipping in LAB, Rep. 142-01, St.A 501; Engeli, *Gustav Böss*, 182.
80. Christian Engeli explains, "The higher the per capita sum (*Einheitssatz*), the lower the portion of local tax income that must be supplied by the tax-wealthy municipalities to the inter-communal *Finanzausgleich*." Engeli, *Gustav Böss*, 181, n.130.
81. His accusations were directed especially at mayors Konrad Adenauer (Cologne), Karl Jarres (Duisburg) and Richard Rive (Halle). In addition to being members of the PST Executive Commitee, all three also occupied seats on the Prussian State Council (*Staatsrat*), to which Böss had looked for support. Engeli, *Gustav Böss*, 182–83 and n.134.
82. Böss to PST Council, 12 May 1927, LAB, Rep. 142-01, St.A 501; also quoted in Engeli, *Gustav Böss*, 184, n.145.
83. PST Council, 9 May 1927, LAB, Rep. 142-01, St.A 501.
84. Especially Konrad Adenauer, who with Karl Jarres was implicated directly by Böss in his interview. In a letter to Mulert on 18 June 1927, Adenauer lamented that the damage done to all the cities by the episode far outweighed the actual financial disadvantages accruing to Berlin from the Finanzausgleich, LAB, Rep. 142-01, St.A 501.
85. Comment of OB Max Brauer (Altona), PST Council, 9 May 1927, LAB, Rep. 142-01, St.A 501.
86. Comments of DST Council member and Berlin city councillor Wilhelm Caspari, PST Council, 9 May 1927, LAB, Rep. 142-01, St.A 501. See also the debate in Berlin city council of 28 April 1927, in *Berlin SVV* (1927), 329–51.
87. Resolution of PST Council, 9 May 1927, LAB, Rep. 142-01, St.A 177.
88. Exec. Committee talks with Böss, 20 June 1927, LAB, Rep. 142-01, St.A 501.
89. See Engeli's comments, *Gustav Böss*, 161–62, 197–201.
90. PST Council talks with Berlin representatives, 20 June 1927, LAB, Rep. 142-01, St.A 501.
91. Berlin's report was forwarded to the PST on 7 July 1927, LAB, Rep. 142-01, St.A 186/II.
92. All in stenographic record to meetings of 20 June 1927, LAB, Rep. 142-01, St.A 501.

93. *Berliner Lokal-Anzeiger*, 26 June 1927, clipping in LAB, Rep. 142-01, St.A 501.
94. PST Council, 26 Nov. 1927, LAB, Rep. 142-01, St.A 186/II; and *Mitt. DST* 21 (1927): col. 514.
95. The sole exceptions originated in the course of the negotiations over the Advisory Board and Gilbert's anti-municipal statements. See materials in LAB, Rep. 142-01, St.B 1631 and 2784/II; and Exec. Committee, 3 Dec. 1927, St.A 177. Also Upmeier, "Schachts Kampf," in Hansmeyer, ed., *Kommunale Finanzpolitik*, 160–79.
96. Circulars of 20 and 23 Nov. 1927, LAB, Rep. 142-01, St.B 1631.
97. Chap. 5.
98. Relevant files are LAB, Rep. 142-01, St.B 3612-13 and 3765-70.
99. Mulert to Brüning and Dietrich, 20 Nov. 1930; and Brüning to Mulert, 30 Jan. 1931, both in LAB, Rep. 142-01, St.B 3765.
100. DST Council circular on "Kommunalkredit" to all member-cities, 5 Nov. 1929, LAB, Rep. 142-01, St.A 163.
101. Mulert, "Die Lage der deutschen Städte gegen Ende des Rechnungsjahres 1931," speech to PST/DST Councils, 12 Feb. 1932, LAB, Rep. 142-01, St.A 774.
102. On the Kreditausschüsse: DST Exec. Committee meetings of 19 Oct. and 1 Dec. 1929, LAB, Rep. 142-01, St.A 397; "Kurzfristige Verschuldung der Gemeinden, kommunale Kreditausschüsse," decree of Prussian Ministries of Interior and Finance, 14 Feb. 1930, *Ministerial-Blatt für die Preussische innere Verwaltung* (Ausgabe A), 91, Nr. 8 (19 Feb. 1930): cols. 115–22; articles in *Mitt. DST* 24 (1930): 109–10, 394–95, 577; DST, *25 Jahre*, 30; and Mulert to Managing Director, Badischer Städteverband, 25 June 1930, LAB, Rep. 142-01, St.B 3615. On their use by the DST in later negotiations, see, e.g., DST Council to Reich Finance Minister, 5 July 1930, St.B 3771.
103. Of the many possible examples, see the meeting of DST representatives with Brüning and Reich ministers in the Chancellery, 10 Aug. 1931, LAB, Rep. 142-01, St.B 3765, and published in *Quellen zur Ära Brüning*, doc. 284, 2:873-81; and Mulert to Reich Chancellor Kurt von Schleicher, 3 Dec. 1932, St.B 3765.
104. Dietrich to Mulert, 21 April 1931, LAB, Rep. 142-01, St.B 3765. On Dietrich and Luther, see James, *German Slump*, 103.
105. See the comments of Matzerath, *Nationalsozialismus*, 98.
106. See Mulert to Severing, 6 Aug. 1931, LAB, Rep. 142-01, St.B 3613; and Mulert's account of his meeting with Severing and Höpker-Aschoff the same day, St.B 3612. Also Bertram, *Staats- und Kommunalpolitik*, 109.
107. See Mulert's submission to Schleicher of 3 Dec. 1932, designed to acquaint him with the cities' problems and demands, LAB, Rep. 142-01, St.B 3765.
108. Frankfurt City Councillor Max Michel to DST, 22 Feb. 1933, LAB, Rep. 142-01, St.A 5.
109. PST circulars of 6, 8, and 10 Feb. 1933, LAB, Rep. 142-01, St.A 370.
110. Mulert circular to Prussian provincial Städtetage, 1 Mar. 1933, LAB, Rep. 142-01, St.B 3613.
111. Members were City councillors Lippert (Berlin), Florian (Düsseldorf), and Dönnecke (Leipzig), and Oberbürgermeister Siebert (Lindau), LAB, Rep. 142-01, St.A 282.
112. Meetings of DST Exec. Committee, 17 Mar. 1933, LAB, Rep. 142-01, St.A 282; and DST Working Committee, 28 Mar. 1933, St.A 162 (quotation). Also Bracher et al., *Machtergreifung*, 451.
113. DST Exec. Committee, 17 Mar. 1933, LAB, Rep. 142-01, St.A 282; Circular of Working Committee to DST member-cities, 30 March 1933, St.A 162. The

meeting with Hitler apparently took place on 5 May; see Mulert's report to Working Committee of 6 May 1933, St.A 162.

114. Chronology is unfortunately vague here. On the RSB's important role, see chap. 3; and materials in LAB, Rep. 142-01, St.A 42. Also Bracher et al., *Machtergreifung*, 454; and Matzerath, *Nationalsozialismus*, 99. On Hitler's limited involvement, ibid., 102.
115. See esp. Mulert's notes of 28 April and 6 May 1933, LAB, Rep. 142-01, St.A 42. His reservations were shared by Haekel. Meeting of the RSB's Working Committee, 25 Apr. 1933, St.A 42.
116. They were Kurt G.A. Jeserich (the Nazi-appointed head of the Kommunalwissenschaftliches Institut of Berlin University, now the foremost historian of administration in Germany), Ralf Zeitler, and Volkmar Hopf. See DST Deputy Albert Meyer-Lülmann to Salomon, leader of Schlesischer Städtetag, 7 June 1933, LAB, Rep. 142-01, St.A 42; also Matzerath, *Nationalsozialismus*, 103. On Fiehler, see Jeserich, ed., *Persönlichkeiten der Verwaltung*, 455–57.
117. The declarations are reproduced in full in Ziebill, *Geschichte*, 60. The standard history of the Gemeindetag is still Matzerath, *Nationalsozialismus*.
118. On the accusations against Mulert, see the newspaper clippings and declaration of Heinrich Sahm in LAB, Rep. 200-34, Acc. 2955, Nr. 16. Mulert's principles and leadership came under sharp attack in Eike von Repkow [pseud.], "Nüchterne kommunalpolitik. Eine Entgegnung an Herrn Dr. Oskar Mulert," *Mitteilungsblatt der Nationalsozialisten in den Parlamenten und gemeindlichen Vertretungskörpern* 6 (1933): 113–15.
119. Voluminous correspondence of DST Council members in April and May notifying DST of their failure to get reelected, LAB, Rep. 142-01, St.A 427/II.
120. Schulz, "Die Anfänge des totalitären Massnahmenstaates," in Bracher et al., *Machtergreifung*, 451–52.
121. For example, see Reichstag NSDAP Fraktion leader Hans Fabricius to Mulert, 27 April 1933, LAB, Rep. 142-01, St.A 162.
122. Correspondence in LAB, Rep. 142-01, St.A 162.
123. Bracher et al., *Machtergreifung*, 451–52, 455; and Schulz, *Zwischen Demokratie*, 3: 490. For Mulert's thoughts on self-government in the Brüning years, see his "Finanzausgleich," *Kommunales Jahrbuch* 3 (1932): 53–54.
124. Oskar Thomas (Stettin) to Mulert, 20 Mar., and Mulert's reply, 25 Mar. 1933, both in LAB, Rep. 142-01, St.A 370.
125. Mulert's memo to DST Deputy Albert Meyer-Lülmann, 6 May 1933, LAB, Rep. 142-01, St.A 42.
126. Bracher et al., *Machtergreifung*, 458.

CHAPTER 3

1. Of the 63,556 incorporated municipalities in Germany in 1925, only 245 were free of Kreis control (*kreisfrei*), *Verwaltungsaufbau*, 102–05. Official statistics described the urban landscape in 1925 as follows:

Rural communes (*Gemeinden*)	pop. under 2,000	60,126
Rural cities (*Landstädte*)	2,000–4,999	2,249
Small cities (*Kleinstädte*)	5,000–19,999	920
Medium cities (*Mittelstädte*)	20,000–99,999	216
Large cities (*Grossstädte*)	over 100,000	45

Statistisches Jahrbuch für das Deutsche Reich, 1929, 8–9.

2. Bracher et al., *Machtergreifung*, 450. The standard accounts of the Spitzenverbände repeat each other to a great degree: Albert Meyer-Lülmann, "Gemeinde- und Städteverbände," in *Handwörterbuch der Kommunalwissenschaften*, ed. Josef Brix et al. (Jena: Gustav Fischer, 1922), 261–84; Böttcher, *Die kommunalen Reichsspitzenverbände*; Volker Viergutz, "Die kommunalen Spitzenverbände: Zu ihrer Geschichte und ihrer archivalischen Überlieferung," in *Berlin in Geschichte und Gegenwart* (*Jahrbuch des Landesarchivs Berlin*, 1983), 53–74; Christian Engeli, "Quellen zur Geschichte der kommunalen Spitzenverbände," *Die alte Stadt: Zeitschrift für Stadtgeschichte, Stadtsoziologie und Denkmalpflege* 5 (1978): 409–21; and Kurt G.A. Jeserich, "Kommunalverwaltung und Kommunalpolitik," in Jeserich et al., eds., *Deutsche Verwaltungsgeschichte*, 4: 503–11.
3. Townships did not belong directly to the LGT, which instead acted as an umbrella organization for the regional associations. The Association of Prussian Provinces was also considered a communal association, and fused with the others in 1933 in the *Deutsche Gemeindetag*. See Jeserich, "Kommunalverwaltung," 4:510–11; Viergutz, "Die kommunalen Spitzenverbände," 64–66; and Bianca Welzing, *Verband der preussischen Provinzen: Repositur 142/6*, Findbuch Nr. 20 (Landesarchiv Berlin, 1996), i–vi.
4. For example, "Kurze Notizen zu den Verhandlungen des Deutschen Landgemeindetages in der Kroll-Oper am 16. November 1928," typescript, BA-Lichterfelde, R1501/25095. For examples of rural attitudes to big cities, see Shelley Baranowski, *The Sanctity of Rural Life: Nobility, Protestantism and Nazism in Weimar Prussia* (Oxford and New York: Oxford University Press, 1995), 102–14.
5. *Verwaltungsaufbau*, 102–05.
6. See the essays by Georg-Christoph von Unruh and Wolfgang Hofmann in Jeserich et al., eds., *Deutsche Verwaltungsgeschichte*, 3: 560–644; Unruh, "Der Kreis im 19. Jahrhundert zwischen Staat und Gesellschaft," in *Kommunale Selbstverwaltung im Zeitalter der Industrialisierung*, ed. Helmuth Croon et al. (Stuttgart: W. Kohlhammer, 1971), 97; Engeli and Haus, eds., *Quellen zum modernen Gemeindeverfassungsrecht*, 467; and Klaus von der Groeben and Hans-Jürgen von der Heide, *Geschichte des Deutschen Landkreistages* (Cologne and Berlin: Grote, 1981), 118–32.
7. Considering the residual importance of the Kreise in the administrative landscape after the First World War, and their heuristic potential for exploring tensions between traditional and modern, they have been strangely neglected by historians. See Jeserich, "Kommunalverwaltung," 4:498–99; and Roger H. Wells, *German Cities: A Study of Contemporary Municipal Politics and Administration* (Princeton, N.J.: Princeton University Press, 1932), 23.
8. Regulations formulated in September 1922 prohibited the domination of the national congress by any single member. Prussia's strength was limited to twenty-six of the seventy-two seats on the governing central committee, the most important decision-making body of the congress. But the influence of the LKT's Prussian "big brother" remained strong: the central office in Berlin was headquarters for both associations, and they shared the same executive officer. The official history of the LKT nonetheless asserts blithely that internal relations between its various elements were generally good. Von der Groeben, *Geschichte*, 37–38.
9. Hugo Lindemann et al., eds., *Kommunales Jahrbuch* (Neue Folge),(Jena, 1931/32), 3:41; von der Groeben, *Geschichte*, 30–55, 76–153.
10. Von der Groeben, *Geschichte*, 28.

11. A revealing reason for the relatively late founding of the Prussian association. The Landräte felt uncomfortable with the possibility of creating an institution that in all likelihood would be forced to oppose the Prussian government at some point. Bismarck's antipathy to such organizations was well known, and it was only when Prussian Minister of the Interior von Loebell assured the Landräte in 1916 that the government had no objection that they finally agreed to found the Verband. Von der Groeben, *Geschichte*, 32.
12. Von der Groeben, *Geschichte*, 43.
13. Von der Groeben, *Geschichte*, 3, quoting LKT Director von Hassel, June 1919.
14. The following greatly simplifies a complicated story, in which organizational name changes, mergers and splits follow in dizzying succession. The *Preussische Landgemeindeverband West* (*Westverband*) was founded in 1922 as an extension of the township associations of Rhineland and Westphalia; it was known after 1927 as the *Preussische Landgemeindetag West*. In the East, the *Verband der preussischen Landgemeinden* (*Ostverband*) was founded in 1902. The most useful account is by insider Bruno Krey,"Kurze Geschichte des Preussischen Landgemeinde-Verbandes und der Verschmelzungs-Verhandlungen mit dem Preussischen Landgemeindetage," *Die Landgemeinde* 30, no. 18 (1921): 209–21, and no. 19 (1921): 227–44. Also Böttcher, *Die kommunalen Reichsspitzenverbände*, 6–7; Josef Göb, *Die Gemeinden in Staat und Gesellschaft, dargestellt in der Geschichte des Rheinischen Gemeindetages, des Preussischen Landgemeindetages West und des Gemeindetages Nord-Rhein* (Siegburg: Reckinger & Co, 1966); and idem, *50 Jahre Deutsche Kommunalpolitik* (Cologne: W. Kohlhammer/Deutscher Gemeindeverlag, 1966).
15. Göb, *50 Jahre*, 19.
16. Verband preussischer Landgemeinden to RMdI, 6 April 1926, BA-Lichterfelde, R 1501/ 25371.
17. Haekel Denkschrift of 13 Mar. 1928, LAB, Rep. 142-03, RSB 308; Elsas's note of 4 May 1928, LAB, Rep. 142-01, St.A 109. In a note to Belian of 10 May 1928, Haekel mentioned a vote of 5:3, with one abstention and two absences, RSB 306; and Gereke to RMdI, 30 April 1928, BA-Lichterfelde, R 1501/ 25324.
18. See his memoirs, *Ich war königlich-preussischer Landrat* (Berlin: Union Verlag, 1970), esp. 92–97, 133–35; also Jeserich, "Kommunalverwaltung," 4:510, n.68; and *Wer ist wer? 1950*, 11th ed. (Berlin: Arani, 1951), 178.
19. Gereke to RMrdI, 30 April 1928, BA-Lichterfelde, R 1501/ 25324. Gereke reminded Mulert that when the Westverband had been running the LGT prior to 1928, it had opposed allowing the East to attend. Later that year, however, he softened his position, suggesting in the interests of parity and cooperation that the other Prussian state and provincial associations (the Association of Prussian Provinces and his own Ostverband) be invited separately as well. With the exception of the latter, this arrangement prevailed until 1933. Conference of 14 May 1925; and correspondence of 1 Mar., 22 Nov. and 25 Nov. 1929, all in LAB, Rep. 142-01, St.A 109.
20. RSB President Haekel's memo of 13 Mar. 1928, LAB, Rep. 142-03, RSB 308.
21. The documentary record implies that Mulert and the DST had a much closer understanding with the West than with the Ostverband, perhaps a combined result of Grossstadt sympathy for the industrial Ruhr and of Gereke's unpredictability, as well as Mulert's close working relationship with Konrad Adenauer and Karl Jarres, both Oberbürgermeister of Rhenish cities. See

Mulert's kindly note to Alfred Schmoll, leader of the Westverband, inviting him informally to attend a meeting of association leaders, 7 Oct. 1929, LAB, Rep. 142–01, St.A 109.

22. Quoted in Hans Albert Berkenhoff, *Zur Verbandsgeschichte des Deutschen Städtebundes* (Göttingen: Otto Schwartz, 1964), 25.
23. In a circular of 13 Mar. 1928, RSB president Haekel listed the approximate number of inhabitants represented under each association's umbrella: DST 30 million; LKT 24 million; LGT 20 million; RSB 8–9 million. See LAB, Rep. 142-03, RSB 308. Similar numbers are in *Kommunales Jahrbuch*, Neue Folge (1931), 2:43–47 and (1932), 3:38–43.
24. See chap. 4.
25. Wolfgang R. Krabbe, *Die deutsche Stadt im 19. und 20. Jahrhundert: Eine Einführung* (Göttingen: Vandenhoeck & Ruprecht, 1989), 95–98; Hein Hoebink, "Städtischer Funktionswandel und Gebietsreform in der Weimarer Republik," in *Die Städte Mitteleuropas im 20. Jahrhundert*, ed. Wilhelm Rausch (Linz: Österr. Arbeistkreis für Stadtgeschichtsforschung et al., 1984), 71–86; and Wells, *German Cities*, 178–80.
26. *Der Reichsstädtebund zum Gesetzentwurf über die kommunale Neugliederung des rheinisch-westfälischen Industriegebiets* (Berlin: n.p., 1929); Berkenhoff, *Verbandsgeschichte*, 31; Hein Hoebink, *Mehr Raum-mehr Macht: Preussische Kommunalpolitik und Raumplanung im rheinisch-westfälischen Industriegebiet, 1900–1933* (Essen: Klartext, 1989), 176–77.
27. Belian to Haekel, 27 Aug. 1928, LAB, Rep. 142-03, RSB 332. The article in question was by Oberbürgermeister Russell of Koblenz, "Gegenwartsaufgaben einer rheinischen Mittelstadt," *Mitt. DST* 22 (1928): cols. 827–34.
28. For the DST, relevant materials are collected in LAB, Rep. 142-01, St.A 42, 303/I and 303/II; for the Reichsstädtebund in LAB, Rep. 142-03, RSB 302, 308, 325, 331, and 332.
29. Compare to the DST's 32 million, Engeli, "Quellen," 416, n. 23. Also preliminary report for DST Council of 14 Sep. 1923, LAB, Rep. 142-01, St.A 739; Haekel to Mulert, 19 May 1933, St.A 303/II; Hans Albert Berkenhoff, *Der Deutsche Städtebund* (Bonn: Harald Boldt, 1970), 19–20, 23–24.
30. Berkenhoff, *Verbandsgeschichte*, 23, 53–54.
31. In 1922, 849 of the RSB's 1,026 member towns were Prussian; ten years later, 906 out of 1,569. Meyer-Lülmann, "Gemeinde- und Städteverbände," 269; and *Kommunales Jahrbuch* (Neue Folge, 1932), 3:40.
32. See the comments of Engeli, "Zur Geschichte der regionalen Städtetage," 186–89; *Kommunale Rundschau*, 1 Aug. 1910; and Berkenhoff, *Verbandsgeschichte*, 11–17.
33. Chairman Saalmann, Bürgermeister of Pless, speaking at the second RSB congress of 10–11 Oct. 1911 in Brandenburg, quoted in Berkenhoff, *Verbandsgeschichte*, 19.
34. Berkenhoff, *Verbandsgeschichte*, 17–18.
35. See pp. 71–74.
36. Correspondence in LAB, Rep. 142-01, St.B 1146; and Bertram, *Staats- und Kommunalpolitik*, 91.
37. Beckstein, *Städtische Interessenpolitik*, 410.
38. At that time, the LGT had not yet assumed its final form. The "national" township association attending the meeting was founded in 1919 as the *Verband der grösseren Preussischen Landgemeinden*, representing East Prussian towns with more than ten thousand inhabitants. Neither the Ost- nor the Westverband were included in this version of the LGT. Their national association, founded in 1923, absorbed the remnants of the first one. See

Meyer-Lülmann, "Gemeinde- und Städteverbände," 269; also the account by former Westverband leader Kuth, quoted at length in Göb, *50 Jahre*, 3–6; and Gereke, *Ich war*, 95–97, 133–35.

39. For details, see their joint petition of two weeks previous (31 Oct. 1923) to the Reich Ministry of Finance, the Reichstag and the Reichsrat, printed in *Mitt. DST* 10 (1923): cols. 205–09.
40. Quoted in Ziebill, *Geschichte*, 231. The RSB used the same universalizing rhetoric: the problem of how to increase municipal revenue was ultimately one "of the continued existence or of the ruin of German cities." Quoted in Beckstein, *Städtische Interessenpolitik*, 411.
41. Recorded in "Gemeinschaftliche ausserordentliche Hauptversammlung des Deutschen Städtetages und des Reichsstädtebundes im Reichstagsgebäude zu Berlin am 11. November 1921," *Mitt. DST* 8 (1921): cols. 421–25.
42. Specific party positions surveyed in Beckstein, *Städtische Interessenpolitik*, 411.
43. The only discussion of any consequence covering these two developments is in Bertram, *Staats- und Kommunalpolitik*, 91–93.
44. Von Achenbach to Böss, 25 Jan. 1923, LAB, Rep. 142-01, St.B 1146.
45. Not a new notion. Before the First World War, the RSB and the PST had considered the idea of a merger. After some deliberation, the PST Council rejected such a move, choosing instead to cooperate with the RSB on a case-by-case basis. Directly after the war, DST managing director Hans Luther and his successor, Bromberg OB Paul Mitzlaff, again discussed the subject, though without following it up. Mitzlaff memo, history of DST/RSB relations 1919–24, 27 May 1926? (dated from location in file), LAB, Rep. 142-01, St.A 303/II; also Ziebill, *Geschichte*, 283.
46. Letter of 17 April 1923, LAB, Rep. 142-01, St.B 1146. See *Mitt. DST* 10 (1923): col. 76; and correspondence in St.B 1146.
47. Representatives from the DST and the Landkreise met on 5 Mar. 1923 to set out conditions and specifics for the Arbeitsgemeinschaft. The proposed allocation of votes (with administrative costs divided accordingly) for the Prussian and the German sections of the Vorstand was to be as follows:

	Deutsche	Preussische
Städtetag	13	8
Verband deutscher Landkreise	10	6
Verband preussischer Provinzen		1
Verband preussischer Landgemeinden	1	
Deutscher Landgemeindetag	2	1

The participants pressed for a speedy merger, wishing to avoid having to wait for ratifying votes from their respective assemblies. At least one informed observer, Dresden OB Bernhard Blüher, believed that creating the Arbeitsgemeinschaft might be possible without convening the Städtetag; not so the merger with the RSB. Constantin to Mitzlaff, 6 Mar. 1923; and Blüher to Mitzlaff, 7 Mar. 1923, both in LAB, Rep. 142-01, St.B 1146.

48. Apparently acceptable to the LKT, though Constantin evinced frustration at the slow pace of the talks, writing Mitzlaff several times in 1923. Mitzlaff's notes of 5 and 9 March and 4 May 1923; Constantin to Mitzlaff, 6 March and 14 August 1923, all in LAB, Rep. 142-01, St.B 1146.
49. A demand stemming from the RSB's predominantly Prussian orientation. See above, n. 31.
50. Haekel's proposal, n.d., LAB, Rep. 142-01, St.A 786/I; and "Verschmelzung DST/RSB," preliminary report and supplement, DST Council, 14 Sep. 1923, St.A 739.

51. Mitzlaff remarked in September 1923 that the informal understanding with Haekel was fundamentally different from the RSB's official demands as presented here, ibid.
52. LAB, Rep. 142-01, St.A 786/I; also Mitzlaff to Constantin, 17 Apr. 1924, St.B 1146; DST/PST joint Councils, 29 May and 14 Sep. 1923, *Mitt. DST* 10 (1923): cols. 122 and 186, respectively.
53. On the RSB's fear of LKT dominance, see Mulert's retrospective analysis, Mulert to Königsberg OB Hans Lohmeyer, 15 Nov. 1926, LAB, Rep. 142-01, St.B 1146.
54. Haekel to DST, 17 May 1924, LAB, Rep. 142-01, St.B 1146.
55. Haekel to Belian and RSB Council, 1 Jan. 1925; and Haekel to Mitzlaff, 13 Nov. 1925, both in NRWHSTA Bes. 50, Nr. 775.
56. Haekel to Belian, 8 Nov. 1926, LAB, Rep. 142-03, RSB 332.
57. Haekel, "Verhältnis zu den übrigen kommunalen Spitzenverbände," preliminary report, RSB Council, 8 Nov. 1926, LAB, Rep. 142-03, RSB 332.
58. Belian to RSB Council, 8 Nov. 1926, LAB, Rep. 142-03, RSB 332.
59. Gerhard Schulz's term, in Bracher et al., *Machtergreifung*, 448.
60. Two major exceptions: First, the associations in 1926 collectively joined the Brussels-based International Union of Cities; hard times by 1930 had led all to resign except the DST, whose own participation was drastically curtailed. (Preliminary report for DST Council, 10 Dec. 1926, LAB, Rep. 142-01, St.A 315; Exec. Committee, 6/7 May 1930, St.A 3, as well as those of 14 Apr. and 4 May 1932, St.A 7). Second, the associations in 1928 formally collaborated on the communal administration of health care. (Materials in St.B 1148; also the lengthy preliminary report for DST Council, 17 Jan. 1930, St.A 336/I; and *Mitt. DST* 22 [1928]: cols. 271–72; 529–30; 748–50).
61. Motto of the Prussian newspaper, *Die Landgemeinde*.
62. On the power struggles between DST Chairman Gustav Böss and the new president, Mulert, see above, chap 2. That similar tensions existed between RSB leaders is suggested by a note of 24 Apr. 1928, in which Belian pointed out to Haekel that vice president Albrecht Voigt was not being given enough duties, responsibilities or confidence by Haekel. Note of 24 Apr. 1928, LAB, Rep. 142-03, RSB 332.
63. See especially the list of 13 June 1933, compiled in the process of the DST's absorption into the Gemeindetag, in LAB, Rep. 142-01, St.B 3764; also Ziebill, *Geschichte*, 56.
64. Constantin sent all materials documenting the Arbeitsgemeinschaft negotiations to the DST one week after Mulert took office, noting that in the conditions of post-inflation Germany any renewed effort along the same lines would require a different approach. He left further pursuit of the question up to Mulert. Constantin to Mulert, 11 Mar. 1926, LAB, Rep. 142-01, St.B 1146. Within a month, Mitzlaff submitted his summary of the DST's relations with the RSB, 1919–24, undated memo, St. A 303/II.
65. Mulert to Lohmeyer, 15 Nov. 1926; and Elsas's note of 22 Dec. 1926, both in LAB, Rep. 142-01, St.B 1146.
66. See especially materials in LAB, Rep. 142-01, St.A 109.
67. Conference of 7 Mar. 1925, LAB, Rep. 142-01, St.A 109; and Mulert's note on talk of 8 June 1926 with Moll (VbPrProv) and Constantin (LKT), St.B 1146.
68. Summaries in LAB, Rep. 142-01, St.A 109.
69. For example, "Entwurf eines Gesetzes zur Aenderung des Finanzausgleichs für das Rechnungsjahr 1927," DST/LKT/VbPrProv/RSB/LGT to Reichsrat, 1 Dec. 1926, LAB, Rep. 142-01, St.B 2796/II.

70. Conferences of association leaders on 14 Nov. and 7 Dec. 1927, both in LAB, Rep. 142-01, St.A 109.
71. See correspondence in LAB, Rep. 142-01, St.A 303/I. Inter-group relations have been presented in the historiography as invariably positive: Ziebill, *Geschichte*, 286–87; Göb, *Gemeinden*, 141–42; Bertram, *Staats- und Kommunalpolitik*, 92–93; and Berkenhoff, *Verbandsgeschichte*, 20; somewhat more balanced in von der Groeben, *Geschichte*, 49–52.
72. Belian's letters to Mulert, 18 Feb. 1928, and to Dresden OB Wilhelm Külz, 18 Oct.1928, both in LAB, Rep. 142-01, St.A 303/I.
73. Ziebill, *Geschichte*, 284; comments of Hans Luther in LAB, Rep. 142-01, St.A 786/I and II; Luther's letter of 2 Oct. 1917 and Elsas memo of 17 Aug. 1926, both in St.A 527; and alterations to DST regulations detailed in St.A 85.
74. Specifically, the DST proposed that it take in all *kreisfrei* cities in Prussia and, in the other Länder, all cities having over twenty thousand inhabitants. Decision of DST Exec. Committee, 26 Apr. 1926, LAB, Rep. 142-01, St.A 315; Mulert to Haekel, 27 May 1926, St.A 303/II.
75. For example, Mulert's requests of 27 May and 6 July 1926. Although Haekel finally agreed to the plan in August, it was left hanging with no concrete details or timetable appended (correspondence and records in LAB, Rep. 142-01, St.A 303/II). Only one town, Teupitz (pop. 2,223) in Kreis Teltow, subsequently dropped double membership and went to the RSB. DST Exec. Committee, 25 Feb. 1927, St.A 3.
76. The only research of any consequence in RSB archival holdings has been that of Jürgen Bertram, who integrated rather limited findings into a more expansive study. On the mid-1920's shift in the strategies of both RSB and DST, see his *Staats- und Kommunalpolitik*, 99–105.
77. Quoted in Berkenhoff, *Deutsche Städtebund*, 25–26.
78. Bertram, *Staats- und Kommunalpolitik*, 99–103.
79. This had important financial aspects. Belian complained in 1928, at the height of the RSB's struggle with the DST, that the financially weak county towns had to support not only the RSB directly, but also pay fees for indirect membership in the DST *and* support the LKT through their taxes. "The result is that the Städtetag is in the fortunate position of shifting central burdens onto its big member-cities, while the Reichsstädtebund has heavy expenses in various areas of which the Städtetag is completely unaware," Belian to Külz, 18 Oct. 1928, LAB, Rep. 142-01, St.A 303/I.
80. Materials in LAB, Rep. 142-01, St.A 109 and 303/I; and Severing's note of 18 Feb. 1929, BA-Lichterfelde, R 1501/ 25324.
81. Phrase from Carl-Ludwig Holtfrerich, "Economic Policy Options and the End of the Weimar Republic," in *Weimar: Why did German Democracy Fail?*, ed. Ian Kershaw (New York: St. Martin's Press, 1990), 69.
82. The best summary of the communal representation issue in the RWR is in Hofmann, *Städtetag und Verfassungsordnung*, 61–63.
83. *DST Magdeburg, 1927*, 55–56. DST demands, formulated by the Council in its meeting of 2 July 1927, are set out in *Mitt. DST* 21 (1927): cols. 153–54.
84. Mulert's comments in the preliminary report for DST Council of 10 Dec. 1926, in LAB, Rep. 142-01, St.A 315. On Reich institutions for representing the cities and the DST, see below, chap. 5.
85. Elsas's note on their talk of 15 June 1927, LAB, Rep. 142-01, St.B 3763; *DST Magdeburg, 1927*, 55–56.
86. Of the proposed eleven communal representatives, five would go to the DST and three to the LKT. Mulert and Georg Schlüter (LKT) to the Reichstag,

6 Dec. 1927, LAB, Rep. 142-01, St.B 1148. The DST and LKT also agreed at this point to jointly demand a communal representative on the important Advisory Board for Foreign Credit (*Beratungsstelle für Auslandskredit*). See DST Council, 23 Jan. 1928, St.A 751; and Hofmann, *Städtetag und Verfassungsordnung*, 57–58, n.217.

87. Belian to Mulert, 18 Feb. 1928, LAB, Rep. 142-01, St.A 303/I. DST-RSB relations were already strained at this point: on the preceding day, Haekel vetoed Mulert's nomination to the Council of the *Deutsche Sparkasse- und Giroverband*. The same day, DST staffer Franz Memelsdorff greatly angered the RSB by insisting that the DST had received insufficient representation on the administrative committee of the Prussian Welfare Ministry, a claim perceived by the RSB as a power-play made at its expense. St.A 303/I.
88. Mulert to Belian, 22 Feb. 1928, LAB, Rep. 142-01, St.A 303/I. Ironically, at a conference on the same day, the associations resolved to avoid scrapping with one another in public, and to deal collectively with official agencies as far as their different interests permitted. See record of conference in Berlin, 22 Feb. 1928, St.A 109.
89. By October 1928, reports were coming in from the provinces that DST members were being courted by the RSB, even in the larger cities with populations over seventy thousand. When OB Hesse (Dessau) informed the RSB that his city was actually *over* eighty thousand, he was told that Dessau's interests could still be represented by the RSB and in fact, that its size would give it extra clout. See a sample letter of RSB solicitation of 1 Mar. 1928, forwarded to the DST by OB Zülch (Allenstein) on 7 Jan. 1929, and report of Hesse, 10 Oct. 1929, along with other relevant correspondence in LAB, Rep. 142-01, St.A 303/II and LAB, Rep. 143-01, RSB 302.
90. For example, Mulert's accusations of RSB "Expansionspolitik" at the DST/RSB talks of 17 Oct. 1928, LAB, Rep. 142-01, St.A 303/I.
91. Belian to Mulert, 27 Mar. 1928; and his claim that not only was the RSB justified in protecting its interests, but that it had never expressly advocated to DST members that they transfer their allegiance to the RSB, Belian/Mulert conversation of 17 Oct. 1928; both in LAB, Rep. 142-01, St.A 303/I.
92. OB Friedrich Ackermann (Stettin) to Mulert, 21 Aug. 1929, LAB, Rep. 142-01, St.A 303/II.
93. PST internal memo, 7 May 1926, LAB, Rep. 142-01, St.B 1143; DST Exec. Committee resolution, 14 May 1926, St.A 315.
94. Bertram, *Staats- und Kommunalpolitik*, 75.
95. Moss, "Cities in the Inflation," 100–104; Hofmann, *Zwischen Rathaus*, passim.
96. Key were a decree of the Prussian Minister of Welfare (19 Feb. 1921), and a 1923 circular from the Reich Minister of Finance. Reich policy was finalized in the "Gemeinschaftliche Geschäftsordnung der Reichsministerien" of 1926. Bertram, *Staats- und Kommunalpolitik*, 73–80.
97. See especially 1931–32 correspondence relating to the cases of: 1) the town of Luckenwalde; and 2) the Schleswig-Holsteinische Städteverein, both in LAB, Rep. 142-01, St.B 3613; also Bertram, *Staats- und Kommunalpolitik*, 78. On Schleswig-Holstein, see below, 108ff.
98. For example, DST requests for information, 2 Sep. 1924 and 14 Jan. 1927, LAB, Rep. 142-01, St.A 42; and meeting of local association leaders in Berlin, 18 Jan. 1927, St.B 3964b.
99. DST questionnaire of 11 Dec. 1930, LAB, Rep. 142-01, St.B 435.
100. Mulert letter of 23 Mar. 1933, LAB, Rep. 142-01, St.A 42.

101. See the revealing letter by Mulert to OB Hermann Beims (Magdeburg), 12 Oct. 1926, in which he writes tolerantly of the desires of the Kleinstädte to increase their voice in the DST, but closes by remarking that the interests of the metropolises must be protected, LAB, Rep. 142-01, St.A 303/I.
102. Report prepared for annual meeting (Hauptausschuss) of 14 May 1924, LAB, Rep. 142-01, St.A 786/I.
103. Preliminary report, Exec. Committee, 13 Sep. 1929, LAB, Rep. 142-01, St.A 370.
104. For example, correspondence of: OB Kreutz (Cottbus), 15 Aug. 1928, St.A 399; and OB Heydemann (Stralsund), 16 Sep. 1929, LAB, Rep. 142-01, St.A 370.
105. Schleswig-Holsteinischer Städteverein to OB Max Brauer (Altona), 31 May 1926, LAB, Rep. 142-01, St.B 1143. The DST Exec. Committee's resolution was transmitted to the provincial Städtetage on 29 May, see St.B 1143. It had little effect; six months later, without notifying the DST, the Verein submitted its own proposals to the Landtag for alterating the Prussian Finanzausgleich. Memo of 7 Nov. 1926, St.B 1143.
106. For this and what follows, see the extensive record of the council meeting of the Schleswig-Holsteinische Städteverein, 26 Nov. 1932, LAB, Rep. 142-01, St.A 42.
107. Also correspondence between Mulert and Bürgermeister Uhlig of Radeberg, another small town looking to leave the DST in 1931 for financial reasons. In the end, Radeberg elected to stay in. Gerhard Kluge, "Die Rolle des Deutschen Städtetages in der Zeit der Weimarer Republik von 1919 bis 1933, dargestellt an seiner Verhaltensweise in wirtschaftspolitischen Fragen und zum Abbau der Selbstverwaltung durch den imperialistischen Staat" (Ph.D. diss., Leipzig, 1970), 218–19 n.411.
108. For example, the Prussian NVO of 3 Sep. 1932. See protests by the RSB to the Reich Interior Ministry, 4 Sept. 1932, BA-Lichterfelde, R 1501/ 25324; also by the East Prussian Städtetag, 1 Oct. 1932, LAB, Rep. 142-01, St.B 3613; and a list of complaints against Landräte brought by small Prussian towns in meeting with Mulert, 29 Nov. 1932, St.A 42. Mulert recounted his own activities in the matter to Lohmeyer, letter of 14 Feb. 1933, St.A 42.
109. For example, to the RSB; to its local subsidiary; to the provincial Städtetag; to the German and Prussian Städtetage; and finally to the Landkreistag.
110. Mulert's summary report, 22 Dec. 1932, emphasized that the new fee setup for Schleswig-Holstein towns was a unique arrangement not to be extended to other provinces or Länder. LAB, Rep. 142-01, St.A 42.
111. As organizations of urban complexity, the towns claimed they required professional, expert administrators. The recent Prussian Decree on Communal Finance of 2 Nov. 1932 provided not only for supervision of the towns by the local Landrat, but also the appointment of an unsalaried, "honorary" Bürgermeister. The towns rejected both measures. See meeting of 29 Nov. 1932, LAB, Rep. 142-01, St.A 42.
112. DST Exec. Committee, 1 Dec. 1932, St.A 295; PST Council, 3 Dec. 1932, LAB, Rep. 142-01, St.A 42.
113. Meeting of 2 Jan. 1933, LAB, Rep. 142-01, St.A 42; report of DST Exec. Committee, 18 Jan. 1933, St.A 282.
114. Ziebill, *Geschichte*, 287. The informal nature of the "cooperative" makes it difficult to date with certainty. Its name first appears when Mulert, representing the "Arbeitsgemeinschaft der kommunalen Spitzenverbände," wrote Brüning and Dietrich on 20 Nov. 1930 to ask that the associations be consulted in the preparation of legislation affecting local governments, LAB,

Rep. 142-01, St.B 3765. But it is more likely that an agreement evolved quietly over the course of the previous year when DST Credit Committees were set up. See, e.g., DST Exec. Committee, 21 Dec. 1929, St.A 3 and 397; Elsas's note of 4 Jan. 1930, St.A 303/II; and protocol of discussion between Mulert and von Leyden, 22 Oct. 1930, St.B 3771.

115. The full text of the DST's "Sanierungsprogramm" of 13 Aug. 1931 is reproduced in *Mitt. DST* 25 (1931): 401-6. For the towns' protests, see the *Berliner Börsen-Courier*, 22 Aug. 1931 (morning ed.), clipping in LAB, Rep. 142-01, St.B 1148; and RSB summary memo of 24 Aug. 1931, NRWHSTA, Bes. 50–53, Nr. 770.
116. Resolution of Landgemeindetag, quoted in Gereke to Reich Finance Minister Dietrich, 29 Aug. 1931, BA-Lichterfelde, R 1501/ 25324. See also letters to Reich Interior Minister from Reichsstädtebund (17 and 29 Aug. 1931), Landkreistag (18 Aug.), Prussian Landgemeindetag West (27 Aug.), all in ibid.; and Bertram, *Staats- und Kommunalpolitik*, 92–95.
117. *Ostsee Zeitung* (Stettin), 28 Aug. 1931, clipping in LAB, Rep. 142-01, St.B 1148. See also Haekel (?) to RSB Council, 24 Aug. 1931, NRWHSTA, Bes. 50–53, Nr. 770.
118. Prussian Landgemeindetag West to Frick, 18 May 1933, BA-Lichterfelde, R 1501/ 25324.
119. Haekel first met the National Socialist city councillor and later mayor of Munich, Karl Fiehler, in July 1932; they apparently got on very well. Matzerath, *Nationalsozialismus*, 51–52, and 99, n.211. Quotations here from Haekel to Frick, 8 April 1933, BA-Lichterfelde, R 1501/ 25324.
120. Bracher et al., *Machtergreifung*, 454. On the RSB Arbeitsausschuss, relevant materials in LAB, Rep. 142-01, St.A 42, esp. Mulert's description of his meeting on 28 April with a delegation of Nazis from the RSB. A detailed account of Robert Ley's meeting with the association leaders on 22 May 1933 is in a letter of same date from Prussian provinces (VbPrProv) leader von Schenck to Landeshauptleute, LAB, Rep. 142-06, Nr. 52; also Matzerath, *Nationalsozialismus*, 98–104.
121. Hoebink, *Mehr Raum*, 177. Quotation taken from the title of Dietrich Orlow's *Weimar Prussia, 1918–1925: The Unlikely Rock of Democracy* (Pittsburgh: University of Pittsburgh Press, 1986).
122. Bronisch, "Erinnerungen."
123. Bonte, *Werbung für Weimar?*, 56–62.
124. Haekel's memo, 13 Mar. 1928, LAB, Rep. 142-03, RSB 308.
125. Bessel, *Germany after the First World War*, 102.

CHAPTER 4

1. Jürgen Reulecke, "The Ruhr: Centralization vs. Decentralization in a Region of Cities," in *Metropolis, 1880–1940*, ed. Anthony Sutcliffe (London: Mansell, 1984), 386. Hein Hoebink, "Kommunale Neugliederung im rheinisch-westfälischen Industriegebiet 1919–1929," in Düwell et al., eds., *Rheinland-Westfalen im Industriezeitalter*, esp. 3: 51–53.
2. Robert Schmidt, "Der Grosskreis, ein neues städebauliches Problem," *Städtebau* 23 (1928): 66. The designation of "city" was and is unclear, both in everyday usage and, to a lesser degree, in official statistics. Although Prussia unambiguously categorized a community's population as "urban" (*städtisch*) once it reached 2,000, a middle-sized city (*Mittelstadt*) could be anywhere

from 20,000 to 100,000. A "metropolis" (*Grossstadt*), by contrast, was always any city larger than 100,000. See "Die Gemeinden des Deutschen Reichs nach Grössenklassen auf Grund der Volkszählung vom 16. Juni 1925," *Wirtschaft und Statistik* 6 (1926), Sonderheft 3: *Die Gemeinden mit 2000 und mehr Einwohnern*, 5.

3. Düsseldorf Oberbürgermeister Robert Lehr, "Neugliederung im Westen: Die Aufgabe der Grossstadt," *Vossische Zeitung*, 27 Oct. 1928 (morn. ed.), excerpted in *Mitt. DST* 22 (1928): press clippings, col. 1335; Reulecke, "The Ruhr," 386.
4. This chapter owes much to Hein Hoebink's extensive collection of material on the 1929 reform in his *Mehr Raum*, esp. 162–247. Useful surveys are idem, "Städtischer Funktionswandel und Gebietsreform in der Weimarer Republik," in Rausch, ed., *Die Städte Mitteleuropas*, 71–86; and Reulecke, ibid., 381–401.
5. Viktor von Leyden, report of December 1926, quoted in Hoebink, *Mehr Raum*, 183.
6. "Gesetz über die kommunale Neugliederung des rheinisch-westfälischen Industriegebiets: Vom 29. Juli 1929," *Preussische Gesetzsammlung* (*PrGS*) 1929, 91–137; summary in Statistisches Reichsamt, *Wirtschaft und Statistik* 9 (1929): 727–28. For Grzesinski's announcement of 6 December, *Mitt. DST* 22 (1928): cols. 1461–62; and Hoebink, *Mehr Raum*, 184–90.
7. Briefly, Kenneth T. Jackson, *Crabgrass Frontier: The Suburbanization of the United States* (New York and Oxford: Oxford University Press, 1985), esp. 138–56; and more extensively for both U.S. and British cities, Jon C. Teaford, *City and Suburb: The Political Fragmentation of Metropolitan America, 1850–1970* (Baltimore and London: Johns Hopkins University Press, 1979).
8. Standard treatments include Reulecke, *Geschichte der Urbanisierung*; Wolfgang R. Krabbe, "Eingemeindungsprobleme vor dem Ersten Weltkrieg: Motive, Widerstände und Verfahrensweise," *Die alte Stadt* 7 (1980): 368–87; Hoebink and others cited above. A broader approach is found in Anthony McElligott's, *Contested City*, 95–123; Brian Ladd, *Urban Planning and Civic Order in Germany, 1860–1914* (Cambridge, Mass.: Harvard University Press, 1990), 210–27; and Christian Engeli, *Landesplanung in Berlin-Brandenburg: Eine Untersuchung zur Geschichte des Landesplanungsverbandes Brandenburg-Mitte, 1929–1936* (Stuttgart: W. Kohlhammer, 1986).
9. *Mitt. DST* 22 (1928): cols. 1473–74. Horst Matzerath, "Städtewachstum und Eingemeindungen im 19. Jahrhundert," in Reulecke, ed., *Die Deutsche Stadt im Industriezeitalter*, esp. 75; and Krabbe, "Eingemeindungsprobleme," 368–87. For the Weimar years in Prussia, see Victor von Leyden, "Gebietsabgrenzung und Neugliederung der Gemeinden: 1. Preussen," in *Kommunales Jahrbuch*, ed. Hugo Lindemann et al. (Jena, 1931), 2:30–37; and Preussisches Staatsministerium, *Hauptverzeichnis zur Preussischen Gesetzsammlung von 1926 bis 1935* (Berlin, 1937), 314–15.
10. "Gesetz über die Bildung einer neuen Stadtgemeinde Berlin: Vom 27. April 1920," *PrGS* 1920, 123–50, reprinted in Engeli and Haus, eds., *Quellen zum modernen Gemeindeverfassungsrecht*, 579–605. See also Daniel Stewart Mattern, "Creating the Modern Metropolis: The Debate over Greater Berlin, 1890–1920" (Ph.D. diss., Univ. of North Carolina, 1991), 410–94; and Otto Büsch, "Entstehung und Leistung der ersten Berliner Demokratie: Das neue Groß-Berlin als Hauptstadt der Weimarer Repubik," in Büsch and Haus, eds., *Berliner Demokratie*, 1: 6–20.
11. Ladd, *Urban Planning*, 210–27.
12. For example, the terms of Düsseldorf's 1929 contracts with its surrounding towns and counties are detailed in *Bericht über die Verwaltung und den*

Stand der Gemeindeangelegenheiten in Düsseldorf im Jahre 1930 (Düsseldorf, 1931), 81–88. The specific contract between Düsseldorf and the town of Kaiserswerth (5 Feb. 1929) is appended in Hoebink, *Mehr Raum*, 321–31.

13. Peters, *Grenzen*, 100–02; Matzerath, "Städtewachstum," 82–84; Krabbe, "Eingemeindungsprobleme," 377–80; Ladd, *Urban Planning*, 210–27.
14. Krabbe, "Eingemeindungsprobleme", 372–73, 377.
15. Matzerath, "Städtewachstum," 82; on the term *Grossstadtimperialismus*, see Hoebink, "Kommunale Neugliederung," 55.
16. Mattern, "Creating the Modern Metropolis," 449–59.
17. Ladd, *Urban Planning*, 215–18; Krabbe, "Eingemeindungsprobleme," 379–80.
18. In 1822, 1899, and 1917. The cities were finally joined in the 1929 reform. Ursula Rombeck-Jaschinski, "Wie die Gross-Stadt Wuppertal entstand: Der Weg zur kommunalen Neugliederung von 1929," *Geschichte im Westen* 3 (1988): 19–21.
19. Krabbe, "Eingemeindungsprobleme," 377–79; Mattern, "Creating the Modern Metropolis," 110 n.132, and 263–64.
20. Phrase used by Landkreistag president Kurt von Stempel, "Umgemeindung und Kreisverfassung," *Deutsche Tageszeitung* 13 July 1929, excerpted in *Mitt. DST* 23 (1929): press clippings, col. 1039; also Hoebink, *Mehr Raum*, 55.
21. "Gesetz über die Regelung verschiedener Punkte des Gemeindeverfassungsrechts: Vom 27. Dezember 1927," *PrGS* 1927, 211–14, § 1.
22. Hoebink, *Mehr Raum*, 162–63.
23. *Berliner Tageblatt*, 21 Jan. 1928, in *Mitt. DST* 22 (1928): press clippings, cols. 181–82. See Grzesinski's speech to the Landkreistag of 22 June 1928, ibid.: cols. 750–51; and to the Westverband, *Kölnische Volkszeitung*, 5 June 1928 (morning ed.).
24. Von der Groeben, *Geschichte*, 96. On Grzesinski's aims and strategies, see Thomas Albrecht, *Für eine wehrhafte Demokratie: Albert Grzesinski und die preussische Politik in der Weimarer Republik* (Bonn: J.H.W. Dietz, 1999), 203–10; also Hoebink, *Mehr Raum*, 184, 198, 203–04, 244. On the towns' hostility to his objectives, *Kölnische Zeitung*, 15 Jan. 1929 (morning ed.). Not surprisingly, the DST was satisfied with the pro-city sympathies of the Interior Ministry and especially of the communal affairs office. Minutes of conversation between DST Vice President Fritz Elsas and von Leyden, 15 June 1927, LAB, Rep. 142-01, St.B 3763; Hoebink, *Mehr Raum*, 243.
25. Mary Nolan, *Visions of Modernity: American Business and the Modernization of Germany* (Oxford and New York: Oxford University Press, 1994); Lieberman, *From Recovery to Catastrophe*; Lees, *Cities Perceived*, 270–73.
26. Preussischer Städtetag, *Grundfragen der kommunalen Neugliederung: Denkschrift des Preussischen Städtetages* (Berlin: Selbstverlag des Deutschen Städtetages, 1929), 7–8; and OB Russell (Koblenz), "Gegenwartsaufgaben einer rheinischen Mittelstadt," *Mitt. DST* 22 (1928): col. 831. For an American parallel, M. Christine Boyer, *Dreaming the Rational City: The Myth of American City Planning* (Cambridge, Mass. and London: MIT Press, 1983), 171–99.
27. Hoebink, *Mehr Raum*, 22, 163, 188–89, 219, and 237; PST, *Grundfragen*, 43; and "Gross-Gemeinden: Neugestaltung kommunalen Verwaltungs-Organisation," *Frankfurter Zeitung*, 24 Feb. 1928, in *Mitt. DST* 22 (1928): press clippings, col. 318.
28. Von Leyden's report of meeting on 8 June 1928 with PST Council members, GSTAPrKB Rep. 77, Tit. 2779, Nr. 6, Bd. 1. Hoebink, *Mehr Raum*, 190–97,

and relevant maps, 363–419. Local authorities published extensively to support their own claims, surveyed in *Mitt. DST* 23 (1929): cols. 101–03.

29. See, for example, the editorial comments in *Kölnische Zeitung*, 31 Jan. 1929 (morning ed.).
30. Although not all members were convinced of the benefits of consolidation. At a June 1928 meeting in Cologne, PST members expressed concern that previously independent areas, once annexed, should receive adequate representation in the new municipal government and that ways be found to ensure that Bürgers participate fully in their local government. The meeting therefore stressed the need for a "decentralized" metropolitan administration. PST Council, 9 June 1928, LAB, Rep. 142-01, St.A 179; reported at length in *Mitt. DST* 22 (1928): cols. 717–21.
31. PST Council, 26 Nov. 1927 in Duisburg, LAB, Rep. 142-01, St.A 186/II and St.A 634, also reported in *Mitt. DST* 21 (1927): cols. 514–17 (quotation 515); PST, *Grundfragen*, 8, 30–31 (quotations); DST, *25 Jahre*, 11; Hoebink's summary, *Mehr Raum*, 177–79.
32. DST, *25 Jahre*, 37–38.
33. *DST Breslau, 1928*, 34.
34. Strategy discussed at PST Council meeting of 9 June 1928 in Cologne, LAB, Rep. 142-01, St.A 179. See Karl Jarres's opening speech to DST's Rhenish branch, published in *Kölnische Zeitung*, 15 June 1929 (morn. ed.); Göb, *Gemeinden*, 103.
35. Matzerath, "Städtewachstum," 82, n.48.
36. As Grzesinski noted. See his speech to the Prussian LKT of 22 June 1928, reported in *Mitt. DST* 22 (1928): cols. 750–51.
37. Preussischer Landkreistag, *Regionalreform und Kreisverfassung: Gedanken und Vorschläge des Preussischen Landkreistages zur kommunalen Verwaltungsreform* (Berlin: n.p., 1928).
38. LKT, *Regionalreform*, 17–22.
39. LKT, "Landkreise und grossstädtische," 295.
40. *Kölnische Zeitung*, 16 Feb. 1929 (morning ed.); and LKT, "Landkreise und grossstädtische Eingemeindungspolitik," *Zeitschrift für Selbstverwaltung* 12 (1929): 299.
41. Robert Schmidt also viewed counties as viable alternatives to big cities in his "Der Grosskreis"; LKT, "Landkreise und grossstädtische Eingemeindungspolitik," 297. See the article by Düsseldorf district prefect zur Nieden, "Der Industriekreis und sein Verhältnis zur Grossstadt: Das Eingemeindungsproblem," in *Die deutschen Landkreise*, ed. Otto Constantin and Erwin Stein (Berlin-Friedenau: Deutscher Kommunal-Verlag, 1926), vol. 1: *Organisation und praktische Arbeit der Landkreise*, 141–80.
42. For the Reichsstädtebund, see its publications *Kommunale Verwaltungsreform und örtliche Selbstverwaltung* (Berlin: n.p., 1928), and *Der Reichsstädtebund zum Gesetzentwurf*. For the Prussian Landgemeindetag West, which directly represented townships in the Ruhr area, see *Der Preussische Landgemeindetag West zur kommunalen Neugliederung der Regierungsbezirke Düsseldorf, Münster, Arnsberg* (Berlin: n.p., 1928).
43. The counties suggested various legal mechanisms to calm the towns' fears of potential abuse of their enhanced powers, including arbitration and claims for damages. These were eventually codified in the "Einführungsgesetz zu dem Gesetz über die kommunale Neurgliederung des rheinisch-westfälischen Industriegebiets," *PrGS* 1929, §§ 42 and 43. See also LKT, "Landkreise und grossstädtische Eingemeindungspolitik," 303–04.
44. RSB Deputy Kurt Kottenberg, paraphrasing Robert Schmidt. *Berliner Börsen-Zeitung*, 28 April 1928 (evening ed.), in *Mitt. DST* 22 (1928): press clip-

pings, col. 558. See also Gereke, "Die Landgemeinde," in Harms, ed., *Volk und Reich*, 2:421; and the article by Hans Peters in *Preussische Gemeinde-Zeitung*, June 1928, in *Mitt. DST* 22 (1928): press clippings, cols. 692–93.

45. Gereke, "Die Landgemeinde," 420; also speeches by Peters and RSB Vice President Albrecht Voigt at the RSB's annual meeting at Kiel on 22 Aug. 1929, reported in *Mitt. DST* 23 (1929): cols. 1161–62.
46. *Preussische Gemeinde-Zeitung*, June 1929, in *Mitt. DST* 23 (1929): press clippings, col. 652.
47. For example, *Preussische Gemeinde-Zeitung*, July 1928, in *Mitt. DST* 22 (1928): press clippings, cols. 911–12. On the RSB's "weakness" and efforts to increase its parliamentary influence, see Bertram, *Staats- und Kommunalpolitik*, 99–103.
48. Göb, *Gemeinden*, 104; Gereke, "Die Landgemeinde," 424. Cf. LKT, "Landkreise und grossstädtische Eingemeindungspolitik," 304; and Hoebink, *Mehr Raum*, 175. Similar alliances had occurred during the consolidation of Greater Berlin; see Engeli, *Landesplanung in Berlin-Brandenburg*, 39, 43. Generally on the convergence of town-county interest, see Carl Beck, in *Preussische Gemeinde-Zeitung*, July 1928, in *Mitt. DST* 22 (1928): press clippings, cols. 911–12; Stempel in *Kölnische Zeitung*, 29 Oct. 1928 (evening ed.) and 16 May 1929 (morning ed.); von der Groeben, *Geschichte*, 80–81, 96; Ernst Fiedler, "Die rechtliche Stellung der Landgemeinden und kreisangehörigen Städte zu den Landkreisen auf Grund des Einführungsgesetz zum Gesetz über die kommunale Neugliederung des rheinisch-westfälischen Industriegebiets vom 29. Juli 1929" (Ph.D. diss., Breslau, 1930), 57; and Göb, *Gemeinden*, 140.
49. *Kölnische Zeitung*, 22 Aug. 1929 (evening ed.); and Göb *Gemeinden*, 103.
50. Quotations from: *Gelsenkirchener Allgemeine Zeitung*, 17 July 1928, in *Mitt. DST* 22 (1928): press clippings, cols. 874–75; and *Kölnische Zeitung*, 22 (morn. ed.) and 26 Jan. (morn. ed. supp.) and 18 June 1929 (eve. ed.); speech of Hans Peters at RSB member-congress, 22 Aug. 1929, reported in *Mitt. DST* 23 (1929): col. 1161.
51. Göb, *Gemeinden*, 102–03.
52. Statistisches Reichsamt, *Wirtschaft und Statistik* 9 (1929): 727–28; Stephanie Reekers, *Die Gebietsentwicklung der Kreise und Gemeinden Westfalens, 1817–1967* (Münster: Aschendorff, 1977), 125.
53. Statistisches Reichsamt, ibid.: 727–28; and *Mitt. DST* 23 (1929): cols. 1146–51. For population changes in specific areas, Hoebink, *Mehr Raum*, 357–61.
54. Berkenhoff, *Der Deutsche Städtebund*, 28.
55. *Berliner Volkszeitung*, 8 July 1929, in *Mitt. DST* 23 (1929): press clippings, cols. 910–11; *Kölnische Zeitung*, 8 July 1929 (evening ed.).
56. *Vossische Zeitung*, 18 July 1929, in *Mitt. DST* 23 (1929): press clippings, col. 1038.
57. Ibid.
58. McElligott, *Contested City*, 104–5.
59. *Bayerische Kurier*, 28 Jan. 1928, excerpted in *Mitt. DST* 22 (1928): col. 184.
60. For example, *Kölnische Zeitung*, 31 July and 1 Aug. 1929 (morning eds.).
61. Staatsgerichtshof decision of 11 Dec. 1929, in *Die Rechtsprechung des Staatsgerichtshofs für das Deutsche Reich und des Reichsgerichts auf Grund Artikel 13 Absatz 2 der Reichsverfassung*, ed. Hans-Heinrich Lammers and Walter Simons (Berlin: Georg Stilke, 1930), 2:99–109, esp. 99–100, 105. Also *Kölnische Zeitung*, 20 July 1929 (morn. ed.); Hoebink, *Mehr Raum*, 218 n.364; and Rombeck-Jaschinski, "Wie die Grossstadt Wuppertal entstand," 32–33.

62. In the "Einführungsgesetz," *PrGS* 1929, 137–49, § 43. This nullified § 4 of the old eastern Kreisordnung governing Auskreisung, now subject to the 1927 law. See Fiedler, "Rechtliche Stellung," 45–60.
63. Fiedler, "Rechtliche Stellung," 59–60.
64. PST, *Grundfragen*, 18; von der Groeben, *Geschichte*, 82. A county was required to seek agreement with all towns under its jurisdiction before invoking supervisory powers, Hoebink, *Mehr Raum*, 231.
65. Fiedler, "Rechtliche Stellung," 45–53.
66. According to von der Groeben, *Geschichte*, 82, and Jacob, *German Administration*, 105.
67. See, e.g., Werner Johe, "Territorialer Expansionsdrang oder wirtschaftliche Notwendigkeit? Die Gross-Hamburg-Frage," *Zeitschrift des Vereins für hamburgische Geschichte* 64 (1978): 149–80. Also commentary by Wiedenfeld, "Eingemeindungen und Umgemeindungen," *Staats- und Selbstverwaltung* 16 (1935): 315; and Wolfgang Bernhardt, "Die Gemeindliche Gebietsreform und das Selbstverwaltungsrecht: Eine vergleichende Studie über die Reformbestrebungen der Weimarer Republik, des Dritten Reiches und Nordrhein Westfalens" (Ph.D. diss., Westfälischen Wilhelms-Universität zu Münster, 1972).
68. Noakes,"Oberbürgermeister and Gauleiter," 202–03.
69. For example, Prussian Interior Minister Ludwig Grauert to Reich Interior Ministry (Hans Fabricius), 13 July 1933, BA-Lichterfelde, R 1501/ 25095.
70. As contemporaries realized. See DST analyst Herbert Meyer, "Gebietsabgrenzung und Neugliederung der Gemeinden," in *Kommunales Jahrbuch*, ed. Hugo Lindemann et al. (Jena, 1932), 3:32; Reekers, *Gebietsentwicklung*, 125; and Hoebink, *Mehr Raum*, 246.
71. Horst Romeyk, *Verwaltungs- und Behördengeschichte der Rheinprovinz, 1914–1945* (Düsseldorf: Droste, 1985), 31–32, 316–39.
72. Jürgen W. Falter and Michael H. Kater, "Wähler und Mitglieder der NSDAP: Neue Forschungsergebnisse zur Soziographie des Nationalsozialismus 1925 bis 1933," *Geschichte und Gesellschaft* 19 (1993): 165–67 (quotation 165). More discussion of small-town voter support is in Jürgen W. Falter, *Hitlers Wähler* (Munich: C.H. Beck, 1991), 163–68. In his *Contested City*, 120–23, Anthony McElligott argues that "consolidation battles" in Altona and its suburbs mobilized protest votes that eventually benefitted the Nazis.
73. Hoebink, *Mehr Raum*, 233–34. The beginnings of a more precise social and political history of anti-urbanism in Weimar can be seen in Alexander Wilde, "Republikfeindschaft in der Berliner Bevölkerung und der Wandel der kommunalen Selbstverwaltung um 1931," in *Beiträge zur Geschichte der Berliner Demokratie, 1919–1933/1945–1985*, ed. Otto Büsch (Berlin, 1988), 107–42; Skyler Arndt-Briggs, "The Construction and Practice of Place in Weimar Republic Berlin" (Ph.D. diss., Univ. of Massachusetts Amherst, 2000); and most fully in McElligott, *Contested City*.
74. For example, Reekers, *Gebietsentwicklung*, 125; Hoebink, *Mehr Raum*, 232–33. For a positive verdict on the long-term effects of the reform, see Frank Theile, "Die Folgewirkungen der kommunalen Neugliederung des rheinisch-westfälischen Industriegebiets in den Jahren 1926 bis 1929, untersucht an Beispielen des östlichen Ruhrgebiets" (Ph.D. diss., Ruhr-Universität Bochum, 1970), esp. 141–52.
75. David A. Johnson, *Planning the Great Metropolis: The 1929 Regional Plan of New York and Its Environs* (London: E & FN Spon, 1996).

CHAPTER 5

1. Arnold Brecht quoted in James, *German Slump*, 46. See also the essay by Hermann Pünder, state secretary in the Reich Chancellery, 1926–32, "Das Reich und die Länder," in *Zehn Jahre Deutsche Geschichte, 1918–1928* (Berlin: Otto Stolllberg, 1928), esp. 81.
2. DNVP deputy von Wilmowsky, as recounted in an article by Reich Interior Minister Carl Severing for the Social Democratic newspaper *Vorwärts*, 8 Oct. 1927, and excerpted in *Mitt. DST*, 21 (1927), Sonderheft "Reichspolitik und Städte": press clippings, col. 96.
3. Patrick Wagner, "Feindbild 'Berufsverbrecher': Die Kriminalpolizei im Übergang von der Weimarer Republik zum Nationalsozialismus," in Bajohr et al., eds., *Zivilisation und Barbarei*, 229.
4. For example, a list dated 23 Dec. 1927 outlining "the twenty-one most important newspaper articles on reform" covers only the period Sept.–Dec. 1927, LAB, Rep. 142-01, St. B 3239a.
5. Mulert, "Wege zum Reichsaufbau," *Frankfurter Zeitung*, 21 Oct. 1928, in *Mitt. DST*, 22 (1928), press clippings, cols. 1331–35; and Leipzig city councillor Walter Leiske, "Regionale Reichsreform," *Mitt. DST*, 23 (1929), col. 49. The many Reichsreform proposals were comprehensively surveyed by Reichssparkommissar Friedrich Saemisch, "Vorschläge zur Reichsreform," GSTAPrKB, Rep. 77, Tit. 253a, Nr. 52, BeiAkten III, 2: 64–163. Also Otto Sartorius, *Neuordnung von Verfassung und Verwaltung in Reich und Ländern* (Hanover: Wirtschaftswissenschaftliche Gesellschaft zum Studium Niedersachsens, e.V., 1928); and Ludwig Biewer, *Reichsreformbestrebungen in der Weimarer Republik. Fragen zur Funktionalreform und zur Neugliederung im Südwesten des Deutschen Reiches* (Frankfurt am Main, Bern, and Cirencester,U.K.: Peter Lang, 1980).
6. Schulz, *Zwischen Demokratie*; cf. Willibalt Apelt, Saxony's Interior Minister 1928–30, *Geschichte der Weimarer Verfassung*, 2d ed. (Munich: Biederstein, 1964), esp. 369–439.
7. Ziebill, *Geschichte*; and more focused, Hofmann, *Städtetag und Verfassungsordnung.*
8. Engeli, "Zur Geschichte," 173–74; Beckstein, *Städtische Interessenpolitik*, 23.
9. Deutscher Städtetag, *Verhandlungen des sechsten Deutschen Städtetages am 25. und 26. September 1924 in Hannover* (Berlin, 1924), 79. For a survey of relief activities in the cities in 1922–23, see *Mitt. DST*, 10 (1923), cols. 214–18.
10. See Josef Wysocki, "Kommunalpolitische Fakten. Der neue gesetzliche Rahmen des kommunalen Handelns," in Hansmeyer, ed., *Kommunale Finanzpolitik*, 23–28. Also Ziebill, *Geschichte*, 355–57, 362–64; Hofmann, *Städtetag und Verfassungsordnung*, 69; Engeli, "Städte und Staat," 167–69. The cities did demand a thorough-going reform of the Reich's system of tax procurement and revenue distribution (*Finanzausgleich*). See, e.g., the petition sent to the Reichsrat on 9 Feb. 1922 by the DST Council, with lengthy proposals for altering the States Tax Law, published in *Mitt. DST*, 9 (1922), cols. 49–67.
11. DST Council, 10 Dec. 1926, LAB, Rep. 142-01, St.A 315, published in shortened form in *Mitt. DST*, 21 (1927), cols. 1–4. Adenauer quotation from meeting of 24 Aug. 1931, St.B 3612.
12. Various records and summaries of this important meeting are in LAB, Rep. 142-01, St.A 315 and 467 (the latter contains a stenographic record), and

in St.B 3964b. A summary report was published in *Mitt. DST*, 21 (1927), cols. 1–4.

13. *Mitt. DST*, 21 (1927), cols. 295–96. Attendees listed in *DST Magdeburg, 1927*, 6–31. The following account, unless noted otherwise, is based on this report.
14. *DST Magdeburg, 1927*, 54–56. On the RWR, see Hofmann, *Städtetag und Verfassungsordnung*, 61–63. The model for the ministerial communal office was the section for communal affairs in the Prussian Interior Ministry of which Mulert had been director, 1920–25, LAB, Rep. 142-01, St.B 3964b. On the Reichsrat, see Arnold Brecht, *Mit der Kraft des Geistes: Lebenserinnerungen* (Stuttgart: Deutsche Verlags-Anstalt, 1967), 2: *1927–1967*, 32–38.
15. *DST Magdeburg, 1927*, 54, 57.
16. Press release for DST Council meeting of 10 and 11 Dec. 1928, printed in full in *Mitt. DST*, 22 (1928), cols. 1485–87. Mulert's care in presentation was obvious from the beginning: see *Bayerische Staatszeitung*, 24 Sept. 1927, and *Bayerischer Kurier*, 3 Oct. 1927, both in *Mitt. DST*, 21 (1927), Sonderheft "Reichspolitik und Städte": press clippings, cols. 80–81 and 92–93, respectively.
17. *DST Breslau, 1928*, 46–49.
18. Excerpts published in *Mitt. DST*, 21 (1927), Sonderheft "Reichspolitik und Städte": cols. 73–104; and 22 (1928), Sonderheft "Reichsaufbau und Selbstverwaltung": cols. 112–32.
19. For example, *München-Augsburger Abendzeitung*, 27 Sept. 1928; *Bayerische Staatszeitung*, 26 Sept. and 1 Oct. 1928; *Der Deutsche Süden*, 10 Oct. 1928; all in *Mitt. DST*, 22 (1928), Sonderheft "Reichsaufbau und Selbstverwaltung": press clippings, cols. 114, 117, 124, 129.
20. *Berliner Tageblatt*, 27 Sept. 1927, in *Mitt. DST*, 21 (1927), Sonderheft "Reichspolitik und Städte": press clippings, col. 87.
21. Bund zur Erneuerung des Reichs, *Reich und Länder: Vorschläge, Begründung, Gesetzentwürfe* (Berlin: G. Stilke, 1928). Individual cities were also angling for a better position via the coming reforms. See the survey of reform activity in *Dresdener Anzeiger* of 12 Oct. 1928, in *Mitt. DST*, 22 (1928), press clippings, col. 1331; Albrecht, *Wehrhafte Demokratie*, 155–290.
22. Gilbert's memo of 10 Oct. 1927 and the German government's reply were published in a supplement to the *Bericht des Generalagenten für Reparationszahlungen* (Berlin: Reimar Hobbing, 1928), vol. 4: report of 10 Dec. 1927. The memo was also published in full by the *New York Times*, 6 Nov. 1927, and is discussed in Schulz, *Zwischen Demokratie*, 1: 568–74.
23. Schacht, *Eigene oder geborgte Währung*, 22. On the connections between Gilbert and Schacht, and the cities' efforts to isolate and deal with each individually, see Frankfurt lord mayor Ludwig Landmann to Mulert, 29 July 1927, and talks between DST Vice President Fritz Elsas and Ministerial Director Zarden of the Reich Finance Ministry, 4 Aug. 1927, both in LAB, Rep. 142-01, St.B 1631. Also McNeil, *American Money*, 171–91.
24. Materials in LAB, Rep. 142-01, St.B 3239a; Vorbericht for DST Council meeting of 24 Jan. 1928, ibid., St.A 548 /I; *Vorwärts*, 27 Sept. 1927; and Sartorius, *Neuordnung*, 60–69. On Bavaria, see D.R. Dorondo, *Bavaria and German Federalism: Reich to Republic, 1918–33; 1945–49* (New York: St. Martin's, 1992).
25. See particularly the Reich cabinet meetings of 3 October and 20 December 1927, in Karl Dietrich Erdmann, Wolfgang Mommsen, and Walter Vogel, eds., *Akten der Reichskanzlei. Weimarer Republik* (Boppard am Rhein:

H. Boldt, 1968), vol. 15: *Die Kabinette Marx*, part 2: 2. *Juni 1927 bis Juni 1928*, docs. 307 (946–49) and 380 (1172–77), respectively.

26. The schedule and organization of the conference were as follows: 1) The initial conference met only once, 16–18 Jan. 1928, creating 2) a Constitution Committee, which convened once on 4 May and again on 22 Oct. 1928. The latter created, in turn, 3) two sub-committees—one for territorial reorganization and the other for administrative jurisdictions—which met four times in July and Oct. 1929. The sub-committees submitted their findings back to 4) the Constitution Committee for its third and final meeting on 21 June 1930. Conference proceedings are summarized in Franz Albert Medicus, *Reichsreform und Länderkonferenz. Die Beratungen und Beschlüsse der Länderkonferenz und ihrer Ausschüsse* (Berlin: C. Heymann, 1930). See more generally Schulz, *Zwischen Demokratie*, 1: 564–612; and Brecht, *Mit der Kraft des Geistes*, 2: 59–99. The cities' interests in the conference are analysed in Hofmann, *Städtetag und Verfassungsordnung*, 103–11.
27. The cities were not without sympathizers in high places. Reich Auditor Friedrich Saemisch, who sat on the small committee that originally set conference structure and protocol, tried early but failed to get them admitted. See (Lohmeyer's?) note of 14 Jan. 1928, LAB 142/1, St.B 3769; and Schulz, *Zwischen Demokratie*, 1: 577–84.
28. DST Council, 23 Jan. 1928, LAB, Rep. 142-01, St.A 751.
29. All of Mulert's nominees to the conference subcommittees (Saemisch, Karl Jarres, Carl Severing) were rejected. DST Exec. Committee, 26 Oct. 1928, LAB, Rep. 142-01, St.A 195; Hofmann, *Städtetag und Verfassungsordnung*, 105; and Bertram, *Staats- und Kommunalpolitik*, 111.
30. "Die Arbeit der Länderkonferenz. Neue Ausschussberatungen," *Mitt. DST*, 22 (1928), cols. 1175–77.
31. The following summary is taken from DST, *Vorschläge zur Abgrenzung der Zuständigkeiten zwischen Reich, Ländern und Gemeinden: Dem Verfassungsausschuss der Länderkonferenz überreicht vom Deutschen Städtetag im Juni 1929* (Berlin: Selbstverlag des Deutschen Städtetages, 1929). The full text was also published in *Mitt. DST* 23 (1929), cols. 1119–26.
32. The states' authority in this respect would remain, however. DST, *Vorschläge zur Abgrenzung*, 6.
33. See the extensive materials in LAB, Rep. 142-01, St.B 3617; also report of PST Council, 9 Feb. 1929, ibid., St.A 179; and *Mitt. DST* 23 (1929), cols. 144–48.
34. Hensel, *Kommunalrecht*, 78–89; and Wells, *German Cities*, 33–63.
35. An initial bill of 1925 failed; it is printed in "Entwurf einer Reichsstädteordnung," *Mitt. DST* 12 (Oct. 1925), Sonderbeilage. Cf. with the later version of 1929, Engeli and Haus, eds., *Quellen zum modernen Gemeindeverfassungsrecht*, 659–62; Böhret, *Aktionen*, 161–71; and Krabbe, "Tendenz," 75–94.
36. Cf. the situation in Altona in McElligott, *Contested City*, 136.
37. See Mulert, "Kommunalkredit," a circular to DST member-cities of 5 Nov. 1929, in LAB, Rep. 142-01, St.A 163; and idem, "Verantwortung!," *Mitt. DST*, 24 (1930), 1–5.
38. Karl Maly, *Geschichte der Frankfurter Stadtverordnetenversammlung* (Frankfurt am Main: Waldemar Kramer, 1992–95), vol. 2, *1901–1933: Das Regiment der Parteien*, 526–34; and (W.H.) Timothy Moss, "Crisis of Self-Government? The Berlin City Representative Assembly, 1929–1931" (M.Phil. thesis, Oxford, 1984).
39. Deutscher Städtetag, *Reichsstädteordnung. Entwurf und Begründung* (Berlin: Selbstverlag des Deutschen Städtetages, 1930); idem, *Jahresversammlung*

des Deutschen Städtetages. Frankfurt am M., 27. September 1929 (hereafter *DST Frankfurt/M, 1929*) (Berlin: Selbstverlag des Deutschen Städtetages, n.d. [1929]), 27, 30, 52; and Oskar Mulert, "Reichsstädteordnung," *Mitt. DST*, 24 (1930), 169–71.

40. Party positions outlined in *DST Frankfurt/M, 1929*, 53–54 (DDP), 58–59 (DVP), 62 (SPD). The DST noted a "strong" swing among Bürgermeister in favor of unicameral government, DST Exec. Committee, 6 May 1930, LAB, Rep. 142-01, St.A 3. The SPD's position was complicated by its Berlin councillors' resistance to increasing mayoral powers, Engeli, *Gustav Böss*, 164–65.
41. For example, *Bayerische Staatszeitung*, 23 Mar. 1930, in *Mitt. DST* 24 (1930), press clippings, 254.
42. The small towns' first object in a new Gemeindeordnung was to secure freedom from state supervision by the Regierungspräsidenten. Albrecht Voigt (Managing Vice President of the Reichsstädtebund), "Die Deutschen Mittel- und Kleinstädte," *Zeitschrift für Kommunalwirtschaft*, 19, Nr. 16 (special issue, 1929), 926–31; also Böttcher, *Die kommunalen Reichsspitzenverbände*, 37–38.
43. *Deutsche Selbstverwaltung*, Aug. 1930, and *Magdeburgische Zeitung*, 13 May 1930, both in *Mitt. DST* 24 (1930), press clippings, 309, 314.
44. Hofmann, *Städtetag und Verfassungsordnung*, 105–06; cf. Ziebill, *Geschichte*, 365–66.
45. Ewald Löser, "Zwei Jahre Länderkonferenz," *Mitt. DST*, 24 (1930), 18–19. The final proposal for a "Reichsreform Law," submitted by Otto Braun to Chancellor Kurt von Schleicher in December 1932, is published in Brecht's memoirs, *Mit der Kraft des Geistes*, 2: 95–98; English version in idem, *Federalism and Regionalism*, 168–85.
46. "Tausend Verwaltungsgemeinschaften in Deutschland—Eine Denkschrift des Reichsinnenministeriums," *Mitt. DST*, 22 (1928), cols. 1319–21.
47. Brecht, *Mit der Kraft des Geistes*, 2: 93, translation here from the English edition, *The Political Education of Arnold Brecht: An Autobiography, 1884–1970* (Princeton, N.J.: Princeton University Press, 1970), 301. Also Orlow, *Weimar Prussia, 1925–1933*, 109–29. On Brüning and the cities, see Dieter Rebentisch, "Kommunalpolitik, Konjunktur und Arbeitsmarkt," in *Verwaltungsgeschichte: Aufgaben, Zielsetzungen, Beispiele*, ed. Rudolf Morsey (Berlin: Duncker & Humblot, 1977), 122–32. An interesting postscript is added by Gerhard Schulz, "Sand gegen den Wind: Letzter Versuch zur Beratung einer Reform der Weimarer Reichsverfassung im Frühjahr 1933," *Vierteljahrshefte für Zeitgeschichte*, 66 (1996), 298–319.
48. Stenographic report of DST Council, 22 Sept. 1927, LAB, Rep. 142-01, St.A 541/I.
49. Ibid. In addition to Beims, the SPD was represented by Altona mayor Max Brauer; Jarres was a prominent member of the DVP and Adenauer of the Zentrum. Of the southern Oberbürgermeister, Luppe belonged to the DDP and Scharnagl to the BVP. See Rebentisch, "Selbstverwaltung," 93. Although Mulert was a member of the DVP from 1926 onward, he kept it quiet; even his party associates considered him a "blank page" politically. Hofmann, *Städtetag und Verfassungsordnung*, 43 n.139.
50. SPD commentator Paul Hertz labelled both the cities and their program "vorwärtsdrängend." *Gewerkschaftszeitung: Organ des Allgemeinen deutschen Gewerkschaftsbundes*, 8 Oct. 1927, in *Mitt. DST* 21 (1927), Sonderheft

"Reichspolitik und Städte": press clippings, cols. 75–76. Hertz reported on the DST's Magdeburg conference in *Vorwärts*, 27 Sept. 1927.

51. DST Council, 22 Sept. 1927, LAB, Rep. 142-01, St.A 541/I.
52. According to Paul Hertz, the southern Social Democrats were the major stumbling block to Mulert's plans, *Vorwärts,* 27 Sept. 1927; also Hofmann, *Städtetag und Verfassungsordnung*, 74.
53. Hofmann, ibid., 74, 99.
54. Ibid., 95–96.
55. Heinrich Scharp, "Die Städte in der Republik," *Deutsche Republik*, 26 Oct. 1928, in *Mitt. DST*, 22 (1928), Sonderheft "Reichsaufbau und Selbstverwaltung": press clippings, col. 130. See also Brecht's comment in *Mit der Kraft des Geistes*, 2: 62. For examples from the press, see *Berliner Börsencourier,* 20 Oct. 1927 and *Kölnische Zeitung,* 25 Sept. 1928, both in *Mitt. DST*, 21 (1927), Sonderheft "Reichspolitik und Städte": press clippings, col. 100; and 22 (1928), Sonderheft "Reichsaufbau und Selbstverwaltung": press clippings, cols. 113–14, respectively.
56. First priority was the pending Young Plan negotiations. Löser's note, 23 Jan. 1930, LAB, Rep. 142-01, St.B 195. See also "Reichsreform wird vertagt," *Hannoverscher Kurier*, Nr. 568/69, 5 Dec. 1929.
57. Reich Finance Minister Hermann Dietrich, quoted in Gerhard Schulz, *Zwischen Demokratie*, 3: 265.
58. Oskar Mulert, "Finanzausgleich,"in *Kommunales Jahrbuch*, ed. Hugo Lindemann et al. (Jena, 1932), 3: 53–54.
59. On the financial policies of the Reich and states toward the communes after 1930 generally, see first Rebentisch, "Kommunalpolitik" in Morsey, ed., *Verwaltungsgeschichte*; and James, *Reichsbank and Public Finance*, 261–85.
60. Mulert's circular to DST member cities of 29 Aug. 1931, LAB, Rep. 142-01, St.B 3692; reprinted in Maurer and Wengst, eds., *Politik und Wirtschaft in der Krise*, 2: 926–29, doc. 298. See also Gerhard Schulz's assessment of Mulert, in *Zwischen Demokratie*, 3: 264–65, 490.
61. For example, Orlow, *Weimar Prussia*, 247–68.
62. Reich Finance Ministry meeting, 1930, quoted in James, *German Slump*, 103.
63. DST Council meeting of 3 Feb. 1933, the last before the "coordination" (*Gleichschaltung*) of all communal associations by the Nazis in late May. LAB, Rep. 142-01, St.A 340 and 734.
64. See their illuminating comments during a 15 Dec. 1930 meeting in the Reich Finance Ministry concerning the emergency in communal finance, LAB, Rep. 142-01, St.B 3766; published in Maurer and Wengst, eds., *Politik und Wirtschaft in der Krise*, doc. 177, 1: 508–12.
65. Brecht, *Mit der Kraft des Geistes*, 2: 92–95; idem, *Federalism and Regionalism*, Appendix F, 168–70.
66. For example, in the first meeting of the DST's Committee for Administrative and Constitutional Reform, 22 Mar. 1927, stenographic record in LAB, Rep. 142–01, St.A 92.
67. For example, Pünder, "Das Reich," 81.
68. "...nur ein Vorwärts," *DST Breslau, 1928*, 30. Quoted, for example, in *Vorwärts*, 26 Sept. 1928; also in *Dortmunder Zeitung* of 29 Sept. 1928, and *Der deutsche Volkswirt* of 28 Sept. 1928, both of the latter in *Mitt. DST*, 22 (1928), Sonderheft "Reichsaufbau und Selbstverwaltung": press clippings, cols. 122 and 125, respectively.

CHAPTER 6

1. James, *German Slump*, 108.
2. John Teaford, *The Twentieth-Century American City: Problem, Promise, and Reality* (Baltimore: Johns Hopkins University Press, 1986), 44–56.
3. Lieberman, *From Recovery to Catastrophe*, passim.
4. See the comments of Engeli, "Städte und Staat," 170–71.
5. See here esp. Applegate's suggestive essay, "Democracy or Reaction?" 264–65.
6. Cf. Moss, "Cities in the Inflation," 4 and 113.

Select Bibliography

I. ARCHIVAL SOURCES

A. Landesarchiv Berlin (LAB)

1. B Rep. 142-01 Acc. St.A

Nr. 3 Engerer Vorstand: Protokolle, 1927–30
5 Kulturausschuss: Sitzungen u. Protokolle, 1929–30
7 Engerer Vorstand: Protokolle, 1931–32
33 Sitzungen: VS DST / PST (1926–27)
34 Sitzungen: VS DST / PST (1926)
42 Städteverbände (1900–33)
75 Sitzungen: VS PST (1931)
85 Satzungen: Alterations
99 Sitzungen: VS DST (1932)
109 Besprechungen: Geschäftsleiter der kommunalen Spitzenverbände
132 Sitzungen: VS PST (1931–32)
136 VS Sitzungen (DST: 1920–26)
140 Engerer Vorstand: Sitzungen, 1931
156 Engerer Vorstand: Sitzungen, 1926–33
162 DST Arbeitsausschuss (1933)
163 Sitzungen: VS DST (1929)
165 Engerer Vorstand: Sitzungen, 1930–31
170 Sitzungen: VS DST (1932)
177 Engerer Vorstand: Sitzungen, 1927
179 VS Sitzungen (PST: Protokolle only, 1924–31)
186/I Sitzungen: VS PST (1927)
186/II Berlin Conflict w/ DST, 1927 - Sitzungen: VS PST (1927)
195 Engerer Vorstand: Protokolle, 1927–30
239 Sitzungen: VS DST (1929)
244 Bericht über die Tätigkeit der Verbände
282 Engerer Vorstand: Sitzungen, 1933
286 Engerer Vorstand: Sitzungen, 1929–30
295 Engerer Vorstand: Protokolle, 1932–33
302 Sitzungen: VS DST (1928)
303/I Verhältnis zum Reichsstädtebund
303/II Verhältnis zum Reichsstädtebund
311 Sitzungen: VS PST (1932–32)
315 Engerer Vorstand: Sitzungen, 1922–26

327/I Hauptausschuss: Preparations and Proceedings
327/II Hauptausschuss: Preparations and Proceedings
336/I Sitzungen: VS DST (1930)
336/II Sitzungen: VS DST (1930)
340 Sitzungen: VS DST (1932–33)
370 VS DST —Personalien (1925–33)
397 Engerer Vorstand: Sitzungen, 1929
398/I Sitzungen: VS DST (1927 - Vorberichte only)
398/II Sitzungen: VS DST (1927)
399 VS DST – Personalien (1927–31)
401 Kulturausschuss: Personalien, 1929–32
427/I VS DST - Personalien (1925–32)
427/II Personalien: VS DST (1927–33)
464 Hauptausschuss: Preparations and Proceedings
467 Sitzungen: VS DST (1926–27)
493/II Sitzungen: VS DST / PST (1932)
501 Berlin Conflict w/ DST, 1927
507/I Hauptausschuss: Preparations and Proceedings
507/II Hauptausschuss: Preparations and Proceedings
527 Hauptausschuss: Preparations and Proceedings\PST Satzungen
531 Besprechungen: Geschäftsführer der Landes- u. Prov. Städtetage (1920–33)
538 Sitzungen: VS DST (1928)
541/I Sitzungen: VS DST (1927)
541/II Sitzungen: VS DST (1927)
590/II Vorstandssitzungen (1924)
602 Engerer Vorstand: Sitzungen, 1931–32
617 Sitzungen: VS DST (1931)
619 Sitzungen: VS DST (1926)
634 Sitzungen: VS DST / PST (1927–28; DST VS 1929)
654 VS Sitzungen (DST: September–December 1925)
734 Sitzungen: VS DST (1931–33)
739 Vorstandssitzungen (1923)
751 Sitzungen: VS DST (1927–28)
752 Sitzungen: VS DST (1928–30)
774 Sitzungen: VS PST (1931–33)
786/I Hauptausschuss: Preparations and Proceedings
786/II Hauptausschuss: Preparations and Proceedings
842/I VS Sitzungen (PST: October–December 1925)
842/II VS Sitzungen (PST: March–June 1925)
900 VS Sitzungen (DS /PST: May–June 1925)

2. *B Rep. 142-01, Acc. St.B*

Nr. 435 Staatskommissare (1930–32)
525 Erfolge der Städtetagsarbeit (1931–32)
1141 Zuschüsse aus Reichsfonds
1142 Übersicht über Verordnungen in Reich u. Preussen
1143 Verhältnis zu den (Land/Prov.) Städtetagen
1144 Vertretung durch Spitzenverbände
1145 Kritik der Selbstverwaltung
1146 Arbeitsgemeinschaft (kommunaler Spitzenverbände)
1147 Arbeitsgemeinschaft der Städte

1148 Arbeitsgemeinschaft der kommunalen Spitzenverbände
1149 Persönlichkeiten = Materialversorgung
1530 Reparationsverhandlungen
1631 Reparationsagent und Städte (1924–29)
1796 Mulert vs. Schacht
1835 Zuständige Staatsbehörde für Gemeindeaufsicht
1836 Verwaltungsberichte (wartime)
1837 Dauer der Amtzeit (städtische Ausschussmitglieder)
1838 Lieferung der Schiedsmannszeitung durch die Stadt
1839 Anerkennungen für ausscheidende Schiedsmänner
1840-41 Ausstellung von Armutszeugnissen für Schiedsmannsangelegenheiten / Schiedsmännergebühr
1842 Verteilung der Stellen der Wohlfahrtspfleger u. Waisenräte
2014 Stadt und Land
2784/I Anleihen (1924–25)
2784/II Finanzausgleich (1927–29)
2796/I Finanzausgleich (1926)
2796/II Finanzausgleich (1926–27)
3611 Staatsausschuss
3612 Fühlungnahme mit den einzelnen Pr. Ministerien
3613 Fühlungnahme mit dem Pr. Ministerium des Innern
3614 Preussischer Landtag: Kommissionen; Verhandlungen
3615 Interfraktioneller Ausschuss — Preussischer Landtag
3616 Fühlungnahme mit Staatsratsmitgliedern
3617 Kommunale Beiräte in Preussen
3763 Reichswirtschaftsrat — Vertreter
3764 Vertreter der Städte in Beiräten und Ausschüssen
3765 Allgemeine Fühlungnahme mit Reichskanzler u. Regierung
3766 Fühlungnahme mit dem Reichsfinanzministerium
3767 Fühlungnahme mit dem Reichsministerium des Innern
3768 Fühlungnahme mit dem Reichsarbeitsministerium
3769 Fühlungnahme mit dem Reichssparkommissar
3770 Fühlungnahme mit dem Reichswirtschaftsministerium
3771 Vertretung der Städtische Interessen auf Einzelgebieten
3964a Selbstverwaltung — (Clippings) — 1927/28
3964b (DST) Vertretung im Parlament
3964b Arbeitsgemeinschaft der kommunalen Spitzenverbände
3964c (DST) Vertretung im Parlament
3964d (DST) Vertretung im Parlament
3964g Selbstbeschränkungmassnahmen der Gemeinden
3964h Einschränkung der Selbstverwaltung
3964i (DST) Vertretung in Parlament
4214 Schriftverkehr der Gemeinden mit Zentralbehörden (bezw. Reichsbahn)
4215 Randstädte in der Nähe von Staatsstädten (1932)
4216 Nachbarbeziehungen zwischen Grossstädten und Randgemeinden
4217 Einberufung der neugewählten Stadtverordnete

3. *B Rep. 142-03 Reichsstädtebund*

Nr. 302 DST/PST (1925–32)
303 Arbeitsgemeinschaft kommunaler Spitzenverbände (1931)
306 Landgemeindetag
308 Preussischer Landgemeindetag West

325	Sparaktion der kleineren Städte
331	Kreditausschüsse
332	Kommunale Spitzenverbände

4. *E Rep. 200-34 Nachlass Oskar Mulert*

Acc.2955	Nr.	15	Nachlass Mulert
		16	Nachlass Mulert — Charges and Dismissal

5. *E Rep. 200-92 Nachlass Heinrich Sahm*

Acc.3737 Nr 2 Diary, 1934–35

B. Bundesarchiv (BA), Berlin-Lichterfelde

R 1501/	PA/ 9278-81	Oskar Mulert - Personnel files
	25095	Selbstverwaltung der Gemeinden und Gemeindeverbände (1926–33) - Landgemeindetag (1928–33)
	25324	Interfraktioneller Ausschuss des Reichstags für kommunal politische Angelegenheiten
	25324	Landgemeindetag (1928–33)
	25324	Reichsstädtebund (1926–33)
	25324	Landkreistag (1929–33)
	25324	Verband preussischer Provinzen (1928–33)
	25371	Heranziehung von Spitzenorganisationen bei Vorbereitung wirtschaftliche Massnahmen

C. Geheimes Staatsarchiv Preussischer Kulturbesitz, Dahlem (GSTAPrKB)

Hauptamt	I, Rep. 77	Ministerium des Innern
Acc	Tit. 253a	Nr. 44 Bd. 1 Deutscher Einheitsstaat
		Nr. 52 Bd. 1-2 Reichsverfassung
	Tit. 311	Nr. 276 Bd. 1 Angelegenheiten... kommunalen Gebiete
	Tit. 2025	Nr. 18 Bd. 1 Bessere Gestaltung des Verhältnisses zwischen dem Reich und den Ländern
	Tit. 2779	Nr. 6, Bd. 1-2 Kommunale Verwaltungsreform: Das Problem der Grossgemeinde
		Nr. 7, Bd. 1 Die Schaffung eines kommunalpolitischen Ausschusses im Reichstage

D. Nordrhein-Westfälisches Hauptstaatsarchiv, Düsseldorf (NRWHSTA)

Bes.50-53	Nr.	766	Reichsstädtebund
		768	Rheinischer Städtebund
		769	Rheinischer Städtebund
		770	Reichsstädtebund
		774	Rheinischer Städtebund
50		2	Rheinischer Städtetag/Deutscher Gemeindetag

5	Preussischer Landgemeindetag West/Deutscher Gemeindetag
775	Reichsstädtebund
778	Reichsstädtebund

E. Stadtarchiv Düsseldorf (DüssStaA)

Sig. III	Nr. 1376	Vereinigung der Finanzdezernenten grösserer deutscher Städte (1928–30)
	9980	Finanz-Dezernenten der grösseren westdeutschen Städte
	9981-82	Verschiedenes
VII	1000-1005	Akten der städtischen Kunstsammlungen
XXIV	880-884	Bericht über Finanzausschußsitzungen

II. PUBLISHED SOURCES

Albrecht, Thomas. *Für eine wehrhafte Demokratie: Albert Grzesinski und die preussische Politik in der Weimarer Republik*. Bonn: J.H.W. Dietz, 1999.

Allen, William Sheridan. *The Nazi Seizure of Power: The Experience of a Single German Town, 1922–1945*. New York: Franklin Watts, 1984.

Alter, Peter, ed. *Im Banne der Metropolen: Berlin und London in den zwanziger Jahren* (Veröffentlichungen des Deutschen Historischen Instituts London, vol. 29). Göttingen and Zürich: Vandenhoeck & Ruprecht, 1993.

Apelt, Willibalt. *Geschichte der Weimarer Verfassung*, 2d ed. Munich: Biederstein, 1964.

Applegate, Celia. *A Nation of Provincials: the German Idea of Heimat*. Berkeley and Los Angeles: University of California Press, 1990.

———. "Democracy or Reaction? The Political Implications of Localist Ideas in Wilhelmine and Weimar Germany." In *Elections, Mass Politics, and Social Change in Modern Germany: New Perspectives*, ed. Larry Eugene Jones and James Retallack. Cambridge: Cambridge University Press, 1992.

Arndt-Briggs, Skyler. "The Construction and Practice of Place in Weimar Republic Berlin." Ph.D. diss., University of Massachusetts, Amherst, 2000.

Bajohr, Frank, et al., eds. *Zivilisation und Barbarei: Die widersprüchlichen Potentiale der Moderne: Detlev Peukert zum Gedenken*. Hamburg: Christians, 1991.

Balderston, Theo. *The Origins and Course of the German Economic Crisis, November 1923 to May 1932* (Schriften zu Historischen Kommission zu Berlin, vol. 2. Beiträge zu Inflation und Wiederaufbau in Deutschland und Europa, 1914–1924). Berlin: Haude & Spener, 1993.

Baranowski, Shelley. *The Sanctity of Rural Life: Nobility, Protestantism, and Nazism in Weimar Prussia*. Oxford and New York: Oxford University Press, 1995.

Beckstein, Hermann. *Städtische Interessenpolitik: Organisation und Politik der Städtetage in Bayern, Preussen und im Deutschen Reich, 1896–1923*. Düsseldorf: Droste, 1991.

Bergmann, Klaus. *Agrarromantik und Grossstadtfeindschaft* (Marburger Abhandlungen zur politischen Wissenschaft, 20). Meisenheim a. Glan: Hain, 1971.

Berkenhoff, Hans Albert. *Zur Verbandsgeschichte des Deutschen Städtebundes* (Schriftenreihe des Deutschen Städtebundes, vol. 3). Göttingen: Otto Schwartz, 1964.

———. *Der Deutsche Städtebund.* Bonn: Harald Boldt, 1970.

Berman, Marshall. *All That Is Solid Melts Into Air: The Experience of Modernity.* New York: Simon and Schuster, 1988.

Bernhardt, Wolfgang. "Die gemeindliche Gebietsreform und das Selbstverwaltungsrecht: Eine vergleichende Studie über die Reformbestrebungen der Weimarer Republik, des Dritten Reiches und Nordrhein-Westfalens." Ph.D. diss., Westfälischen Wilhelms-Universität zu Münster, 1972.

Bertram, Jürgen. *Staats- und Kommunalpolitik: Notwendigkeit und Grenzen ihrer Koordinierung.* Stuttgart: W. Kohlhammer, 1967.

Bessel, Richard J. *Germany after the First World War.* Oxford: Clarendon Press, 1993.

Biewer, Ludwig. *Reichsreformbestrebungen in der Weimarer Republik. Fragen zur Funktionalreform und zur Neugliederung im Südwesten des Deutschen Reiches.* Frankfurt am Main, Bern, and Cirencester, U.K.: Peter Lang, 1980.

Blachly, F.F. and M.E. Oatman. *The Government and Administration of Germany.* Baltimore: Johns Hopkins University Press, 1928.

Blackbourn, David and Geoff Eley. *The Peculiarities of German History: Bourgeois Society and Politics in Nineteenth-Century Germany.* Oxford: Oxford University Press, 1984.

Blaich, Fritz. "Möglichkeiten und Grenzen kommunaler Wirtschaftspolitik während der Weltwirtschaftskrise 1929 bis 1932." *Archiv für Kommunalwissenschaften* 9 (1970): 92–108.

———. *Die Wirtschaftskrise 1925-26 und die Reichsregierung: von der Erwebslosenfürsorge zur Konjunkturpolitik.* Kallmünz: Lassleben, 1977.

Blüher, Bernhard. "Municipal Administration: Measures for Simplifying Them and Reducing Their Cost." *Annals of Collective Economy* 4 (1928): 181–92.

Böhret, Carl. *Aktionen gegen die "kalte Sozialisierung," 1926–1930: Ein Beitrag zum Wirken ökonomischer Einflussverbände in der Weimarer Republik.* Berlin: Duncker & Humblot, 1966.

Böttcher, Oskar. *Die kommunalen Reichsspitzenverbände.* Berlin-Friedenau: Deutscher Kommunal-Verlag, 1932.

Bonte, Achim. *Werbung für Weimar? Öffentlichkeitsarbeit von Grossstadtverwaltungen in der Weimarer Republik.* Mannheim: Palatium Verlag, 1997.

Bracher, Karl Dietrich, Wolfgang Sauer, and Gerhard Schulz. *Die nationalsozialistische Machtergreifung: Studien zur Errichtung des totalitären Herrschaftssystems in Deutschland 1933/34.* Cologne and Opladen: Westdeutscher Verlag, 1960.

Brecht, Arnold. *Prelude to Silence: The End of the German Republic.* New York: Oxford University Press, 1944.

———. *Federalism and Regionalism in Germany: The Division of Prussia.* Oxford: Oxford University Press, 1945.

———. *Mit der Kraft des Geistes: Lebenserinnerungen*, Zweite Hälfte: 1927–1967. Stuttgart: Deutsche Verlags-Anstalt, 1967.

———. *The Political Education of Arnold Brecht: An Autobiography, 1884–1970.* Princeton: Princeton University Press, 1970.

Brunn, Gerhard. "Berlin (1871–1939)-Megalopolis Manqué?" In *Megalopolis: The Giant City in History*, ed. Theo Barker and Anthony Sutcliffe. New York: St. Martin's, 1993.

Bühler, Ottmar and Chr. Kerstiens, eds. *Die Behördenorganisationen des Ruhrgebiets und die Verwaltungsreform: Heutiger Stand und künftige Entwicklung des Reichs-, Staats- und Selbstverwaltungsbehörden des Ruhrgebiets*. Essen: G.D. Baedeker, 1926.

Büsch, Otto. *Geschichte der Berliner Kommunalwirtschaft in der Weimarer Epoche*. Berlin: Walter de Gruyter, 1960.

———, ed. *Beiträge zur Geschichte der Berliner Demokratie: 1919–1933/1945–1985*. Berlin: Colloquium Verlag, 1988.

Büsch, Otto and Wolfgang Haus. *Berliner Demokratie, 1919–1985*, vol. 1: *Berlin als Hauptstadt der Weimarer Republik, 1919–1933*. Berlin and New York: Walter de Gruyter, 1987.

Bund zur Erneuerung des Reichs. *Reich und Länder: Vorschläge, Begründung, Gesetzentwürfe*. Berlin: G. Stilke, 1928.

Caplan, Jane. *Government without Administration: State and Civil Service in Weimar and Nazi Germany*. Oxford: Clarendon Press, 1988.

Clingan, C. Edmund. "Breaking the Balance: The Debate over Emergency Unemployment Aid in Weimar Germany, 1925–6." *Journal of Contemporary History* 29 (1994): 371–84.

Constantin, Otto and Erwin Stein, eds. *Die deutschen Landkreise*, 2 vols. Berlin-Friedenau: Deutscher Kommunal-Verlag, 1926.

———, eds. *Monographien deutscher Landkreise*, 6 vols. Berlin: Deutscher Kommunal-Verlag, 1925–31.

Crew, David F. "The Pathologies of Modernity: Detlev Peukert on Germany's Twentieth Century." *Social History* 17 (1992): 319–28.

———. *Germans on Welfare: From Weimar to Hitler*. New York: Oxford University Press, 1998.

Davis, Belinda. *Home Fires Burning : Food, Politics, and Everyday Life in World War I Berlin*. Chapel Hill: University of North Carolina Press, 2000.

Dawson, William Harbutt. *Municipal Life and Government in Germany*. London: Longmans, 1914.

Delius, Walter. "Die Notverordnungen und ihre Auswirkungen auf die Gemeinden." *Zeitschrift für Kommunalwirtschaft* 21 (1931): 1257–77.

Deutscher Städtetag. *Verhandlungen des Sechsten Deutschen Städtetages am 25. und 26. September 1924 in Hannover*. Berlin: Selbstverlag der Geschäftsstelle des Deutschen Städtetages, 1924.

———. *Städte, Staat, Wirtschaft: Denkschrift des Deutschen Städtetages*. Berlin: n.p., 1926.

———. *Jahresversammlung des Deutschen Städtetages am 17. und 18. September 1926 in Stettin*. Berlin: Selbstverlag des Deutschen Städtetages, 1927.

———. *Siebenter Deutscher Städtetag: Magdeburg, 23. September 1927*. Berlin: Selbstverlag des Deutschen Städtetages, 1927.

———. *Jahresversammlung des deutschen Städtetages, 1928 in Breslau* (Schriftenreihe des deutschen Städtetages, Heft 4). Berlin: Selbstverlag des Deutschen Städtetages, 1928.

———. *Jahresversammlung des Deutschen Städtetages: Frankfurt am M., 27. September 1929*. Berlin: Selbstverlag des Deutschen Städtetages, n.d. [1929].

———. *Vorschläge zur Abgrenzung der Zuständigkeiten zwischen Reich, Ländern und Gemeinden: Dem Verfassungsausschuss der Länderkonferenz überreicht vom Deutschen Städtetag im Juni 1929*. Berlin: Selbstverlag des Deutschen Städtetages, 1929.

———. *Achter Deutscher Städtetag: Dresden, 26. September 1930*. Berlin: Selbstverlag des Deutschen Städtetages, n.d. [1930].

——. *Reichsstädteordnung: Entwurf und Begründung* (Schriftenreihe des Deutschen Städtetages no. ll). Berlin: Selbstverlag des Deutschen Städtetages, 1930.

——. *25 Jahre Gemeinschaftsarbeit deutscher Städte*. Berlin: Selbstverlag des Deutschen Städtetages, 1930.

——. *Der Städtetag*. Title varies: *Mitteilungen der Zentralstelle des Deutschen Städtetages* 1–7 (1905–1920); *Mitteilungen des Deutschen Städtetages* 8–21 (1922–Sept. 1927); *Der Städtetag: Mitteilungen des Deutschen Städtetages* 21–26 (Oct. 1927–1932); *Der Städtetag: Zeitschrift für deutsche Kommunalpolitik* 27 (Jan.–June 1933); *Der Gemeindetag: Zeitschrift für deutsche Kommunalpolitik* 27–39 (July 1933–1945).

Dorondo, D.R. *Bavaria and German Federalism: Reich to Republic, 1918–33; 1945–49*. New York: St. Martin's, 1992.

Dülffer, Jost et al. *Hitlers Städte: Baupolitik im Dritten Reich, eine Dokumentation*. Cologne and Vienna: Böhlau, 1978.

Dülffer, Jost. "NS-Herrschaftssystem und Stadtgestaltung: Das Gesetz zur Neugestaltung deutscher Städte vom 4. Oktober 1937." *German Studies Review* 12 (1989): 69–89.

Düsseldorf (Stadt). *Stenographische Berichte der Stadtverordneten-Versammlung*. Stadt Düsseldorf, 1909–32.

Eley, Geoff, ed. *Society, Culture, and the State in Germany, 1870–1930*. Ann Arbor: University of Michigan, 1996.

Elsas, Fritz. "Gegenwartsfragen der Kommunalpolitik." *Zeitschrift für Kommunalwirtschaft* 18 (1928): 1267–74.

——. *Auf dem Stuttgarter Rathaus, 1915–1922: Erinnerungen von Fritz Elsas (1890–1945)* (Veröffentlichungen des Archivs der Stadt Stuttgart, vol. 47). Stuttgart: Klett-Cotta, 1990.

Engeli, Christian. *Gustav Böss: Oberbürgermeister von Berlin, 1921–1930*. Stuttgart: W. Kohlhammer, 1971.

——. "Quellen zur Geschichte der kommunalen Spitzenverbände." *Die alte Stadt: Zeitschrift für Stadtgeschichte, Stadtsoziologie und Denkmalpflege* 5 (1978): 409–21.

——. "Zur Geschichte der regionalen Städtetage." *Archiv für Kommunalwissenschaften* 19 (1980): 173–99.

——. "Städte und Staat in der Weimarer Republik: Hans Herzfeld zum Gedenken." In *Kommunale Selbstverwaltung—Idee und Wirklichkeit: 20. Arbeitstagung in Mannheim*, ed. Bernhard Kirchgässner and Jörg Schadt. Sigmaringen: Jan Thorbecke, 1983.

——. *Landesplanung in Berlin-Brandenburg: Eine Untersuchung zur Geschichte des Landesplanungsverbandes Brandenburg-Mitte, 1929–1936*. Stuttgart: W. Kohlhammer, 1986.

Engeli, Christian and Wolfgang Haus, eds. *Quellen zum modernen Gemeindeverfassungsrecht in Deutschland* (Schriften des Deutschen Instituts für Urbanistik, no. 45). Stuttgart: W. Kohlhammer, 1975.

Epstein, Klaus. *Matthias Erzberger and the Dilemma of German Democracy*. Princeton, N.J.: Princeton University Press, 1959.

Erdmann, Karl Dietrich et al., eds. *Akten der Reichskanzlei: Weimarer Republik*, 13 vols. Boppard am Rhein: H. Boldt, 1968.

Evans, Richard J. *Death in Hamburg: Society and Politics in the Cholera Years, 1830–1910*. Harmondsworth: Penguin, 1987.

Evans, Richard J. and Dick Geary, eds. *The German Unemployed*. London and Sydney: Croom Helm, 1987.

Fairbairn, Brett. "History from the Ecological Perspective: Gaia Theory and the Problem of Cooperatives in Turn-of-the-Century Germany." *American Historical Review* 99 (1994): 1203–39.

Falter, Jürgen W. *Hitlers Wähler*. Munich: C.H. Beck, 1991.

Falter, Jürgen W. and Michael H. Kater. "Wähler und Mitglieder der NSDAP: Neue Forschungsergebnisse zur Soziographie des Nationalsozialismus 1925 bis 1933." *Geschichte und Gesellschaft* 19 (1993): 155–77.

Feldman, Gerald D. "The Weimar Republic: A Problem of Modernization?" *Archiv für Sozialgeschichte* 26 (1986): 1–26.

———. *The Great Disorder: Politics, Economics, and Society in the German Inflation, 1914–1924*. New York and Oxford: Oxford University Press, 1993.

Feldman, Gerald D. et al., eds. *Die Anpassung an die Inflation/The Adaptation to Inflation*. Berlin and New York: Walter de Gruyter, 1986.

Finke, Alfred. "Hagener Eingemeindungsfragen." In *Die Stadt Hagen (Westf.)* (Monographien deutscher Städte, vol. 26), ed. Erwin Stein. Berlin: Deutscher Kommunal-Verlag, 1928.

Föllmer, Moritz and Rüdiger Graf, eds. *Die "Krise" der Weimarer Republik: Zur Kritik eines Deutungsmusters*. Frankfurt and New York: Campus Verlag, 2005.

Forsthoff, Ernst. *Die Krise der Gemeindeverwaltung im heutigen Staat*. Berlin: Junker & Dünnhaupt, 1932.

Freund, Friedrich Th. W. "Die Entwürfe zu den neuen preussischen Verfassungsgesetzen für Städte und Landgemeinden." *Deutsche Juristen-Zeitung* 27, 15/16 (1922): cols. 487–92.

Frisby, David. *Fragments of Modernity: Theories of Modernity in the Work of Simmel, Kracauer and Benjamin*. Cambridge, Mass.: MIT Press, 1986.

———. *The Alienated Mind: The Sociology of Knowledge in Germany, 1918–33*. London: Routledge, 1992.

Fritzsche, Peter. "Weimar Populism and National Socialism in Local Perspective." In *Elections, Mass Politics, and Social Change in Modern Germany: New Perspectives*, ed. Larry Eugene Jones and James Retallack. Cambridge: Cambridge University Press, 1992.

———. *Reading Berlin 1900*. Cambridge, Mass.: Harvard University Press, 1996.

Gay, Peter. *Weimar Culture: the Outsider as Insider*. New York: Harper & Row, 1968.

Die Gemeinde: Halbmonatsschrift für sozialistische Arbeit in Stadt und Land, 1924–33.

Gereke, Günther. "Die Landgemeinde." In *Volk und Reich der Deutschen: Vorlesungen gehalten in der Deutschen Vereinigung für Staatswissenschaftliche Fortbildung*, ed. Bernhard Harms. Berlin: Reimar Hobbing, 1929.

———. *Ich war königlich-preussischer Landrat*. Berlin: Union Verlag, 1970.

Göb, Josef. *50 Jahre Deutsche Kommunalpolitik*. Cologne: W. Kohlhammer/Deutscher Gemeindeverlag, 1966.

———. *Die Gemeinden in Staat und Gesellschaft, dargestellt an der Geschichte des Rheinischen Gemeindetages, des Preussischen Landgemeindetages West und des Gemeindetages Nord-Rhein*. Siegburg: Reckinger & Co., 1966.

Grassmann, Siegfried. *Hugo Preuss und die deutsche Selbstverwaltung*. Lübeck and Hamburg: Matthiesen Verlag, 1965.

Groeben, Klaus von der and Hans-Jürgen von der Heide. *Geschichte des Deutschen Landkreistages* (Der Kreis, vol. 5). Cologne and Berlin: Grote, 1981.

Grzesinski, Albert Carl. *Inside Germany*. New York: Dutton, 1939.

Gunlicks, Arthur B. *Local Government in the German Federal System*. Durham, N.C.: Duke University Press, 1986.

Haekel, Gotthold. "Kommunale Verbände: Reichsstädtebund." In *Kommunales Jahrbuch*, ed. Hugo Lindemann, Otto Most and Oskar Mulert. Jena: Gustav Fischer, 1931.

Haekel, Gotthold and Erwin Stein, eds. "Die deutschen Mittel- und Kleinstädte." *Zeitschrift für Kommunalwirtschaft* 19 (no. 16 [special issue], Aug. 1929). Berlin-Friedenau: Deutscher Kommunal-Verlag, 1929.

Hamilton, Richard F. *Who Voted for Hitler?* Princeton, N.J.: Princeton University Press, 1982.

Hansmeyer, Karl-Heinrich, with Gisela Upmeier, Josef Wysocki, and Hermann Dietrich-Troeltsch. *Kommunale Finanzpolitik in der Weimarer Republik*. Stuttgart: W. Kohlhammer, 1973.

Harms, Bernhard, ed. *Volk und Reich der Deutschen: Vorlesungen gehalten in der Deutschen Vereinigung für Staatswissenschaftliche Fortbildung*, 3 vols. Berlin: Reimar Hobbing, 1929.

——, ed. *Recht und Staat im Neuen Deutschland: Vorlesungen gehalten in der Deutschen Vereinigung für Staatswissenschaftliche Fortbildung*, 2 vols. Berlin: Reimar Hobbing, 1929.

Harvey, David. *Consciousness and the Urban Experience: Studies in the History and Theory of Capitalist Urbanization*. Baltimore: Johns Hopkins University Press, 1985.

Haus, Wolfgang. "Staatskommissare und Selbstverwaltung, 1930–1933." *Der Städtetag* (Neue Folge), 9 (March 1956): 96–97.

Haxthausen, Charles W. and Heidrun Suhr, eds. *Berlin: Culture and Metropolis*. Minneapolis: University of Minnesota Press, 1990.

Heffter, Heinrich. *Die Deutsche Selbstverwaltung im 19. Jahrhundert: Geschichte der Ideen und Institutionen*. Stuttgart: W. Kohlhammer, 1969, 2d ed.

Heindl, W. *Die Haushalte von Reich, Ländern und Gemeinden in Deutschland von 1925 bis 1933: Öffentliche Haushalte und Krisenverschärfung*. Frankfurt am Main: Lang, 1984.

Hensel, Albert. *Kommunalrecht und Kommunalpolitik in Deutschland*. Breslau: Ferdinand Hirt, 1928.

Hensel, Walther. *3 x Kommunalpolitik, 1926-1964: Ein Beitrag zur Zeitgeschichte*. Cologne and Berlin: Grote, 1970.

Herf, Jeffrey. *Reactionary Modernism: Technology, Culture, and Politics in Weimar and the Third Reich*. Cambridge: Cambridge University Press, 1984.

——. "Reaktionäre Modernisten und Berlin: Die Ablehunung der kosmopolitischen Metropole." In *Im Banne der Metropolen: Berlin und London in den zwanziger Jahren* (Veröffentlichungen des Deutschen Historischen Instituts London, Bd. 29), ed. Peter Alter. Göttingen and Zürich: Vandenhoeck & Ruprecht, 1993.

Hermand, Jost and Frank Trommler. *Die Kultur der Weimarer Republik*. Munich: Nymphenburger Verlagshandlung, 1978.

Herzfeld, Hans. *Demokratie und Selbstverwaltung in der Weimarer Epoche* (Schriftenreihe des Vereins zur Pflege Kommunalwissenschaftlicher Aufgaben e.V., Bd. 2). Stuttgart: W. Kohlhammer, 1956.

Hirsch, Paul. *Gemeindesozialismus: eine Kursusdisposition*. Berlin: Zentralbildungsausschuss der Sozialdemokratischen Partei Deutschlands, 1920.

Hoebink, Hein. "Städtischer Funktionswandel und Gebietsreform in der Weimarer Republik." In *Die Städte Mitteleuropas im 20. Jahrhundert*, ed. Wilhelm Rausch. Linz/Donau: Österr. Arbeistskreis für Stadtgeschichtsforschung et al., 1984.

———. "Kommunale Neugliederung im rheinisch-westfälischen Industriegebiet, 1919–1929: Ziele und Aufgaben aus der Sicht der Staatsregierung." In *Rheinland-Westfalen im Industriezeitalter*, vol. 3: *Vom Ende der Weimarer Republik bis zum Land Nordrhein-Westfalen*, ed. Kurt Düwell and Wolfgang Köllmann. Wuppertal: Peter Hammer, 1984.

———. *Mehr Raum-mehr Macht: preussische Kommunalpolitik und Raumplanung im rheinisch-westfälischen Industriegebiet 1900–1933*. Essen: Klartext, 1989.

Hofmann, Wolfgang. "Plebiszitäre Demokratie und kommunale Selbstverwaltung in der Weimarer Republik."*Archiv für Kommunalwissenschaften* 4 (1965): 264–81.

———. *Städtetag und Verfassungsordnung: Position und Politik der Hauptgeschäftsführer eines kommunalen Spitzenverbandes* (Schriftenreihe des Vereins für Kommunalwissenschaften, vol. 13). Stuttgart: W. Kohlhammer, 1966.

———. "The Public Interest Pressure Group: The Case of the Deutsche Städtetag." *Public Administration* 45 (1967): 245–59.

———. "Prussian Town Councils in the 19th Century as Representative Institutions." In *Liber Memorialis Georges de Lagarde* (Studies Presented to the International Commission for the History of Representative and Parliamentary Institutions, vol. 38). Louvain and Paris: Nauwelaerts, 1968.

———. *Zwischen Rathaus und Reichskanzlei: Die Oberbürgermeister in der Kommunal- und Staatspolitik des Deutschen Reiches von 1890 bis 1933* (Schriften des Deutschen Instituts für Urbanistik, no. 46). Stuttgart: W. Kohlhammer, 1974.

———. "Die Entwicklung der kommunalen Selbstverwaltung von 1848 bis 1918." In *Handbuch der kommunalen Wissenschaft und Praxis*, vol. 1: *Grundlagen*, ed. G. Püttner. Berlin, Heidelberg, New York: Springer, 1981.

Holtfrerich, Carl-Ludwig. "The Modernisation of the Tax System in the First World War and the Great Inflation, 1914–1923." In *Wealth and Taxation in Central Europe: The History and Sociology of Public Finance*, ed. Peter-Christian Witt. Leamington Spa, Hamburg, New York: Berg, 1987.

Hong, Young-Sun. *Welfare, Modernity, and the Weimar State, 1919–1933*. Princeton, N.J.: Princeton University Press, 1998.

Hüttenberger, Peter. *Düsseldorf: Geschichte von den Anfängen bis ins 20. Jahrhundert*, vol. 3: *Die Industrie- und Verwaltungsstadt (20. Jahrhundert)*. Düsseldorf: Patmos, 1989.

Iggers, Georg G., ed. *The Social History of Politics: Critical Perspectives in West German Historical Writing Since 1945*. New York: St. Martin's, 1985.

Jachmann, Hans. "Düsseldorf in der Weltwirtschaftskrise." Ph.D. diss., Düsseldorf, 1988.

Jackson, Kenneth T. *Crabgrass Frontier: The Suburbanization of the United States*. Oxford and New York: Oxford University Press, 1985.

Jacob, Herbert. *German Administration since Bismarck: Central Authority versus Local Autonomy*. New Haven and London: Yale University Press, 1963.

James, Harold. *The Reichsbank and Public Finance in Germany, 1924–1933: A Study of the Politics of Economics during the Great Depression*. Frankfurt am Main: Fritz Knapp, 1985.

———. *The German Slump: Politics and Economics, 1924–1931*. New York: Oxford University Press, 1986.

———. "Municipal Finance in the Weimar Republic." In *The State and Social Change in Germany, 1880–1980*, ed. W.R. Lee and Eve Rosenhaft. New York, Oxford, and Munich: Berg, 1990.

Jaskot, Paul B. *The Architecture of Oppression: The SS, Forced Labor and the Nazi Monumental Building Economy*. London: Routledge, 2000.

Jelavich, Peter. *Berlin Cabaret*. Cambridge, Mass.: Harvard University Press, 1993.

Jeserich, Kurt G.A. and Helmut Neuhaus, eds. *Persönlichkeiten der Verwaltung: Biographien zur deutschen Verwaltungsgeschichte, 1648–1945*. Stuttgart, Berlin, and Cologne: W. Kohlhammer, 1991.

Jeserich, Kurt G.A., Hans Pohl, and Georg-Christoph von Unruh, eds. *Deutsche Verwaltungsgeschichte*, 6 vols. Stuttgart: Deutsche Verlags-Anstalt, 1980–1985.

John, Jürgen. "Deutscher Städtetag (DstT), 1905–1933." In *Lexicon zur Parteiengeschichte: Die bürgerlichen und kleinbürgerlichen Parteien und Verbände in Deutschland (1789–1945)*, ed. Dieter Fricke et al. Leipzig: VEB Bibliographisches Institut, 1984.

———. "'Unitarischer Bundesstaat,' 'Reichsreform' und 'Reichsneugliederung' in der Weimarer Republik." In *"Mitteldeutschland": Begriff - Geschichte - Konstrukt*, ed. Jürgen John. Rudolstadt and Jena: Hain, 2001.

Johnson, David A. *Planning the Great Metropolis: The 1929 Regional Plan of New York and Its Environs*. London: E & FN Spon, 1996.

Jursch, Hermann. "The Organization of Municipal Loans in Germany." *Annals of Collective Economy* 3 (1927): 321–27.

Kaes, Anton et al., eds. *The Weimar Republic Sourcebook*. Berkeley, Los Angeles, and London: University of Califonia Press, 1994.

Kershaw, Ian, ed. *Weimar: Why did German Democracy Fail?* New York: St. Martin's Press, 1990.

Kluge, Gerhard. "Die Rolle des Deutschen Städtetages in der Zeit der Weimarer Republik von 1919 bis 1933, dargestellt an seiner Verhaltensweise in wirtschaftspolitischen Fragen und zum Abbau der Selbstverwaltung durch den imperialistischen Staat." Ph.D. diss., Leipzig, 1970.

Koch, H.W. *A Constitutional History of Germany in the Nineteenth and Twentieth Centuries*. London: Longman, 1984.

Köllmann, Wolfgang. "The Process of Urbanization in Germany at the Height of the Industrialization Period." *Journal of Contemporary History* 4, no. 3 (1969): 59–76. Reprinted in *The Urbanization of European Society in the Nineteenth Century*, ed. Andrew Lees and Lynn Lees. Lexington, Mass.: Heath, 1976.

———. *Bevölkerung in der industriellen Revolution: Studien zur Bevölkerungsgeschichte Deutschlands*. Göttingen: Vandenhoeck & Ruprecht, 1974.

Koshar, Rudy. "Against the 'Frightful Leveller': Historic Preservation and German Cities, 1890–1914." *Journal of Urban History* 19, no. 3 (1993): 7–29.

Köttgen, Arnold. *Die Krise der kommunalen Selbstverwaltung*. Tübingen: J.C.B. Mohr, 1931.

Krabbe, Wolfgang R. "Eingemeindungsprobleme vor dem Ersten Weltkrieg: Motive, Widerstände und Verfahrensweise." *Die alte Stadt* 7 (1980): 368–87.

———. *Die deutsche Stadt im 19. und 20. Jahrhundert: Eine Einführung*. Göttingen: Vandenhoeck & Ruprecht, 1989.

———. "Die Tendenz zur autoritären Kommunalverfassung: Preussen, Deutschland und das Rheinland 1920–1935." In *Preussen und die rheinischen Städte*, ed. Margret Wensky. Cologne: Rheinland-Verlag, 1994.

Krey, Bruno. "Kurze Geschichte des Preussischen Landgemeinde-Verbandes und der Verschmelzungs-Verhandlungen mit dem Preussischen Landgemeindetage." *Die Landgemeinde,* 30, nos. 18–19 (1921): 209–221, 227–44.

Ladd, Brian. *Urban Planning and Civic Order in Germany, 1860–1914.* Cambridge, Mass.: Harvard University Press, 1990.

Lammers, Hans-Heinrich and Walter Simons, eds. *Die Rechtsprechung des Staatsgerichtshofs für das Deutsche Reich und des Reichsgerichts auf Grund Artikel 13 Absatz 2 der Reichsverfassung*, 2 vols. Berlin: Georg Stilke, 1930.

Lane, Barbara Miller. *Architecture and Politics in Germany, 1918–1945.* Cambridge, Mass.: Harvard University Press, 1985.

Laqueur, Walter. *Weimar: A Cultural History, 1918–1933.* London: Weidenfeld & Nicolson, 1974.

Leaman, Jeremy. "The Gemeinden as Agents of Fiscal and Social Policy in the Twentieth Century: Local Government and State-form Crises in Germany." In *The State and Social Change in Germany, 1880–1980*, ed. W.R. Lee and Eve Rosenhaft. New York, Oxford, and Munich: Berg, 1990.

Lee, J.J. "Aspects of Urbanization and Economic Development in Germany, 1815–1914." In *Towns in Societies: Essays in Economic History and Historical Sociology*, ed. Philip Abrams and E.A. Wrigley. Cambridge: Cambridge University Press, 1978.

Lees, Andrew. *Cities Perceived: Urban Society in European and American Thought, 1820–1940.* New York: Columbia University Press, 1985.

———. "Berlin and Modern Urbanity in German Discourse, 1845–1945." *Journal of Urban History* 17 (1991): 153–80.

Lehnert, Detlef. *Kommunale Politik, Parteiensystem und Interessenkonflikte in Berlin und Wien, 1919–1932.* Berlin: Haude & Spener, 1991.

Leyden, Viktor von. "Gebietsabgrenzungen und Neugliederung der Gemeinden I: Preussen." In *Kommunales Jahrbuch* (Neue Folge), ed. Hugo Lindemann, Otto Most and Oskar Mulert. Jena: Gustav Fischer, 1931.

Lichtenstein, Herta. *Die Finanzwirtschaft der Deutschen Grossstädte von 1925 bis 1931; ein Beitrag zu dem Problem des Finanzausgleichs.* Jena: Gustav Fischer, 1933.

Lieberman, Ben. "From Recovery to Instability: Municipal Politics and Social Provision in Weimar Germany, 1924–1930." Ph.D. diss., University of Chicago, 1992.

———. "Luxury or Public Investment? Productivity and Planning for Weimar Recovery." *Central European History* 26 (1993): 195–213.

———. "Testing Peukert's Paradigm: The 'Crisis of Classical Modernity' in the 'New Frankfurt,' 1925–1930." *German Studies Review* 17 (1994): 287–303.

———. *From Recovery to Catastrophe: Municipal Stabilization and Political Crisis in Weimar Germany.* New York and Oxford: Berghahn, 1998.

Lohmeyer, Hans. "Die Entwicklung des deutschen Gemeindeverfassungsrechts seit der Revolution." *Deutsche Juristen-Zeitung* 30, no. 5 (1925): cols. 407–11.

Lüben, Kurt. "Raum und Verwaltungsgrenzen im niederrheinisch-westfälischen Wirtschaftsgebiet." *Erde und Wirtschaft: Vierteljahrsschrift für Wirtschaftsgeographie und ihre praktische Anwendung* 5, no. 2 (1931): 49–67.

Luther, Hans. *Im Dienste des Städtetages*. Berlin: Schriftenreihe des Vereins zur Pflege kommunalwirtschaftlicher Aufgaben, 1959.

Luther, Hans et al., eds. *Zukunftsaufgaben der deutschen Städte*. Berlin: Deutscher Kommunal-Verlag, 1922.

Maly, Karl. *Geschichte der Frankfurter Stadtverordnetenversammlung*. Frankfurt am Main: Waldemar Kramer, 1992–95, 2 vols.

Mangoldt, Karl von. *Das Grossstadtproblem und die Wege zu seiner Lösung*. Berlin, Stuttgart, and Leipzig: Pontos-Verlag, 1928.

Mattern, Daniel Stewart. "Creating the Modern Metropolis: The Debate over Greater Berlin, 1890–1920." Ph.D. diss., University of North Carolina, 1991.

Matzerath, Horst. *Nationalsozialismus und kommunale Selbstverwaltung*. Stuttgart: W. Kohlhammer, 1970.

———. "Von der Stadt zur Gemeinde: Zur Entwicklung des rechtlichen Stadtbegriffs im 19. und 20. Jahrhundert." *Archiv für Kommunalwissenschaften* 13 (1974): 17–46.

———. "Städtewachstum und Eingemeindungen im 19. Jahrhundert." In *Die Deutsche Stadt im Industriezeitalter: Beiträge zur modernen deutschen Stadtgeschichte*, ed. Jürgen Reulecke. Wuppertal: Peter Hammer, 1978.

———. "The Influence of Industrialization on Urban Growth in Prussia (1815–1914)." In *Patterns of European Urbanization since 1500*, ed. H. Schmal. London: Croom Helm, 1981.

———. "Die Zeit des Nationalsozialismus." In *Handbuch der kommunalen Wissenschaft und Praxis*, vol. 1: *Grundlagen*, ed. G. Püttner. Berlin, Heidelberg, New York: Springer, 1981.

———. "Berlin, 1890–1940." In *Metropolis, 1890–1940*, ed. Anthony Sutcliffe. London: Mansell, 1984.

Maurer, Ilse and Udo Wengst, eds. *Politik und Wirtschaft in der Krise 1930–1932: Quellen zur Ära Brüning*, 2 vols. Düsseldorf: Droste, 1980.

McElligott, Anthony. "Crisis in the Cities: the Collapse of Weimar." *History Today* 43 (1993): 18–24.

———. *Contested City: Municipal Politics and the Rise of Nazism in Altona, 1917–1937*. Ann Arbor: University of Michigan Press, 1998.

———. ed. *The German Urban Experience, 1900–1945: Modernity and Crisis*. London and New York: Routledge, 2001.

McKibben, David. "Who Were the German Independent Socialists? The Leipzig City Council Election of 6 December 1917." *Central European History* 25 (1992): 425–43.

McNeil, William C. *American Money and the Weimar Republic: Economics and Politics on the Eve of the Great Depression*. New York: Columbia University Press, 1986.

Medicus, Franz Albrecht, ed. *Reichsreform und Länderkonferenz: Die Beratungen und Beschlüsse der Länderkonferenz und ihrer Ausschüsse*. Berlin: C. Heymann, 1930.

Merkl, Peter. "Urban Challenge under the Empire." In *Another Germany: A Reconsideration of the Imperial Era*, ed. Joachim Remak and Jack R. Dukes. Boulder, Colo. and London: Westview Press, 1988.

Mertens, Paul. "Eingemeindungsprobleme des Landkreises Essen und seiner Gemeinden." In *Der Landkreis Essen* (Monographien Deutscher Landkreise, vol. 4), ed. Otto Constantin and Erwin Stein. Berlin: Deutscher Kommunal-Verlag, 1926.

Meyer, Herbert. "Kommunale Verbände." In *Kommunales Jahrbuch*, ed. Hugo Lindemann, Otto Most and Oskar Mulert. Jena: Gustav Fischer, 1931.

Meyer-Lülmann, Albert. "Gemeinde- und Städteverbände." In *Handwörterbuch der Kommunalwissenschaften*, ed. Josef Brix et al. Jena: Gustav Fischer, 1922.

Ministerial-Blatt für die preussische innere Verwaltung.

Mitzlaff, Paul. "German Cities since the Revolution of 1918." *National Municipal Review* 15, no. 11, supp. (Nov. 1926): 677–91.

Moeller, Robert G., ed. *Peasants and Lords in Modern Germany: Recent Studies in Agricultural History*. Boston: Allen & Unwin, 1986.

Moss, (W.H.) Timothy. "Crisis of Self-Government? The Berlin City Representative Assembly, 1929–1931." M.Phil. thesis, Oxford, 1984.

———. "Cities in the Inflation: Municipal Government in Berlin, Cologne, and Frankfurt am Main during the Early Years of the Weimar Republic." Ph.D. diss., Oxford, 1992.

———. "Der Spielraum und die Leistungen kommunaler Sozialpolitik nach dem Ersten Weltkrieg." *Archiv für Kommunalwissenschaften* 32 (1993): 280–99.

Mulert, Oskar. "Die Entwicklung der Selbstverwaltung." In *Zehn Jahre Deutsche Geschichte, 1918–1928*. Berlin: Otto Stollberg, 1928.

———. "The Economic Activities of German Municipalities." *Annals of Collective Economy* 5 (1929): 209–70.

———. "Die Stadtgemeinde." In *Volk und Reich der Deutschen: Vorlesungen gehalten in der Deutschen Vereinigung für Staatswissenschaftliche Fortbildung*, ed. Bernhard Harms. Berlin: Reimar Hobbing, 1929.

Newcomer, Mabel. *Central and Local Finance in Germany and England*. New York: Columbia University Press, 1937.

Nipperdey, Hans Carl, ed. *Die Grundrechte und Grundpflichten der Reichsverfassung*, 3 vols. Berlin: Reimar Hobbing, 1930.

Noakes, Jeremy. "Oberbürgermeister and Gauleiter: City Government between Party and State." In *Der "Führerstaat"—Mythos und Realität: Studien zur Struktur und Politik des Dritten Reiches*, ed. Gerhard Hirschfeld and Lothar Kettenacker. Stuttgart: Ernst Klett, 1981.

Nolan, Mary. *Visions of Modernity: American Business and the Modernization of Germany*. New York: Oxford University Press, 1994.

Orlow, Dietrich. *Weimar Prussia, 1918–1925: The Unlikely Rock of Democracy*. Pittsburgh: University of Pittsburgh Press, 1986.

———. *Weimar Prussia, 1925–1933: The Illusion of Strength*. Pittsburgh: University of Pittsburgh Press, 1991.

Peters, Hans. *Grenzen der kommunalen Selbstverwaltung in Preussen: Ein Beitrag zur Lehre vom Verhältnis der Gemeinden zu Staat und Reich*. Berlin: Julius Springer, 1926.

Peukert, Detlev J.K. *The Weimar Republic: The Crisis of Classical Modernity*. London: Allen Lane, The Penguin Press, 1991.

Piesche, Margarete. "Die Rolle des Reparationsagenten Seymour Parker Gilbert während der Weimarer Republik (1924–1930)." *Jahrbuch für Geschichte* 18 (1978): 135–69.

Pogge von Strandmann, Hartmut. "The Liberal Power Monopoly in the Cities of Imperial Germany." In *Elections, Mass Politics, and Social Change in Modern Germany: New Perspectives*, ed. Larry Eugene Jones and James Retallack. Cambridge: Cambridge University Press, 1992.

Poor, Harold Lloyd. "City versus Country: Anti-urbanism in the Weimar Republic." *Societas - A Review of Social History* 6 (1976): 177–92.

Preussischer Landkreistag. *Regionalreform und Kreisverfassung: Gedanken und Vorschläge des Preussischen Landkreistages zur kommunalen Verwaltungsreform*. Berlin: n.p., 1928.

———. "Landkreise und grossstädtische Eingemeindungspolitik." *Zeitschrift für Selbstverwaltung* 12 (1929): 289–304.

Preussischer Landgemeindetag West. *Der Preussische Landgemeindetag West zur kommunalen Neugliederung der Regierungsbezirke Düsseldorf, Münster, Arnsberg*. Berlin: n.p., 1928.

Preussischer Städtetag. *Jahresversammlung des Preussischen Städtetages: Magdeburg, 24. September 1927*. Berlin: Selbstverlag des Deutschen Städtetages, n.d. [1927].

———. *Jahresversammlung des Preussischen Städtetages: Breslau, 26. September 1928*. Berlin: Selbstverlag des Deutschen Städtetages, n.d. [1928].

———. *Jahresversammlung des Preussischen Städtetages: Frankfurt a. M., 28. September 1929*. Berlin: Selbstverlag des Deutschen Städtetages, n.d. [1929].

———. *Grundfragen der kommunalen Neugliederung: Denkschrift des Preussischen Städtetages*. Berlin: Selbstverlag des Deutschen Städtetages, 1929.

———. *Elfter Preussischer Städtetag: Dresden, 27. September 1930*. Berlin: Selbstverlag des Deutschen Städtetages, n.d. [1930].

Preuss, Hugo. *Gemeinde, Staat, Reich als Gebietskörperschaften*. Aalen: Scientia Verlag, 1964 (1889).

Preussische Gesetzsammlung (1890–1933).

Pünder, Hermann. "Das Reich und die Länder." In *Zehn Jahre Deutsche Geschichte, 1918–1928*. Berlin: Otto Stollberg, 1928.

———. "Zusammenarbeit mit Heinrich Brüning in der Reichskanzlei 1930–1932." In *Staat, Wirtschaft und Politik in der Weimarer Republik: Festschrift für Heinrich Brüning*, ed. Ferdinand A. Hermens and Theodor Schieder. Berlin: Duncker & Humblot, 1967.

Rebentisch, Dieter. "Kommunalpolitik, Konjunktur und Arbeitsmarkt in der Endphase der Weimarer Republik." In *Verwaltungsgeschichte: Aufgaben, Zielsetzungen, Beispiele*, ed. Rudolf Morsey. Berlin: Duncker & Humblot, 1977.

———. "Industrialisierung, Bevölkerungswachstum und Eingemeindungen: Das Beispiel Frankfurt am Main, 1870-1914." In *Die Deutsche Stadt im Industriezeitalter: Beiträge zur modernen deutschen Stadtgeschichte*, ed. Jürgen Reulecke. Wuppertal: Peter Hammer, 1978.

———. "Die Selbstverwaltung in der Weimarer Zeit." In *Handbuch der kommunalen Wissenschaft und Praxis*, vol. 1: *Grundlagen*, ed. G. Püttner. Berlin, Heidelberg, New York: Springer, 1981.

———. "Programmatik und Praxis sozialdemokratischer Kommunalpolitik in der Weimarer Republik." *Die alte Stadt: Zeitschrift für Stadtgeschichte, Stadtsoziologie und Denkmalpflege* 12 (1985): 33–56.

Reekers, Stephanie. *Die Gebietsentwicklung der Kreise und Gemeinden Westfalens, 1817–1967*. Munster: Aschendorff, 1977.

Reichsarbeitsgemeinschaft deutscher Föderalisten. *Die Kommunale Neuentwicklung im Ruhrgebiet als Etappe zur diktatorischen grosspreussischen Zentralisation* (Schriften der Reichsarbeitsgemeinschaft deutscher Föderalisten, Heft 4). Cologne: Reichs- und Heimat-Verlag, 1929.

Reichsstädtebund. *Kommunale Verwaltungsreform und örtliche Selbstverwaltung*. Berlin: n.p., 1928.

———. *Der Reichsstädtebund zum Gesetzentwurf über die kommunale Neugliederung des rheinisch-westfälischen Industriegebiets*. Berlin: n.p., 1929.

Repkow, Eike von [pseud.], "Nüchterne kommunalpolitik. Eine Entgegnung an Herrn Dr. Oskar Mulert." *Mitteilungsblatt der Nationalsozialisten in den Parlamenten und gemeindlichen Vertretungskörpern* 6 (1933): 113–15.

Reulecke, Jürgen. "Wirtschaft und Bevölkerung ausgewählter Städte im Ersten Weltkrieg (Barmen, Düsseldorf, Essen, Krefeld)." In *Die Deutsche Stadt im Industriezeitalter: Beiträge zur modernen deutschen Stadtgeschichte*, ed. Jürgen Reulecke. Wuppertal: Peter Hammer, 1978.

———. "Zur städtischen Finanzlage in den Anfangsjahren der Weimarer Republik." *Archiv für Kommunalwissenschaften* 21 (1982): 199–219.

———. "The Ruhr: Centralization vs. Decentralization in a Region of Cities." In *Metropolis, 1890–1940*, ed. Anthony Sutcliffe. London: Mansell, 1984.

———. *Geschichte der Urbanisierung in Deutschland.* Frankfurt am Main: Suhrkamp, 1985.

———. "Die Auswirkungen der Inflation auf die städtischen Finanzen." In *Die Nachwirkungen der Inflation auf die deutsche Geschichte, 1924–1933* (Schriften des Historischen Kollegs, Kolloquien 6), ed. Gerald D. Feldman. Munich: Oldenbourg, 1985.

———. "Federal Republic of Germany." In *Modern Urban History Research in Europe, USA and Japan: a Handbook*, ed. Christian Engeli and Horst Matzerath. Oxford, Munich, and New York: Berg, 1989.

Reulecke, Jürgen and Gerhard Brunn, eds. *Metropolis Berlin: Berlin im Vergleich europäischer Hauptstädte im 19. und 20. Jahrhundert.* Bonn and Berlin: Bouvier, 1992.

Ribhegge, Wilhelm. "Die Systemfunktion der Gemeinden: Zur deutschen Kommunalgeschichte seit 1918." In *Kommunale Demokratie: Beiträge für die Praxis der kommunalen Selbstverwaltung*, ed. Rainer Frey. Bonn-Bad Godesberg: Neue Gesellschaft, 1976.

———. "Die politische Kultur der Stadt: Zur historischen Rolle der deutschen Städte." *Die alte Stadt* 21 (1994): 131–49.

Rössler, Mechtild. "'Area Research' and 'Spatial Planning' from the Weimar Republic to the German Federal Republic: Creating a Society with a Spatial Order under National Socialism." In *Science, Technology and National Socialism*, ed. Monika Renneberg and Mark Walker. Cambridge: Cambridge University Press, 1994.

Rombeck-Jaschinski, Ursula. "Wie die Grossstadt Wuppertal entstand: Der Weg zur kommunalen Neugliederung von 1929." *Geschichte im Westen* 3 (1988): 19–34.

Romeyk, Horst. *Verwaltungs- und Behördengeschichte der Rheinprovinz, 1914–1945.* Düsseldorf: Droste, 1985.

Roth, Nadine Leeann. "Metamorphoses: Urban Space and Modern Identity, Berlin 1870–1933." Ph.D. diss., University of Toronto, 2003.

Sartorius, Otto. *Neuordnung von Verfassung und Verwaltung in Reich und Ländern.* Hanover: Wirtschaftswissenschaftliche Gesellschaft zum Studium Niedersachsens, e.V., 1928.

Sauer, Wolfgang. "Weimar Culture: Experiments in Modernism." *Social Research* 39 (1972): 254–84.

Schacht, Hjalmar. *Eigene oder geborgte Währung.* Leipzig: Quelle & Meyer, 1927.

Schmid, Manfred, ed. *Fritz Elsas, ein Demokrat im Widerstand: Zeugnisse eines Liberalen in der Weimarer Republik.* Gerlingen: Bleicher, 1999.

Schmitt, Carl. *Der Hüter der Verfassung.* Tübingen: J.C.B. Mohr, 1931.

Schubert, Dirk. "Grossstadtfeindschaft und Stadtplanung: Neue Anmerkungen zu einer alten Diskussion." *Die alte Stadt* 13 (1986): 22–41.

Schulte, Albert. "The Financial Significance of the Gainful Activities of German Municipalities." *Annals of Collective Economy* 7 (1931): 183–94.
Schulz, Gerhard. *Zwischen Demokratie und Diktatur. Verfassungspolitik und Reichsreform in der Weimarer Republik*, 3 vols. Berlin: Walter de Gruyter, 1963, 1987, 1991.
Schwabe, Klaus, ed. *Oberbürgermeister* (Büdinger Forschungen zur Sozialgeschichte 1979). Boppard am Rhein: Harald Boldt, 1981.
Seidel, Johannes. *Die Haushaltspläne der deutschen Gemeinden* (Finanzwissenschaftliche und volkswirtschaftiche Studien, vol. 27). Jena: Gustav Fischer, 1933.
Sennett, Richard. *Flesh and Stone: The Body and the City in Western Civilization.* New York: Norton, 1994.
Sheehan, James J. "Liberalism and the City in 19th-century Germany." *Past and Present* no. 51 (1971): 116–37.
———. *German Liberalism in the Nineteenth Century.* Chicago: University of Chicago Press, 1978.
———. *German History, 1770–1866.* Oxford and Toronto: Oxford University Press, 1989.
Silverman, Dan P. "A Pledge Unredeemed: The Housing Crisis in Weimar Germany." *Central European History* 3 (1970): 112–39.
Simmel, Georg. *The Sociology of Georg Simmel*, ed. Kurt H. Wolff. Glencoe, Ill.: Free Press, 1950.
Smith, Michael Peter. *The City and Social Theory.* Oxford: Basil Blackwell, 1980.
Sprenger, Heinrich. *Heinrich Sahm: Kommunalpolitiker und Staatsmann.* Cologne: Grote, 1969.
Staats- und Selbstverwaltung: Zeitschrift für Staats- und Kommunalverwaltungen und -beamte, Fachblatt für Gesetzes- und praktische Verwaltungskunde, Büro- und Wirtschaftsführung, 1927–1935.
Statistisches Jahrbuch deutscher Städte, 1890–1915; 1927–1933.
Statistisches Reichsamt. *Die Gemeinden mit 2000 und mehr Einwohnern im Deutschen Reich* (*Wirtschaft u. Statistik* 6 [1926], Sonderheft 3). Berlin, 1926.
———. *Verwaltungsaufbau, Steuerverteilung und Lastenverteilung im Deutschen Reich* (Einzelschriften zur Statistik des Deutschen Reichs, no. 6). Berlin: Reimar Hobbing, 1929.
———. *Statistik des Deutschen Reichs*, vol. 387: *Kommunale Finanzwirtschaft.* Berlin: Reimar Hobbing, 1931.
Stein, Erwin, ed. *Monographien deutscher Städte*, 39 vols. Berlin: Deutscher Kommunal-Verlag, 1912–33.
———, ed. *Monographien Deutscher Landgemeinden.* Berlin: Deutscher Kommunal-Verlag, 1925.
———. "The German Municipal Association." *Public Management* 9 (1927): 516–46.
Steinmetz, George. *Regulating the Social: The Welfare State and Local Politics in Imperial Germany.* Princeton, N.J.: Princeton University Press, 1993.
Steitz, Walter, ed. *Quellen zur deutschen Wirtschafts- und Sozialgeschichte vom ersten Weltkrieg bis zum Ende der Weimarer Republik.* Darmstadt: Wissenschaftliche Buchgesellschaft, 1993.
Stier-Somlo, Fritz. "Das Grundrecht der kommunalen Selbstverwaltung unter besonderer Berücksichtigung des Eingemeindungsrechts." *Archiv des öffentlichen Rechts* (New Series) 17 (1929): 1–93.
Sutcliffe, Anthony. *Towards the Planned City: Germany, Britain, the United States and France, 1780–1914.* New York: St. Martin's, 1981.

Suval, Stanley. *Electoral Politics in Wilhelmine Germany*. Chapel Hill: University of North Carolina Press, 1985.

Swett, Pamela E. *Neighbors and Enemies: The Culture of Radicalism in Berlin, 1929–1933*. Cambridge: Cambridge University Press, 2004.

Taeuber, Conrad. *Migration to and from German Cities, 1902–29*. Rome: Istituto Poligrafico dello Stato, 1932.

Teaford, John C. *City and Suburb: The Political Fragmentation of Metropolitan America, 1850–1970*. Baltimore and London: Johns Hopkins University Press, 1979.

———. *The Twentieth-Century American City: Problem, Promise, and Reality*. Baltimore: Johns Hopkins University Press, 1986.

Terhalle, Fritz. "Geschichte der deutschen öffentlichen Finanzwirtschaft vom Beginn des 19. Jahrhunderts bis zum Schlusse des Zweiten Weltkriegs." In *Handbuch der Finanzwissenschaft*, 2d ed., ed. Wilhelm Gerloff and Fritz Neumark. Tübingen: J.C.B. Mohr, 1952.

Theile, Frank. "Die Folgewirkungen der kommunalen Neugliederung des rheinisch-westfälischen Industriegebiets in den Jahren 1926 bis 1929: untersucht an Beispielen des östlichen Ruhrgebiets." Ph.D. Diss., Ruhr-Universität Bochum, 1970.

Trebilcock, Clive. *The Industrialization of the Continental Powers, 1780–1914*. London: Longman, 1981.

Unruh, Georg-Christoph von. "Der Kreis im 19. Jahrhundert zwischen Staat und Gesellschaft." In *Kommunale Selbstverwaltung im Zeitalter der Industrialisierung* (Schriftenreihe des Vereins für Kommunalwissenschaft, no. 33), ed. Helmuth Croon, Wolfgang Hofmann and Georg-Christoph von Unruh. Stuttgart: W. Kohlhammer, 1971.

Verwaltungsakademie Berlin, ed. *Gegenwartsfragen der Kommunalverwaltung*. Berlin: Reimar Hobbing, 1929.

Viergutz, Volker. "Die kommunalen Spitzenverbände: Zu ihrer Geschichte und ihrer archivalischen Überlieferung." In *Berlin in Geschichte und Gegenwart* (Jahrbuch des Landesarchivs Berlin). Berlin: Landesarchiv Berlin, 1983.

Walker, Mack. *German Home Towns: Community, State, and General Estate 1648–1871*. Ithaca and London: Cornell University Press, 1971.

Ward, Janet. *Weimar Surfaces: Urban Visual Culture in 1920s Germany*. Berkeley: University of California, 2001.

Webb, Steven B. *Hyperinflation and Stabilization in Weimar Germany*. Oxford and New York: Oxford University Press, 1989.

Weber, Adolf. *Hat Schacht Recht? Die Abhängigkeit der deutschen Volkswirtschaft vom Ausland*. Munich and Leipzig: Duncker & Humblot, 1928.

Wehler, Hans-Ulrich. *The German Empire, 1871–1918*. Leamington Spa: Berg, 1985.

Weisbrod, Bernd. "The Crisis of German Unemployment Insurance in 1928/1929 and its Political Repercussions." In *The Emergence of the Welfare State in Britain and Germany, 1850–1950*, ed. Wolfgang J. Mommsen. London: Croom Helm, 1981.

Wells, Roger Hewes. *German Cities: A Study of Contemporary Municipal Politics and Administration*. Princeton: Princeton University Press, 1932.

Wiedenhoeft, Ronald. *Berlin's Housing Revolution: German Reform in the 1920s*. Ann Arbor: University Microfilms International Research Press, 1985.

Winter, Jay and Jean-Louis Robert, eds. *Capital Cities at War: Paris, London, Berlin, 1914–1919*. Cambridge: Cambridge University Press, 1997.

Witt, Peter-Christian. "The Prussian Landrat as Tax Official, 1891–1914: Some Observations on the Political and Social Function of the German Civil Service during the Wilhelmine Empire." In *The Social History of Politics: Critical Perspectives in West German Historical Writing since 1945*, ed. Georg Iggers. New York: Berg/St. Martin's, 1985.

———. "Tax Policies, Tax Assessment and Inflation: Towards a Sociology of Public Finances in the German Inflation, 1914–1923." In *Wealth and Taxation in Central Europe: The History and Sociology of Public Finance*, ed. Peter-Christian Witt. Leamington Spa, Hamburg, New York: Berg, 1987.

Wolffsohn, Michael. "Creation of Employment as a Welfare Policy. The Final Phase of the Weimar Republic." In *The Emergence of the Welfare State in Britain and Germany, 1850–1950*, ed. Wolfgang J. Mommsen. London: Croom Helm, 1981.

Yaney, George L. *The World of the Manager: Food Administration in Berlin during World War I*. New York: Peter Lang, 1994.

Zeck, W. "Staatsaufsicht in Angelegenheiten des Gemeindehaushalts." *Staats- und Selbstverwaltung* 12, no. 4 (Feb. 1931): 65–67.

Ziebill, Otto. *Geschichte des Deutschen Städtetages: Fünfzig Jahre deutsche Kommunalpolitik*, 2nd ed. Stuttgart: W. Kohlhammer, 1956.

Zöllner, Detlev. "Germany." In *The Evolution of Social Insurance, 1881–1981: Studies of Germany, France, Great Britain, Austria and Switzerland*, ed. Peter A. Köhler, et al. Munich, London, New York: Max-Planck-Institut für ausländisches und internationales Sozialrecht, 1982.

Index

For Product Safety Concerns and Information please contact our EU
representative GPSR@taylorandfrancis.com
Taylor & Francis Verlag GmbH, Kaufingerstraße 24, 80331 München, Germany

www.ingramcontent.com/pod-product-compliance
Lightning Source LLC
Chambersburg PA
CBHW050516280326
41932CB00014B/2340

* 9 7 8 0 4 1 5 7 6 2 5 0 2 *